IOWA BIRDS

Ann Johnson
Jim Bangma
Gregory Kennedy

Lone Pine Publishing International

First printed in 2005   10 9 8 7 6 5 4 3 2 1
Printed in Canada

Distributed by Lone Pine Publishing
1808 – B Street NW, Suite 140
Auburn, WA, USA 98001

Website: www.lonepinepublishing.com

Library and Archives Canada Cataloguing in Publication

Johnson, Ann, 1949-
Iowa Birds / Ann Johnson, Jim Bangma, Gregory Kennedy.

ISBN-13: 978-1-55105-461-2
ISBN-10: 1-55105-461-2

1. Birds--Iowa. 2. Bird watching--Iowa. I. Bangma, Jim II. Kennedy, Gregory, 1956- III. Title.

QL684.I6J63 2005   598'.09777   C2005-901470-9

Scanning & Digital Film: Elite Lithographers Co.
Cover Illustration: American Goldfinch by Gary Ross

PC: P1

CONTENTS

ACKNOWLEDGMENTS

This project would not be possible without the talents of Dr. James J. Dinsmore and Dr. Thomas H. Kent. Their untold hours of compiling data and writing *Birds in Iowa* provided us with invaluable information for use in a field guide. We are also indebted to the many members of the Iowa Ornithologists' Union who have generously shared their records over the years so that a picture of bird distribution across the state could become more clear.

Others providing significant contributions to our work include biologists Bruce Ehresman and Pat Schlarbaum of the Iowa Department of Natural Resources Wildlife Diversity Program, who provided critical information on Bird Conservation Regions, status of the state's threatened and endangered species, and information on bird releases and reintroductions. Aspiring attorney Aaron Brees graciously reviewed our text for glaring errors. The definitions of Bird Conservation Regions, or ecological areas, are courtesy of the U.S. North American Bird Conservation Initiative (http://www.nabci-us.org).

We especially thank our patient editors, Carmen Adams and Genevieve Boyer, who provided us guidance and answered all of our questions throughout the project. Working with them has been a pleasure.

One would certainly be remiss in not honoring the memory of Dr. Gladys Black in a field guide written specifically for Iowa. Her influence through *Des Moines Register* birding columns, as well as her willingness to teach anyone within earshot about the birds of Iowa, was instrumental in nurturing an entire generation of birders who now provide the data to make books such as this possible. We think she would be proud of what birding in Iowa has become.

Belted Kingfisher

Snow Goose
size 31 in • p. 20

Canada Goose
size 44 in • p. 21

Tundra Swan
size 54 in • p. 22

Wood Duck
size 17 in • p. 23

Gadwall
size 20 in • p. 24

Mallard
size 24 in • p. 25

Blue-winged Teal
size 15 in • p. 26

Northern Shoveler
size 19 in • p. 27

Northern Pintail
size 23 in • p. 28

Canvasback
size 20 in • p. 29

Ring-necked Duck
size 16 in • p. 30

Lesser Scaup
size 16 in • p. 31

Bufflehead
size 14 in • p. 32

Hooded Merganser
size 17 in • p. 33

Common Merganser
size 25 in • p. 34

Ruddy Duck
size 15 in • p. 35

Ring-necked Pheasant
size 30 in • p. 36

Wild Turkey
size 41 in • p. 37

Northern Bobwhite
size 10 in • p. 38

Common Loon
size 32 in • p. 39

Pied-billed Grebe
size 13 in • p. 40

Western Grebe
size 22 in • p. 41

American White Pelican
size 60 in • p. 42

REFERENCE GUIDE

DIVING BIRDS

Double-crested Cormorant
size 29 in • p. 43

HERONLIKE BIRDS

American Bittern
size 25 in • p. 44

Great Blue Heron
size 51 in • p. 45

Great Egret
size 39 in • p. 46

Green Heron
size 18 in • p. 47

Black-crowned Night-Heron
size 24 in • p. 48

Turkey Vulture
size 29 in • p. 49

BIRDS OF PREY

Osprey
size 23 in • p. 50

Bald Eagle
size 37 in • p. 51

Northern Harrier
size 20 in • p. 52

Cooper's Hawk
size 16 in • p. 53

Broad-winged Hawk
size 16 in • p. 54

Red-tailed Hawk
size 20 in • p. 55

Rough-legged Hawk
size 21 in • p. 56

American Kestrel
size 8 in • p. 57

Peregrine Falcon
size 16 in • p. 58

RAILS, COOTS & CRANES

Sora
size 9 in • p. 59

American Coot
size 14 in • p. 60

Sandhill Crane
size 45 in • p. 61

SHOREBIRDS

Killdeer
size 10 in • p. 62

Lesser Yellowlegs
size 10 in • p. 63

Spotted Sandpiper
size 7 in • p. 64

Least Sandpiper
size 5 in • p. 65

Pectoral Sandpiper
size 9 in • p. 66

Wilson's Snipe
size 11 in • p. 67

American Woodcock
size 11 in • p. 68

Franklin's Gull
size 14 in • p. 69

Ring-billed Gull
size 19 in • p. 70

Herring Gull
size 24 in • p. 71

Caspian Tern
size 21 in • p. 72

Forster's Tern
size 15 in • p. 73

Black Tern
size 9 in • p. 74

Rock Pigeon
size 12 in • p. 75

Eurasian Collared-Dove
size 12 in • p. 76

Mourning Dove
size 12 in • p. 77

Yellow-billed Cuckoo
size 12 in • p. 78

Eastern Screech-Owl
size 8 in • p. 79

Great Horned Owl
size 22 in • p. 80

Barred Owl
size 21 in • p. 81

Common Nighthawk
size 9 in • p. 82

Whip-poor-will
size 9 in • p. 83

Chimney Swift
size 5 in • p. 84

Ruby-throated Hummingbird
size 4 in • p. 85

Belted Kingfisher
size 12 in • p. 86

Red-headed Woodpecker
size 9 in • p. 87

Red-bellied Woodpecker
size 10 in • p. 88

Yellow-bellied Sapsucker
size 8 in • p. 89

WOODPECKERS

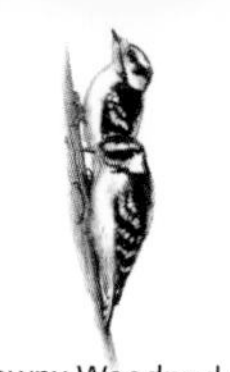
Downy Woodpecker
size 6 in • p. 90

Hairy Woodpecker
size 9 in • p. 91

Northern Flicker
size 13 in • p. 92

Pileated Woodpecker
size 17 in • p. 93

FLYCATCHERS

Eastern Wood-Pewee
size 6 in • p. 94

Willow Flycatcher
size 6 in • p. 95

Eastern Phoebe
size 7 in • p. 96

Great Crested Flycatcher
size 8 in • p. 97

Western Kingbird
size 8 in • p. 98

Eastern Kingbird
size 8 in • p. 99

SHRIKES & VIREOS

Loggerhead Shrike
size 9 in • p. 100

Yellow-throated Vireo
size 5 in • p. 101

Warbling Vireo
size 5 in • p. 102

Red-eyed Vireo
size 6 in • p. 103

JAYS & CROWS

Blue Jay
size 12 in • p. 104

American Crow
size 18 in • p. 105

LARKS & SWALLOWS

Horned Lark
size 7 in • p. 106

Purple Martin
size 7 in • p. 107

Tree Swallow
size 5 in • p. 108

Northern Rough-winged Swallow
size 5 in • p. 109

Cliff Swallow
size 5 in • p. 110

Barn Swallow
size 7 in • p. 111

CHICKADEES, WRENS & NUTHATCHES

Black-capped Chickadee
size 5 in • p. 112

Tufted Titmouse
size 6 in • p. 113

Red-breasted Nuthatch
size 4 in • p. 114

White-breasted Nuthatch
size 6 in • p. 115

Brown Creeper
size 5 in • p. 116

House Wren
size 5 in • p. 117

Marsh Wren
size 5 in • p. 118

Ruby-crowned Kinglet
size 4 in • p. 119

Blue-gray Gnatcatcher
size 4 in • p. 120

Eastern Bluebird
size 7 in • p. 121

Wood Thrush
size 8 in • p. 122

American Robin
size 10 in • p. 123

Gray Catbird
size 9 in • p. 124

Brown Thrasher
size 11 in • p. 125

European Starling
size 8 in • p. 126

Cedar Waxwing
size 7 in • p. 127

Yellow Warbler
size 5 in • p. 128

Yellow-rumped Warbler
size 5 in • p. 129

Palm Warbler
size 5 in • p. 130

Black-and-white Warbler
size 5 in • p. 131

American Redstart
size 5 in • p. 132

Prothonotary Warbler
size 5 in • p. 133

Ovenbird
size 6 in • p. 134

Common Yellowthroat
size 5 in • p. 135

Scarlet Tanager
size 7 in • p. 136

Eastern Towhee
size 8 in • p. 137

American Tree Sparrow
size 6 in • p. 138

Chipping Sparrow
size 5 in • p. 139

Vesper Sparrow
size 6 in • p. 140

SPARROWS, GROSBEAKS & BUNTINGS

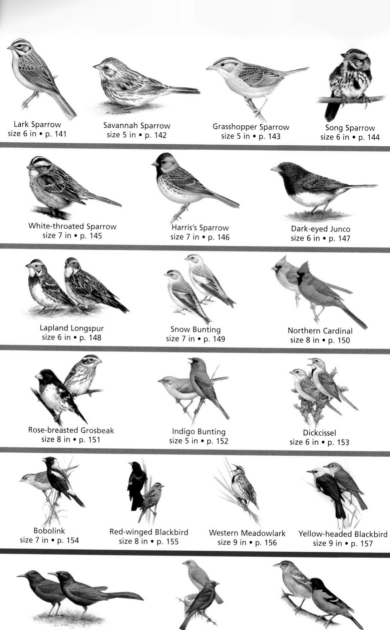

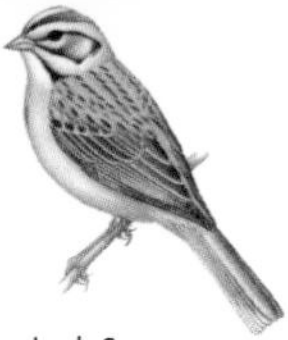

Lark Sparrow
size 6 in • p. 141

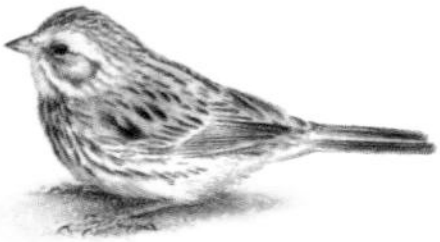

Savannah Sparrow
size 5 in • p. 142

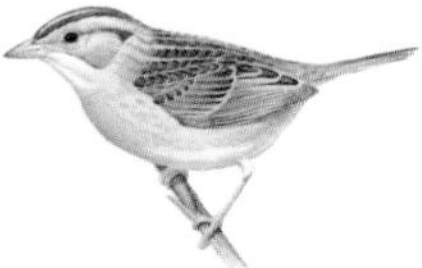

Grasshopper Sparrow
size 5 in • p. 143

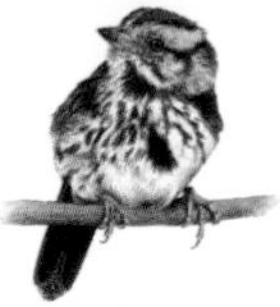

Song Sparrow
size 6 in • p. 144

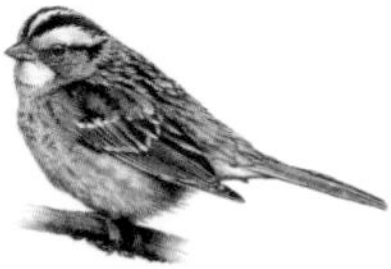

White-throated Sparrow
size 7 in • p. 145

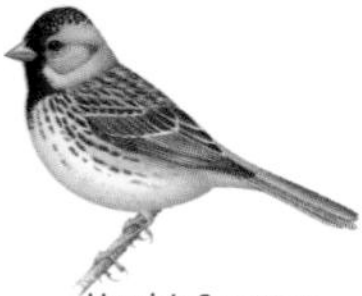

Harris's Sparrow
size 7 in • p. 146

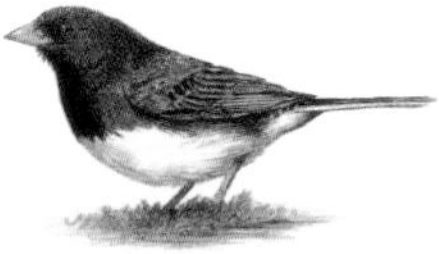

Dark-eyed Junco
size 6 in • p. 147

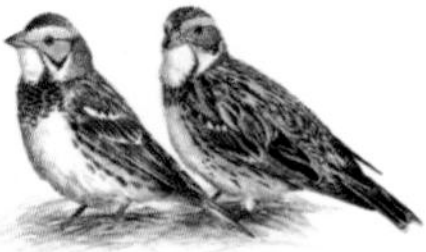

Lapland Longspur
size 6 in • p. 148

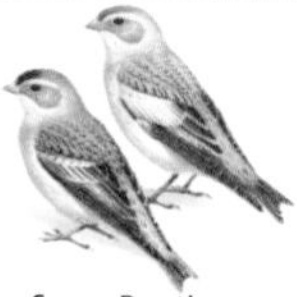

Snow Bunting
size 7 in • p. 149

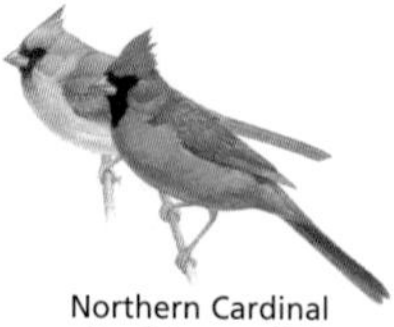

Northern Cardinal
size 8 in • p. 150

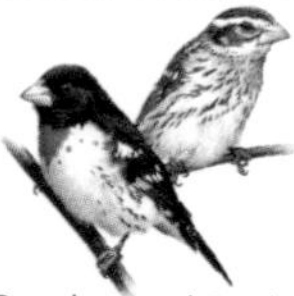

Rose-breasted Grosbeak
size 8 in • p. 151

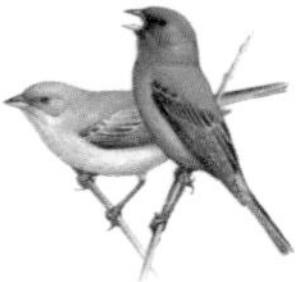

Indigo Bunting
size 5 in • p. 152

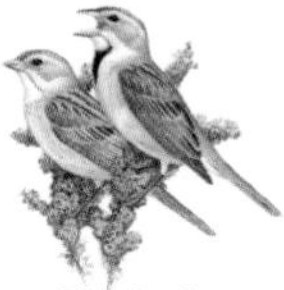

Dickcissel
size 6 in • p. 153

BLACKBIRDS & ALLIES

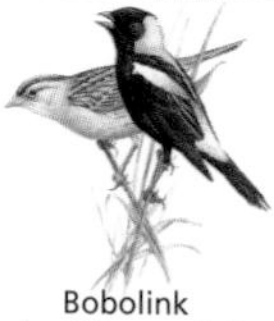

Bobolink
size 7 in • p. 154

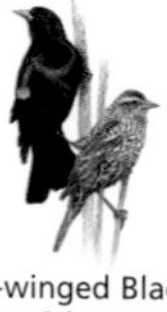

Red-winged Blackbird
size 8 in • p. 155

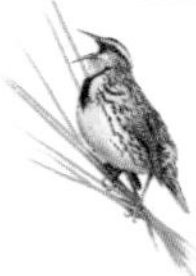

Western Meadowlark
size 9 in • p. 156

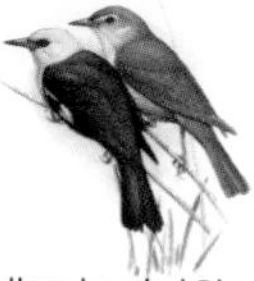

Yellow-headed Blackbird
size 9 in • p. 157

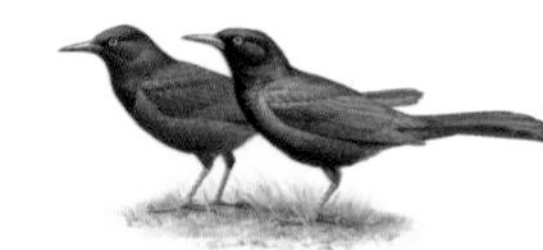

Common Grackle
size 12 in • p. 158

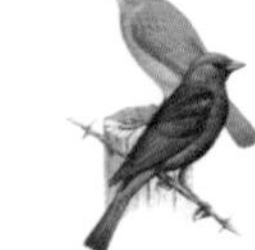

Brown-headed Cowbird
size 7 in • p. 159

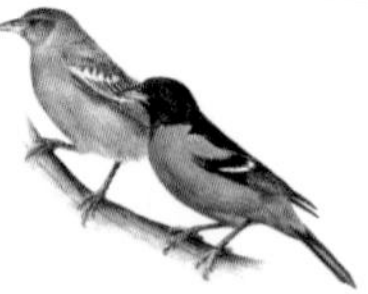

Baltimore Oriole
size 7 in • p. 160

FINCHLIKE BIRDS

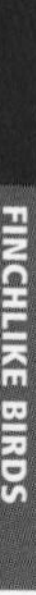

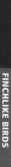

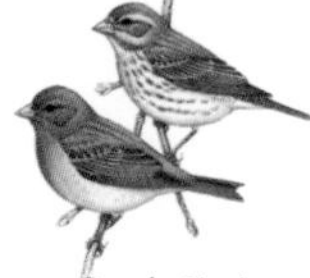

Purple Finch
size 5 in • p. 161

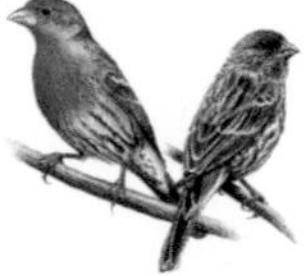

House Finch
size 5 in • p. 162

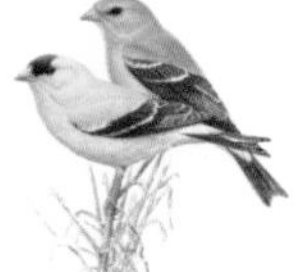

American Goldfinch
size 5 in • p. 163

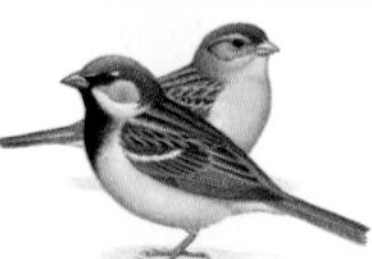

House Sparrow
size 6 in • p. 164

INTRODUCTION

BIRDING IN IOWA

In recent decades, birding has evolved into a worldwide phenomenon that boasts millions of participants. There are many good reasons why it has become such a popular activity. Some people go birding for relaxation and others enjoy the outdoor exercise it affords. Birding can be a rewarding learning experience, an opportunity to socialize with like-minded people and a way to monitor the health of the local environment, pursued at whatever level you desire.

Whether you are just beginning to take an interest in birds or have already learned to identify many species, this field guide has something for you. We have selected 145 of the species you are most likely to encounter in Iowa. A few occur only in specialized habitat, but most species can be found easily throughout the state.

Whether you are looking out your back window or walking along a secluded trail, you will find that there are always birds close by. Birds such as jays and chickadees are our year-round neighbors, prominent at backyard feeders. Some birds, especially waterbirds and songbirds, only visit Iowa in migration and summer to take advantage of abundant food and to raise their young. Others pass through our state on their way to other breeding grounds, and still others, such as the Dark-eyed Junco, are only winter visitors.

Most of the birds featured in this book are common and familiar and can be encountered on a regular basis. A few species are shy and secretive or are restricted to certain habitats, and seeing them can be a noteworthy event.

Iowa has a long tradition of friendly birding. Local birding clubs, Audubon chapters and the statewide Iowa Ornithologists' Union welcome new birders at their many functions throughout the year. Christmas bird counts, breeding bird surveys, feeder surveys, hawk watches and highly popular birding festivals provide a chance for birders of all levels to interact and share their appreciation for birds. Whatever your level of knowledge, there is ample opportunity for you to get involved and learn more.

Iowa is certainly a crossroads for avifauna. The checklist at the back of the book provides a complete list of the species that you might see in the state.

Sandhill Crane

For more information on birding in Iowa, explore:

Iowa Ornithologists' Union
http://www.iowabirds.org

Iowa Audubon Society
http://www.iowaaudubon.org

Iowa Department of Natural Resources
http://www.iowadnr.com/wildlife/files/BCA_index.html

IOWA'S TOP BIRDING SITES

There are hundreds of good birding areas throughout the state. The Iowa Department of Natural Resources (DNR) uses three ecological classifications to define the birding regions within the state: Prairie–Hardwood Transition, Prairie Pothole Region and Eastern Tallgrass Prairie. Within each of these regions, birders will find a great variety of habitats in which to find their representative birds.

The following sites listed for these regions have been selected to represent a broad range of bird communities and habitats, with an emphasis on diversity and accessibility. DNR-designated Bird Conservation Areas are indicated on the map in red.

Prairie–Hardwood Transition Region

1. Upper Mississippi River NWR
2. Effigy Mounds/Yellow River Forest BCA
3. Mines of Spain

Prairie Pothole Region

4. Spirit Lake/Kettleson Hogsback
5. Spring Run Grasslands BCA
6. Ruthven Wildlife Area/Dewey's Pasture
7. Ingham, High and Cunningham Lakes Complex
8. Union Slough NWR
9. Myre Slough
10. Elk Creek Marsh
11. Clear Lake/Ventura Marsh
12. Union Hills BCA
13. Big Wall Lake
14. Blackhawk Lake/Tomahawk Marsh
15. Dunbar Slough
16. Snake Creek Marsh
17. Ledges SP
18. Jester Park/Saylorville Reservoir

Eastern Tallgrass Prairie Region

19. Gitchie Manitou Natural Area
20. Waterman Creek Area
21. Broken Kettle Grasslands BCA
22. Owego Wetlands
23. Moorhead County Park
24. DeSoto NWR
25. Hitchcock Nature Area
26. Forney Lake WA
27. Waubonsie SP
28. Riverton WA
29. Springbrook SP
30. Kellerton Grasslands BCA
31. Medicine Creek
32. Sedan Bottoms
33. Lake Rathbun
34. Stephen's SF
35. Red Rock Reservoir
36. Des Moines–Waterworks Park
37. Shell Rock Greenbelt
38. Big Marsh
39. Sweet Marsh
40. George Wyth SP/Hartman Reserve
41. Backbone SP
42. Iowa River Corridor BCA
43. Coralville Reservoir/Hawkeye WA
44. Hickory Hill Park
45. Cone Marsh
46. Wildcat Den SP
47. Port Louisa NWR
48. Lacey–Keosauqua SP
49. Shimek SF
50. Pool 19–Mississippi River

BCA = Bird Conservation Area
NWR = National Wildlife Refuge
SF = State Forest
SP = State Park
WA = Wildlife Area

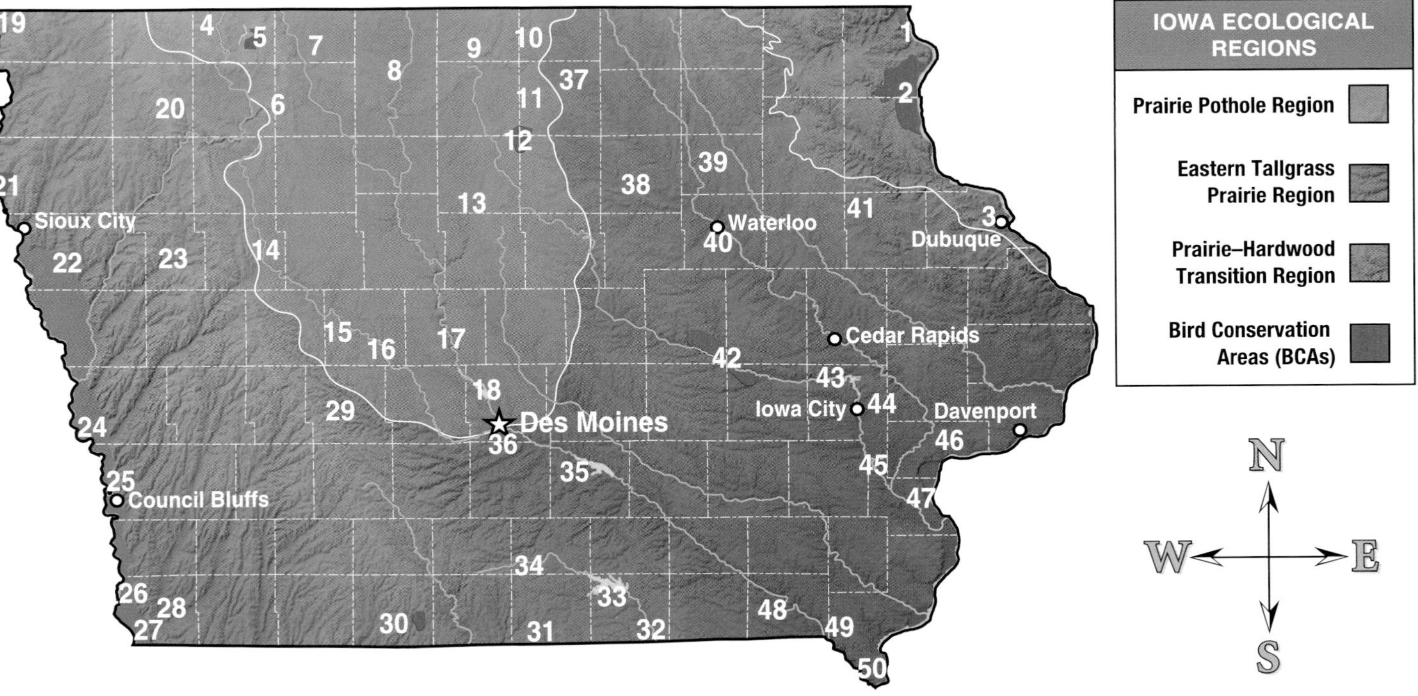
IOWA ECOLOGICAL REGIONS
Prairie Pothole Region
Eastern Tallgrass Prairie Region
Prairie–Hardwood Transition Region
Bird Conservation Areas (BCAs)
N
W
E
S
Sioux City
Waterloo
Dubuque
Cedar Rapids
Iowa City
Davenport
Des Moines
Council Bluffs

THROUGH THE SEASONS IN IOWA

Species diversity in Iowa depends more upon season than geography. Although some of the species described in this book are year-round residents, many only visit during migration or breeding season. Traveling to new areas as the seasons progress will really maximize your birding experiences. For instance, although ducks are widespread during spring migration, in summer they are better observed in the Prairie Pothole Region.

Winter

Many people begin their birding adventures by enticing birds to backyard feeders in winter. Some of Iowa's wintering birds are year-round residents and others just visit our area to escape harsher, more northerly climates.

Some resident birds—for example, the Black-capped Chickadee, Northern Cardinal, Blue Jay, Downy Woodpecker and White-breasted Nuthatch—wear the same plumage throughout the year. Others, such as the American Goldfinch and Eurasian Starling, lose their breeding colors and may even look like an entirely different species. The Dark-eyed Junco and American Tree Sparrow are also common winter visitors.

More northerly locations like the Waterman Area or the Shell Rock Greenbelt may have better odds for unusual visitors, such as the Bohemian Waxwing. Look for the Northern Saw-whet Owl in George Wyth State Park, Ledges State Park and as far south as Stephen's State Forest. The Short-eared Owl often winters in the southern grasslands of Medicine Creek. If the weather is not brutally cold, areas below the dams of the large reservoirs, Coralville, Saylorville, Red Rock and Rathbun, may provide an interesting assortment of wintering raptors, gulls and waterfowl. The largest concentrations, however, are found at the series of locks and dams along the Mississippi River where wintering ducks, such as Common Merganser and Common Goldeneye, might be found in larger numbers. Bald Eagles winter throughout the state, especially along any large river where open water prevails.

Black-capped Chickadee

Spring

Just as the ice is breaking on Iowa's lakes and ponds in late February, spring migrants are making their way to their breeding grounds. Thousands of geese and ducks feed on leftover grain in farm fields, building energy reserves for the long trip north. On a beautiful, early spring day in March you may see up to 500,000 Snow Geese fly over western locations, for example, Forney Lake. Early nesters, such as the Great Horned Owl, are already incubating eggs and Red-tailed Hawks circle in pairs around most woodlots. Nesting and courting Eastern Phoebes and American Woodcocks are also common. The activities of migration are widespread throughout most of the 50 sites listed for the state. A trek to Kellerton BCA is marked on the calendars of most birders and is not to be missed—the anticipation of seeing the dance of the Greater Prairie Chicken can be a great introduction to a new season of birding.

By mid-April the shorebird migration is in full swing. Snow melt and spring floods change the landscape almost daily, and migrants exploit the shallows and mudflats left in their wake. Trips to potholes like Myre and Dunbar Sloughs usually produce the longest list, but migrants are likely to appear on any flooded field. Other favorite shorebird sites are Owego Wetlands, Riverton WA, Hawkeye WA and the upper reaches of Red Rock Reservoir.

Fox, Field, Vesper and Savannah sparrows replace winter's American Tree Sparrow. Tree Swallows compete with Eastern Bluebirds for prime nesting holes, and Juncos disappear.

As spring progresses you may find Sandhill Cranes nesting in Sweet Marsh, at the Upper Mississippi Wildlife Refuge or at Otter Creek Marsh along the Iowa River Corridor. Locally breeding species, such as the Northern Parula and Cerulean, Worm-eating and Kentucky warblers, begin nesting in places like Shimek State Forest, Lacey–Keosauqua State Park and Effigy Mounds/Yellow River Forest Bird Conservation Area.

The highlight of spring for most birders, however, is the frenetic pace of migration in mid-May. Songbirds that have wintered in the tropics arrive to find choice nesting areas; others pass through on their way to the northern bogs. The resident American Goldfinch sheds his drab winter plumage and joins the riot of color that arrives with the warblers, orioles, tanagers, grosbeaks, buntings and flycatchers. Now is the time for big day counts: topping 100 species for the day is not uncommon. Favorite places to bird in May include Ledges, Backbone, Springbrook and George Wyth state parks, Hickory Hill Park in Iowa City, Des Moines–Waterworks Park and Moorehead County Park. Before you know it, spring turns to summer and breeding residents become busy with domestic duties.

Common Grackle

Summer

June is a wonderful time for watching bird behavior. The nesting season starts with males loudly defending a chosen territory, singing high from perches where they watch carefully for intruders. The bustle of summer can be compared to that of migration, with parents busy building nests, incubating eggs and feeding their nestlings.

Pied-billed Grebe

Summer is also the season when available and undisturbed habitat is most important to the species you will see. Find a nice grassland to see Grasshopper Sparrows, Bobolinks, Dickcissels and, if you are lucky, Upland Sandpipers. Medicine Creek Wildlife Area is one of the better places to find nesting Henslow's Sparrows. Black-billed Magpies have nested at Broken Kettle Grasslands Bird Conservation Area. Some species, such as Broad-winged Hawks, Wood Thrushes and Ovenbirds, require uninterrupted stands of timber; wooded parks and forests are ideal places to search for these birds. Other common species, such as Brown Thrashers and Gray Catbirds, seem to be hiding in every hedgerow and edge.

Perhaps some of the most summer fun involves exploring the Prairie Pothole Region. Iowa lies on the southern edge of a huge landform of marshes and puddles where the bulk of North American ducklings are raised. Numbers may not be as great as in the Dakotas and Canada's Prairie Provinces, but broods of Wood Ducks, Blue-winged Teals, Gadwalls and Redheads are fairly common in this area.

Just as summer is settling, fall migration is already beginning. Shorebirds are the champions of long-distance migration, and the first males returning from the Arctic appear in early July. Most of these males are not actively involved in parenting, so they leave the family behind. Shorebirds found later in fall migration are generally females with their young.

Savannah Sparrow

Fall

Although late nesters, such as American Goldfinches, are only just feeding newly fledged young, some birds start moving south in August, providing a sense of seasonal transition. Migration moves at a much slower pace in fall than in spring. Individuals may stop awhile to feed and store energy for the long flight ahead, giving observers more opportunity to study field marks and learn the birds. Rather than being high in the canopy as they are in the spring, warblers are often found at heights that are easier on your neck.

New challenges, however, await you in fall. Some species molt their bright breeding colors, opting instead for a more neutral look in the winter season. Many young shorebirds appear much brighter than their parents because their feathers are newer. The Chestnut-sided Warbler no longer has chestnut sides and a Scarlet Tanager has lost its crimson red plumage. At this time of year, many birds resemble each other and identification becomes more difficult.

The relaxed atmosphere of fall is perfect for special events and festivals. Hawk watches offer an opportunity to volunteer and monitor raptor and songbird movements. The September Pelican Festival at Jester Park entertains about 5000 visitors with at least as many pelicans. The November Rivers & Bluffs Festival in Lansing showcases the staging area for much of the mid-continent population of waterfowl, with hundreds of Tundra Swans stealing the show. On the opposite side of the state, the Snow Goose congregation at DeSoto National Wildlife Refuge in late fall and early winter is also a sight to behold. As winter gets closer and ice sets in, the waterfowl of the Mississippi Flyway continue south to Pool 19 where thousands of Lesser Scaup and Canvasbacks gather to feed on fingernail snails.

Some birds are still slowly moving southward in December. Christmas bird counts generally record a few of these species, primarily waterfowl and gulls, and can include Black-crowned Night-Herons and Snow Buntings. By late December the cycle begins anew. Great Horned Owls are setting up territories while birders search for winter finches and dream of ponds bustling with Pintails.

Peregrine Falcon

ABOUT THE SPECIES ACCOUNTS

This book gives detailed accounts of 145 species of birds that occur regularly in Iowa and can be expected on an annual basis. The order of the birds and their common and scientific names follow the American Ornithologists' Union's *Check-list of North American Birds* (7th edition, July 1998, revised to include the *Forty-fifth Supplement,* 2004).

As well as discussing the identifying features of a bird, each species account also attempts to bring the bird to life by describing its various character traits. Personifying a bird helps us to relate to it on a personal level, though the characterizations should not be mistaken for scientific propositions. Nonetheless, we hope that a lively, engaging text will communicate our scientific knowledge as smoothly and effectively as possible.

One of the challenges of birding is that many species look different in spring and summer than they do in fall and winter, as they switch between breeding and nonbreeding plumages, and immature birds often look different from their parents. This book does not try to describe or illustrate all the different plumages of a species; instead, it focuses on the forms that are most likely to be seen in our area.

ID: It is difficult to describe the features of a bird without being able to visualize it, so this section is best used in combination with the illustrations. Where appropriate, the description is subdivided to highlight the differences between male and female adult birds, breeding and nonbreeding birds and immatures. The descriptions use as few technical terms as possible, favoring easily understood language. Birds may not have "jawlines," "eyebrows" or "chins," but these and other scientifically inaccurate terms are easily understood by all readers. Some of the most common features of birds are pointed out in the Glossary illustration (p. 165).

Size: The size measurement, the average length of the bird's body from bill to tail, is an approximate measurement of the bird as it is seen in nature. The size of larger birds is often given as a range because of variation among individuals. Please note that birds with long tails often have large measurements that do not necessarily reflect "body" size. In addition, wingspan (from wing tip to wing tip) is given.

Habitat: The habitats we have listed describe where each species is most commonly found. In most cases it is a generalized description, but if a bird is restricted to a specific habitat, the habitat is described precisely. Because of the freedom flight gives them, birds can turn up almost anywhere. However, they will usually be found in environments that provide the specific food, water, cover or nesting habitat they require.

Nesting: The reproductive strategies used by different bird species vary: in each species account, nest location and structure, clutch size, incubation period and parental duties are discussed. Remember that birding ethics discourage the disturbance of active bird nests. If you disturb a nest, you may drive off the parents during a critical period or expose defenseless young to predators. The nesting behavior of birds not known to nest in our region is not described.

Feeding: Birds spend a great deal of time foraging for food. If you know what a bird eats and where the food is found, you will have a good chance of finding the bird you are looking for.

Voice: You will hear many birds, particularly songbirds, that may remain hidden from view. Memorable paraphrases of distinctive sounds will aid you in identifying a species. These paraphrases often only loosely resemble the call, song or sound produced by the bird. Should one of our paraphrases not work for you, feel free to make up your own—the creative exercise will reinforce your memory of the bird's vocalizations.

Similar Species: To the extent practicable, similar species and their distinguishing features are briefly discussed. If you concentrate on the most relevant field marks, the subtle differences between species can be reduced to easily identifiable traits. You might find it useful to consult this section when finalizing your identification; knowing the most relevant field marks will speed up the identification process. Even experienced birders can mistake one species for another.

Range Maps: The range map for each species represents the overall range of the species in an average year. Most birds will confine their annual movements to this range, although each year some birds wander beyond their traditional boundaries. These maps do not show differences in abundance within the range—areas of a range with good habitat will support a denser population than areas with poorer habitat. These maps also cannot show small pockets within the range where the species may actually be absent, or how the range may change from year to year.

Unlike most other field guides, we have attempted to show migratory pathways—areas of the region where birds may appear while en route to nesting or winter habitat. Many of these migratory routes are "best guesses" that will no doubt be refined as new discoveries are made. The representations of these pathways do not distinguish high-use migration corridors from areas that are seldom used.

RANGE MAP SYMBOLS

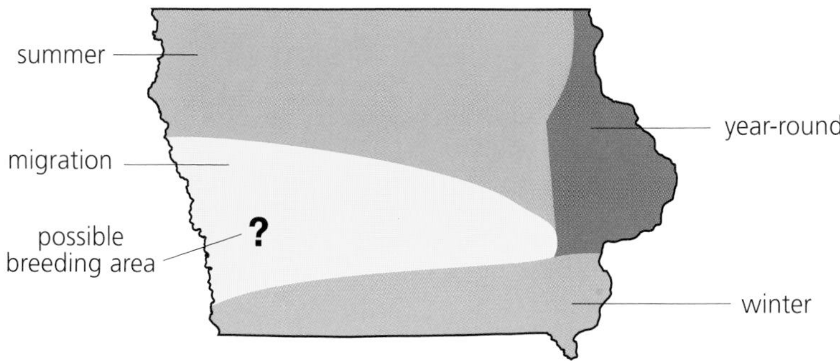

SNOW GOOSE

Chen caerulescens

Over a half million Snow Geese form a great spectacle along the Missouri River drainage during migration. Smaller numbers are seen elsewhere in the state. Landing in farmers' fields, these cackling geese fuel up on waste grain from the previous year's crops. In recent years, the population of Snow Geese has increased dramatically in North America, as they take advantage of human-induced changes in the landscape and in the food supply. • Snow Geese grub for their food, often digging for the parts of plants growing below ground. Their strong, serrated bills are well designed for pulling up the root stalks of marsh plants and gripping slippery grasses. • Unlike Canada Geese, which fly in "V" formations, migrating Snow Geese usually form oscillating, wavy lines. • Until 1983, this bird's two color morphs, white and blue, were considered to be two different species. The scientific name *caerulescens* means "bluish" in Latin and was coined to describe the blue morph.

blue morph

white morph

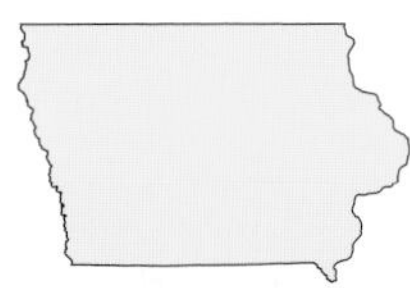

ID: white overall; black wing tips; pink feet and bill; dark "grinning patch" on bill; plumage is occasionally stained rusty red. *Blue morph:* white head and upper neck; dark blue gray body. *Immature:* gray or dusty white plumage; dark bill and feet.

Size: *L* 28–33 in; *W* 4½–5 ft.

Status: abundant migrant along the Missouri R. from early March to mid-April and from November to December; common migrant elsewhere; a few may winter.

Habitat: shallow wetlands, lakes and fields.

Nesting: does not nest in Iowa.

Feeding: grazes on waste grain and new sprouts; also eats aquatic vegetation, grasses, sedges and roots.

Voice: loud, nasal, constant *houk-houk* in flight.

Similar Species: *Ross's Goose:* smaller; shorter neck; lacks black "grinning patch." *Tundra* (p. 22), *Trumpeter* and *Mute swans:* larger; white wing tips. *American White Pelican* (p. 42): much larger bill and body.

Best Sites: Desoto NWR; Forney L.; Riverton WA.

CANADA GOOSE

Branta canadensis

Canada Geese are among the most recognizable birds in our region. Hunted almost to extinction, the "Giant" Canada Goose was once a threatened subspecies, and was reintroduced to Iowa starting in 1964. In recent decades, these large, bold residents have inundated waterfronts, picnic sites, golf courses and city parks. Canada Geese and their various subspecies all migrate through Iowa. Most of the medium-sized subspecies and the recently named Cackling Goose, which is now its own species, are early spring and late fall migrants, only occasionally overwintering in mixed flocks with the resident "Giant." • Canada Goose pairs mate for life and, unlike most birds, the parents do not sever bonds with their young until the beginning of the next year's nesting, almost a year after the young are born, thus increasing the chance of survival for young birds. • Fuzzy goslings seem to compel people, especially children, to get closer. Unfortunately, goose parents can cause harm to unwelcome strangers—hissing sounds and low, outstretched necks are warning signs to look out for.

ID: long, black neck; white "chin strap"; white undertail coverts; light brown underparts; dark brown upperparts; short, black tail.

Size: *L* 37–49 in; *W* 3½–5 ft.

Status: reintroduced; abundant resident.

Habitat: lakeshores, riverbanks, ponds, farmlands, golf courses and city parks.

Nesting: on an island or shoreline; usually on the ground; female builds a nest of plant materials lined with down; female incubates 3–8 white eggs for 25–28 days while the male stands guard.

Feeding: grazes on new sprouts, aquatic vegetation, grass and roots; tips up for aquatic roots and tubers.

Voice: loud, familiar *ah-honk*.

Similar Species: *Cackling Goose:* nearly identical to Canada Goose, but similar to the size of a Mallard. *Greater White-fronted Goose:* brown neck and head; white around base of bill; dark speckling on belly; orange legs; lacks white "chin strap." *Brant:* white "necklace"; black upper breast; lacks white "chin strap." *Snow Goose* (p. 20): blue morph has white head and upper neck. *Double-crested Cormorant* (p. 43): lacks white "chin strap" and undertail coverts; crooked neck in flight.

Best Sites: found statewide in appropriate habitat.

TUNDRA SWAN

Cygnus columbianus

Before the last of the winter's snows have melted, Tundra Swans return to our region, bringing us the first whispers of spring. In fall, thousands gather along the Mississippi River, especially above Lock and Dam #9. • Two other species of swans occur in Iowa. In the 1990s, Trumpeter Swans were released throughout the state and have become locally established. The Mute Swan is found locally; whether these are escaped birds or represent an expansion from the eastern states is debated by birders. Distinguishing between swan species can be made easier by examining the bill: the knobbed orange bill of the Mute Swan is hard to mistake. There is a subtle difference in slope between the bills of the Tundra Swan and the Trumpeter Swan, and the yellow at the base of the Tundra's bill can be more difficult to discern. • In the early 19th century, members of the Lewis and Clark expedition found this bird near the Columbia River, thus its scientific name *columbianus.*

ID: white plumage; large, black bill; black feet; often shows yellow lores; neck is held straight up; upper neck and head have rounded, slightly curving profile. *Immature:* gray brown plumage; gray bill.

Size: *L* 4–5 ft; *W* 6–7 ft.

Status: rare migrant from March to April and from November to December.

Habitat: shallow areas of lakes and wetlands, agricultural fields and flooded pastures.

Nesting: does not nest in Iowa.

Feeding: tips up, dabbles and surface gleans for aquatic vegetation and aquatic invertebrates; grazes for tubers, roots and waste grain.

Voice: high-pitched, quivering *oo-oo-whoo* is constantly repeated by migrating flocks.

Similar Species: *Trumpeter Swan:* larger; loud, buglelike voice; lacks yellow lores; found year-round in marshes and farm ponds. *Mute Swan:* orange bill with black knob on upper base; neck is held in an S-shape with downpointed bill; wings are often held arched over back. *Snow Goose* (p. 20): smaller; black wing tips; shorter neck; pinkish bill. *American White Pelican* (p. 42): large, orange bill; black wing tips.

Best Sites: Upper Mississippi River NWR. *In fall migration:* NE Iowa along Mississippi R.

WOOD DUCK

Aix sponsa

The male Wood Duck is one of the most colorful waterbirds in North America, and books, magazines, postcards and calendars regularly celebrate its beauty. • Truly birds of the forest, Wood Ducks will nest in trees that are a mile or more from the nearest body of water. Newly hatched ducklings often jump 20 feet or more to the ground from their nest cavities to follow their mother. The little bundles of down are not exactly feather light, but miraculously, seldom sustain injury. • Landowners with a tree-lined pond or other suitable wetland may attract a family of Wood Ducks by building a nest box lined with sawdust and equipped with a predator guard. The nest box should be erected close to the wetland shoreline at a reasonable height, usually at least 5 feet from the ground. • The scientific name *sponsa* is Latin for "promised bride," suggesting that the male appears formally dressed for a wedding.

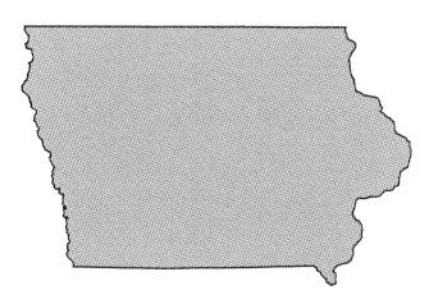

ID: *Male:* glossy, green head with some white streaks; crest is slicked back from crown; white "chin" and throat; white-spotted, purplish chestnut breast; black-and-white shoulder slash; golden sides; dark back and hindquarters. *Female:* white, teardrop-shaped eye patch; mottled brown breast is streaked with white; gray brown upperparts; white belly.

Size: *L* 15–20 in; *W* 30 in.

Status: common migrant and breeder from March to November; rare in winter at pockets of open water.

Habitat: swamps, ponds, marshes, streams and lakeshores with wooded edges.

Nesting: in a hollow, tree cavity or artificial nest box; may be as high as 30 ft up; usually near water; cavity is lined with down; female incubates 9–14 white to buff eggs for 25–35 days.

Feeding: gleans the water's surface and tips up for aquatic vegetation, especially duckweed, aquatic sedges and grasses; eats more fruits and nuts than other ducks.

Voice: *Male:* ascending *ter-wee-wee*. *Female:* squeaky *woo-e-e-k*.

Similar Species: *Hooded Merganser* (p. 33): slim, black bill; black-and-white breast; male has black head with white crest patch. *Harlequin Duck:* rare vagrant; male is blue gray overall with black-and-white patches; female has unstreaked breast and white ear patch.

Best Sites: found statewide in appropriate habitat.

GADWALL

Anas strepera

Male Gadwalls lack the striking plumage of most other male ducks, but they nevertheless have a dignified appearance and a subtle beauty. Once you learn their field marks—a black rump and white wing patches—Gadwalls are surprisingly easy to identify. • Ducks in the genus *Anas*, the dabbling ducks, are most often observed tipping up their hindquarters and submerging their heads to feed, but Gadwalls dive more often than others of this group. These ducks feed equally during the day and night to avoid spending long periods of time sleeping or eating, a strategy that reduces the risk of predation. • Gadwall numbers have greatly increased in this area since the 1950s, and this duck has expanded its range throughout North America. The majority of Gadwalls winter on the Gulf Coast of the United States and Mexico, although increasing numbers overwinter on inland lakes across the country.

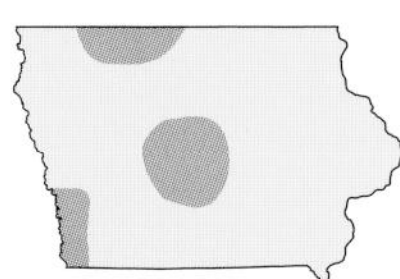

ID: white speculum and belly. *Male:* mostly gray; black hindquarters; dark bill. *Female:* mottled brown; brown bill with orange sides.

Size: *L* 18–22 in; *W* 33 in.

Status: common migrant from mid-March to May and from September to December; uncommon breeder; rare winter visitor.

Habitat: shallow marshes and wetlands, lake borders and beaver ponds.

Nesting: in tall vegetation, sometimes far from water; nest is well concealed in a scraped-out hollow, often with grass arching overhead; nest is made of grass and other dry vegetation and lined with down; female incubates 8–11 white eggs for 24–27 days.

Feeding: dabbles and tips up for aquatic plants; also eats aquatic invertebrates, tadpoles and small fish; grazes on grass and waste grain during migration; one of the few dabblers to dive routinely for food.

Voice: *Male:* simple, singular quack; often whistles harshly. *Female:* high *kaak kaaak kak-kak-kak*, in series and oscillating in volume.

Similar Species: *American Wigeon:* green speculum; white forewing patch; male has white forehead and green swipe trailing from each eye; female has blue or gray bill. *Mallard* (p. 25) and *Northern Pintail* (p. 28): lack white speculum, black hindquarters of male Gadwall and orange sides on female bill.

Best Sites: *Breeding:* Prairie Pothole Region. *In migration:* found statewide. *Winter:* rare in the west.

MALLARD

Anas platyrhynchos

The male Mallard, with his iridescent, green head and chestnut brown breast, is the classic wild duck. Mallards can be seen almost any day of the year, often in flocks and always near open water. These confident birds have even been known to take up residence in local swimming pools. • Wild Mallards will freely mate with domestic ducks, which were originally derived from Mallards in Europe. The resulting offspring, often seen in city parks, are a confusing blend of both parents. • Male Mallards molt after breeding, losing much of their extravagant plumage. This "eclipse" plumage camouflages them during their flightless period, but they are usually wearing their breeding colors again by early fall. • Most people think of the Mallard's quack as the classic duck call, but the female Mallard is one of the only ducks that really "quacks." The scientific name *platyrhynchos* is Greek for "broad, flat bill."

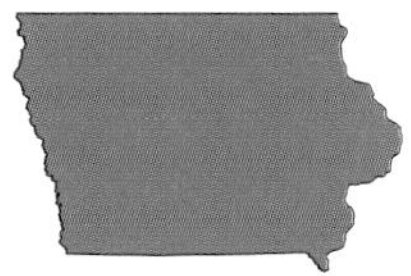

ID: dark blue speculum bordered by white; orange feet. *Male:* glossy, green head; yellow bill; chestnut brown breast; white "necklace"; gray body plumage; black tail feathers curl upward. *Female:* mottled brown overall; orange bill is spattered with black.

Size: *L* 20–27½ in; *W* 35 in.

Status: abundant resident with large concentrations found along the Mississippi R. and below dams of major rivers in winter.

Habitat: lakes, wetlands, rivers, city parks, agricultural areas and sewage lagoons.

Nesting: in tall vegetation or under a bush, often near water; nest of grass and other plant material is lined with down; female incubates 7–10 light green to white eggs for 26–30 days.

Feeding: tips up and dabbles in shallows for the seeds of sedges, willows and pondweeds; also eats insects, aquatic invertebrates, larval amphibians and fish eggs.

Voice: *Male:* deep, quiet quacks. *Female:* loud quacks; very vocal.

Similar Species: *Northern Shoveler* (p. 27): much larger bill; male has white breast. *American Black Duck:* rare; darker than female Mallard with paler head; purple speculum lacks white border. *Common Merganser* (p. 34): blood red bill and white underparts; male lacks chestnut breast.

Best Sites: found statewide in appropriate habitat.

BLUE-WINGED TEAL

Anas discors

The small, speedy Blue-winged Teal is renowned for its aviation skills. This bird's small size and precise, sharp twists and turns in flight make it easier to identify in the field. • Despite the similarity of their names, the Green-winged Teal (*A. crecca*) is not the Blue-winged Teal's closest relative. The Blue-winged Teal is more closely related to the Northern Shoveler and the Cinnamon Teal (*A. cyanoptera*). These birds all have broad, flat bills, pale blue forewings and green speculums. Female Cinnamon Teals and female Blue-winged Teals are so similar in appearance that even expert birders and ornithologists have difficulty distinguishing them. • Blue-winged Teals migrate farther than most ducks, summering as far north as the Canadian tundra and wintering mainly in Central and South America. • The scientific name *discors* is Latin for "without harmony," which might refer to this bird's call as it takes flight, or to its contrasting plumage.

ID: *Male:* blue gray head; white crescent on face; darker bill than female; black-spotted breast and sides. *Female:* mottled brown overall; white throat. *In flight:* blue forewing patch; green speculum.

Size: *L* 14–16 in; *W* 23 in.

Status: common migrant and breeder throughout, from mid-March to mid-October; a few remain in early winter.

Habitat: shallow lake edges and wetlands; prefers areas of short but dense emergent vegetation.

Nesting: in grass along a shoreline or in a meadow; nest is built with grass and a lot of down; female incubates 8–13 white eggs, sometimes tinged with olive, for 23–27 days.

Feeding: gleans the water's surface for sedge and grass seeds, pondweeds, duckweeds and aquatic invertebrates.

Voice: *Male:* soft *keck-keck-keck*. *Female:* soft quacks.

Similar Species: *Green-winged Teal:* female has smaller bill, black-and-green speculum and lacks blue forewing patch. *Northern Shoveler* (p. 27): much larger bill with paler base; male has green head and lacks spotting on body. *Cinnamon Teal:* rare; female is virtually identical to female Blue-winged Teal, but brown is richer and eye line is less distinct.

Best Sites: *Breeding:* Prairie Pothole Region. *In migration:* widespread in appropriate habitat.

NORTHERN SHOVELER

Anas clypeata

The initial reaction upon seeing this bird for the first time is often, "Wow, look at the big bill on that Mallard!", but a closer look will reveal a completely different bird altogether. The Northern Shoveler has an extra large, spoonlike bill that allows it to strain small invertebrates from the water and from the bottoms of ponds. This handsome duck, though a dabbler, is rarely seen tipping up, and is usually spotted in the shallows of ponds and marshes where the mucky bottom is easiest to access. It eats much smaller organisms than do most other waterfowl, and its intestines are elongated to prolong the digestion of the hard-bodied invertebrates in its diet. • The scientific name *clypeata*, Latin for "furnished with a shield," possibly refers to the chestnut patches on the flanks of the male. This species was once placed in its own genus, *Spatula*, the meaning of which needs no explanation.

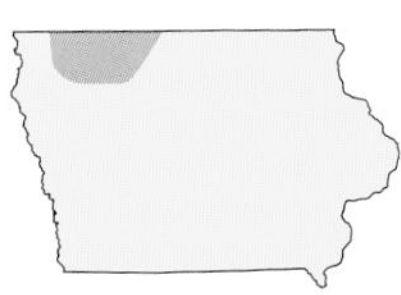

ID: large, spatulate bill; blue forewing patch; green speculum. *Male:* green head; yellow eyes; white breast; chestnut brown flanks. *Female:* mottled brown overall; orange-tinged bill.
Size: *L* 18–20 in; *W* 30 in.
Status: common migrant from March to May and from September through October; uncommon breeder; occasionally winters.
Habitat: shallow marshes, bogs and lakes with muddy bottoms and emergent vegetation, usually in open and semi-open areas.
Nesting: in a shallow hollow on dry ground, usually within 150 ft of water; female builds a nest of dry grass and down and incubates 10–12 pale greenish buff eggs for 21–28 days.
Feeding: dabbles in shallow and often muddy water; strains out plant and animal matter, especially aquatic crustaceans, insect larvae and seeds; rarely tips up.
Voice: generally quiet; occasionally a raspy chuckle or quack, most often heard during spring courtship.
Similar Species: *Mallard* (p. 25): male has chestnut brown breast and white flanks; lacks pale blue forewing patch; blue speculum bordered by white. *Blue-winged Teal* (p. 26): much smaller bill; smaller overall; male has spotted breast and sides.
Best Sites: *Breeding:* Prairie Pothole Region. *In migration:* widespread in appropriate habitat.

NORTHERN PINTAIL

Anas acuta

The trademark of the elegant and graceful male Northern Pintail is its long, tapering tail feathers, which are easily seen in flight and point skyward when the bird dabbles. In our area, only the rare male Long-tailed Duck shares this feature. • Migrating Northern Pintails are often seen in flocks of 20 to 40 birds, but in early spring, flooded agricultural fields attract the largest flocks, with up to 10,000 individuals. Northern Pintails breed earlier than most waterfowl, and in the United States they begin nesting in mid-April. • The Pintail, as well as other ducks and wetland birds, has benefited recently from habitat restoration by public and private organizations throughout the state of Iowa.

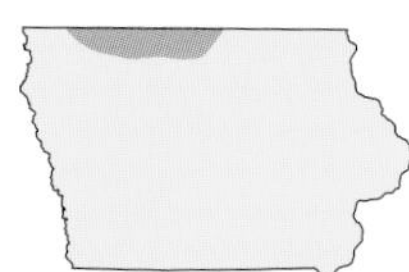

ID: long, slender neck; dark, glossy bill. *Male:* chocolate brown head; long, tapering tail feathers; white of breast extends up sides of neck; dusty gray body plumage; black-and-white hindquarters. *Female:* mottled light brown overall. *In flight:* slender body; brownish speculum with white trailing edge.

Size: *L* 21–25 in; *W* 34 in.

Status: common migrant from early March through mid-April and from early October through mid-December; uncommon breeder; occasionally winters.

Habitat: shallow wetlands, fields and lake edges.

Nesting: in a small depression in low vegetation; nest of grass, leaves and moss is lined with down; female incubates 6–12 greenish buff eggs for 22–25 days.

Feeding: tips up in shallows for the seeds of sedges, willows and pondweeds; also eats aquatic invertebrates and larval amphibians; eats waste grain in agricultural areas during migration; diet is more varied than that of other dabbling ducks.

Voice: *Male:* soft, whistling call. *Female:* rough quack.

Similar Species: male is distinctive. *Mallard* (p. 25) and *Gadwall* (p. 24): females are chunkier, usually have dark or 2-tone bills and lack tapering tail and long, slender neck. *Blue-winged Teal* (p. 26): green speculum; blue forewing patch; female is smaller. *Long-tailed Duck:* rare; head is not uniformly dark; all-dark wings.

Best Sites: *Breeding:* Prairie Pothole Region. *In migration:* Riverton WA; Desoto NWR; Forney L.; Ruthven WA. *Winter:* found in the west.

CANVASBACK

Aythya valisineria

Most male ducks sport richly decorated backs, but that of the male Canvasback is bright and clean, and appropriately appears to be wrapped in white canvas. In profile, the Canvasback casts a noble image—the long bill meets the forecrown with no apparent break in angle, allowing birds of either sex to be distinguished at long range. This bird's back and unique profile are unmistakable field marks. • Canvasbacks are diving ducks that are typically found on large areas of open water. Because these birds prefer large lakes and bays and the deepest areas of wetlands, birders often need binoculars to admire the male's wild red eyes and mahogany head. Over 100,000 stage at Pool 19 on the Mississippi River in migration. • The scientific name *valisineria* refers to one of the Canvasback's favorite foods, wild celery (*Vallisneria americana*).

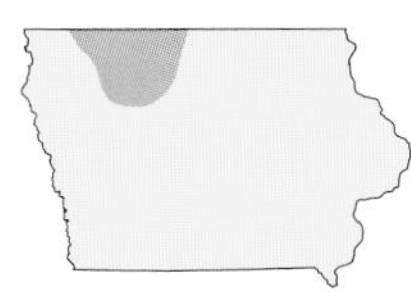

ID: head slopes upward from bill to forehead. *Male:* white back and sides; chestnut brown head; black breast and hindquarters; red eyes. *Female:* profile is similar to male; head and neck are duller brown; gray back and sides.
Size: *L* 19–22 in; *W* 29 in.
Status: uncommon migrant, although abundant at some locations along the Mississippi R.; winters along the Mississippi in varying numbers depending upon availability of open water.
Habitat: marshes, ponds, shallow lakes and other wetlands; large lakes in migration.
Nesting: basket nest of reeds and grass is lined with down and suspended above shallow water in dense stands of cattails and bulrushes; may also nest on dry ground; female incubates 7–9 olive green eggs for up to 29 days.
Feeding: dives to depths of up to 30 ft (average is 10–15 ft); feeds on roots, tubers, the basal stems of plants, including pondweeds, wild celery and bulrush seeds; occasionally eats aquatic invertebrates.
Voice: generally quiet. *Male:* occasional coos and "growls" during courtship. *Female:* low, soft, "purring" quack or *kuck;* also "growls."
Similar Species: *Redhead:* rounded rather than sloped forehead; male has gray back and bluish bill.
Best Sites: *Breeding:* Prairie Pothole Region. *In migration:* found statewide. *Late fall* and *winter:* Pool 19 of Mississippi R.

RING-NECKED DUCK

Aythya collaris

The Ring-necked Duck's distinctive white bill markings and angular head are field marks that immediately strike an observer. After seeing the Ring-necked Duck in the wild, you may wonder why it was not named the "Ring-billed Duck." This bird's name is derived from the scientific name *collaris* (collar), which originated when an ornithologist identified an indistinct cinnamon collar on a museum specimen. • Ring-necked Ducks are generalized feeders and are able to sustain themselves even when resources are low on their common subarctic and boreal nesting grounds. Although Ring-necks are diving ducks, they often behave more like dabbling ducks, frequently tipping up for food, hiding their young in dense vegetation and taking flight directly from the water's surface.

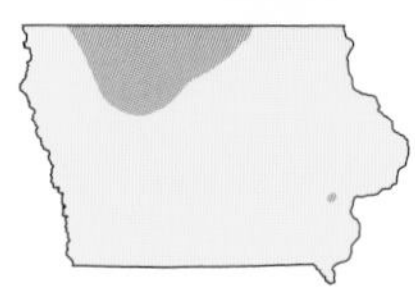

ID: *Male:* angular, dark purple head; black breast, back and hindquarters; white shoulder slash; gray sides; blue gray bill with black-and-white bands at tip; thin, white border around base of bill. *Female:* dark brown overall; white eye ring; dark bill with black-and-white bands at tip; pale crescent on front of face.

Size: *L* 14–18 in; *W* 25 in.

Status: common migrant across the state, most common from early March through April and in October and November; rare breeder; occasional winter resident.

Habitat: reservoirs, shallow wooded ponds, swamps, marshes and sloughs with emergent vegetation.

Nesting: on a floating island or hummock; frequently over water; rarely on a shoreline; bulky nest of grass and moss is lined with down; female incubates 8–10 olive tan eggs for 25–29 days.

Feeding: dives underwater for aquatic vegetation, including seeds, tubers and pondweed leaves; also eats aquatic invertebrates and mollusks.

Voice: seldom heard. *Male:* low-pitched, hissing whistle. *Female:* growling *churr*.

Similar Species: *Lesser Scaup* (p. 31) and *Greater Scaup:* lack white ring near tip of bill; male lacks black back; female has broad, clearly defined white border around base of bill and lacks eye ring. *Redhead:* rounded rather than peaked head; less white on front of face; female has less prominent eye ring.

Best Sites: *Breeding:* Prairie Pothole Region. *In migration:* farm ponds and lakes. *Winter:* along the Mississippi R.

LESSER SCAUP

Aythya affinis

The male Lesser Scaup and its close relative, the Greater Scaup (*A. marila*), mirror the color pattern of an Oreo cookie: they are black at both ends and pale-colored in the middle. Although Greater Scaup and Lesser Scaup may occur together on larger lakes during migration, they tend not to mingle. • The Lesser Scaup is most at home on the lakes of forested areas, but can also be found nesting in marshes. • A member of the *Aythya* genus of diving ducks, the Lesser Scaup leaps up gracefully before diving underwater, where it propels itself with the powerful strokes of its feet. • The scientific name *affinis* is Latin for "adjacent" or "allied"—a reference to this scaup's close association to other diving ducks. "Scaup" may refer to a preferred winter food of this duck—shellfish beds are called "scalps" in Scotland—or it might be a phonetic imitation of one of its calls. • Both the Lesser Scaup and the Greater Scaup are known by the nickname "Bluebill."

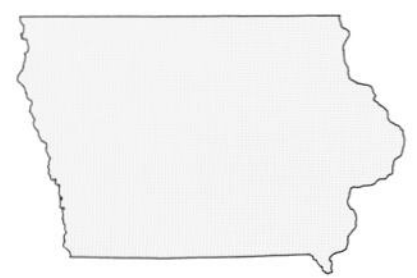

ID: yellow eyes. *Male:* purplish black head; black breast and hindquarters; dusty white sides; grayish back; black-tipped, blue gray bill. *Female:* dark brown overall; well-defined white patch at base of bill.

Size: *L* 15–18 in; *W* 25 in.

Status: abundant migrant from mid-March to mid-April and from mid-October to late November; occasionally winters.

Habitat: lakes, farm ponds, reservoirs, large marshes and rivers.

Nesting: does not nest in Iowa.

Feeding: dives for aquatic invertebrates, mostly mollusks, amphipods and insect larvae; occasionally eats aquatic vegetation.

Voice: alarm call is a deep *scaup. Male:* soft *whee-oooh* in courtship. *Female:* purring *kwah.*

Similar Species: *Greater Scaup:* rounded head; slightly larger bill; longer, white wing flash; male's head is greenish black. *Ring-necked Duck* (p. 30): male has white shoulder slash and black back; female has white-ringed bill. *Redhead:* female has less white at base of bill; male has red head and darker sides. *Canvasback* (p. 29): male has reddish head and uniformly whitish back; female lacks white at base of long sloping bill.

Best Sites: found statewide, especially at Mississippi R. pools.

BUFFLEHEAD

Bucephala albeola

Buffleheads are frequently among the first diving ducks identified by those with a growing awareness of wild waterfowl. They are boldly patterned, resembling few other species on park ponds and urban reservoirs where they are normally abundant. • The great white patch on the rear of the male's head is his most striking feature. Females are somber but appealing, their sooty heads ornamented with a pretty white "cheek" spot. • In migration and winter, the Bufflehead dives for its meals, and if you are lucky, you may catch the entertaining sight of a whole flock diving at once. • The scientific name *Bucephala*, meaning "ox-headed" in Greek, refers to the shape of this bird's head; *albeola* is Latin for "white," a reference to the male's plumage.

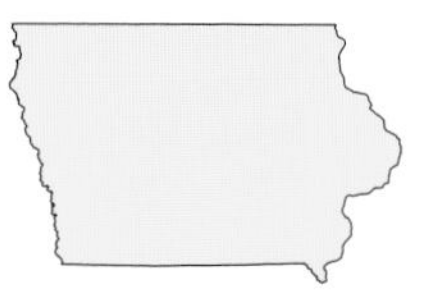

ID: very small, rounded duck; short neck; short, gray bill; white speculum in flight. *Male:* white wedge on back of head; head is otherwise iridescent, dark green or purple, usually appearing black; dark back; white neck and underparts. *Female:* dark brown head; white, oval ear patch; light brown sides.
Size: *L* 13–15 in; *W* 21 in.
Status: common migrant from mid-March to late April and from mid-October to mid-November; a few may winter on open water.
Habitat: open water of lakes, large ponds and rivers.
Nesting: does not nest in Iowa.
Feeding: dives for aquatic invertebrates; takes water boatmen and mayfly and damselfly larvae in summer; favors mollusks, particularly snails, and crustaceans in winter; also eats some small fish and pondweeds.
Voice: *Male:* growling call. *Female:* harsh quack.
Similar Species: *Hooded Merganser* (p. 33): white crest is outlined in black. *Common Goldeneye* and *Barrow's Goldeneye:* males are larger and have white patch between eye and bill. *Other diving ducks* (pp. 29–31): females are much larger. *Harlequin Duck:* rare vagrant; female has several light-colored spots on head.
Best Sites: found statewide in appropriate habitat.

HOODED MERGANSER

Lophodytes cucullatus

Extremely attractive and exceptionally shy, the Hooded Merganser is one of the most sought after ducks from a birder's perspective. • Most of the time the brilliantly colored crest of the male Hooded Merganser is held flat, but he does not hesitate to unfold it when it comes time to attract a mate or signal approaching danger. The drake displays his full range of colors and athletic abilities in elaborate, late-winter courtship displays and chases. It is important that he put on an impressive show because there are usually twice as many males as there are females. • All mergansers have thin bills with small, toothlike serrations to help them keep a firm grasp on slippery prey. The smallest of the mergansers, Hoodies have a more diverse diet than their larger relatives. • Hooded Mergansers first breed at two years of age. Females lay spherically shaped eggs with unusually thick shells.

ID: slim body; crested head; dark, thin, pointed bill. *Male:* black head and back; bold, white crest outlined in black; white breast with 2 black slashes; rusty sides. *Female:* dusky brown body; shaggy, reddish brown crest. *In flight:* small, white wing patches.
Size: *L* 16–18 in; *W* 24 in.
Status: uncommon migrant in April and October through November; uncommon breeder; occasionally winters.
Habitat: wetlands, lakes and rivers. *Breeding:* ponds on woodland edges.
Nesting: usually in a tree cavity 15–40 ft high; may also use nest boxes; cavity is lined with leaves, grass and down; female incubates 10–12 spherical, white eggs for 29–33 days; some females may lay their eggs in other birds' nests, including the nests of other species.
Feeding: very diverse diet; dives for small fish, caddisfly and dragonfly larvae, snails, amphibians and crayfish; also eats acorns.
Voice: low grunts and croaks. *Male:* frog-like *crrrrooo* in courtship display. *Female:* generally quiet; occasionally a harsh *gak* or a croaking *croo-croo-crook.*
Similar Species: *Bufflehead* (p. 32): male lacks black breast and shoulder slashes and black outline around white head crest. *Red-breasted Merganser* and *Common Merganser* (p. 34): females have much longer, orange bill and gray back. *Other diving ducks* (pp. 29–31): females lack crest.
Best Sites: *Breeding:* along the Mississippi R. *In migration:* found statewide.

COMMON MERGANSER

Mergus merganser

Takeoff for flight appears to take great effort for the large Common Merganser as it lumbers along the surface of the water, beating its wings until it gains sufficient speed to become airborne. Once up and away, this great duck flies arrow-straight, low over the water, making broad sweeping turns to follow meandering rivers and lake shorelines. • The Common Merganser is highly social, and often gathers in large groups in winter and during migration. In winter, any source of open water with a fish-filled shoal will support many of these skilled divers. • Common Mergansers breed among forest-edged waterways wherever there are cool, clear and unpolluted lakes and rivers. They are cavity nesters, but will forfeit a suitable cavity and nest on the ground in areas with good fishing. • The Common Merganser is the most widespread and abundant merganser in North America. It also occurs in Europe and Asia, where it is called the "Goosander."

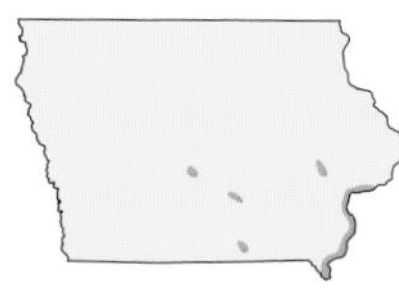

ID: large, elongated body. *Male:* glossy, green head without crest; blood red bill and feet; white body plumage; black stripe on back; dark eyes. *Female:* rusty neck and crested head; clean white "chin" and breast; orange bill; gray body; orangish eyes. *In flight:* shallow wingbeats; body is compressed and arrowlike.
Size: *L* 22–27 in; *W* 34 in.
Status: common migrant and winter resident from November through May.
Habitat: large rivers and deep lakes.
Nesting: does not nest in Iowa.
Feeding: dives to depths of 30 ft for small fish, usually whitefish, trout, suckers, perch and minnows; young eat aquatic invertebrates and insects.
Voice: *Male:* harsh *uig-a,* like a guitar twang. *Female:* harsh *karr karr.*
Similar Species: *Red-breasted Merganser:* male has shaggy, green crest and spotted, red breast; female lacks clean white throat. *Common Loon* (p. 39): dark bill; white-spotted back. *Mallard* (p. 25): male has chestnut brown breast and yellow bill. *Common Goldeneye:* male has white "cheek" patch and stubby, dark bill.
Best Sites: Saylorville; Red Rock; Coralville; Rathbun; Mississippi R.

RUDDY DUCK

Oxyura jamaicensis

The clown of the wetlands, the male Ruddy Duck displays energetic courtship behavior with comedic enthusiasm. The small male vigorously pumps his bright blue bill, almost touching his breast. The *plap, plap, plap-plap-plap* of the display increases in speed to its hilarious climax: a spasmodic jerk and sputter. • Female Ruddies lay up to 10 eggs at a time—a remarkable feat considering that their eggs are bigger than those of a Mallard, and that a Mallard is significantly larger than a Ruddy Duck. Females take part in an unusual practice of dumping some of their eggs into a communal "dummy" nest, which gathers as many as 60 eggs that will receive no motherly care. • Some people might imagine birding paradise as a deep, lush green forest or a dense, marshy wetland, but birders searching for Ruddy Ducks might find a sewage lagoon a worthwhile place to visit.

breeding

breeding

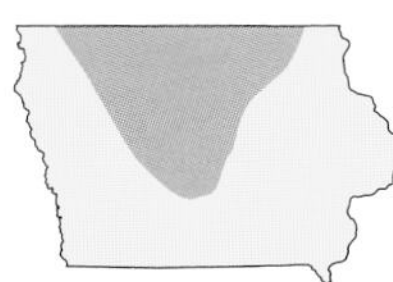

ID: large bill and head; short neck; long, stiff tail feathers (often held upward). *Breeding male:* white "cheek"; chestnut red body; blue bill; black tail and crown. *Female:* brown overall; dark "cheek" stripe; darker crown and back. *Nonbreeding male:* similar to female, but with white "cheek."
Size: *L* 15–16 in; *W* 18½ in.
Status: common migrant with peaks in April and November; uncommon breeder.
Habitat: *Breeding:* shallow marshes with dense emergent vegetation and muddy bottoms. *In migration* and *winter:* sewage lagoons and lakes with open, shallow water.
Nesting: in cattails, bulrushes or other emergent vegetation; female suspends a woven platform nest over water; may use an abandoned duck or coot nest, muskrat lodge or exposed log; female incubates 5–10 rough, whitish eggs for 23–26 days; occasional brood parasite.
Feeding: dives for seeds of pondweeds, sedges, bulrushes and the leafy parts of aquatic plants; also eats a few aquatic invertebrates.
Voice: *Male: chuck-chuck-chuck-chur-r-r-r* during courtship display. *Female:* generally silent.
Similar Species: *Cinnamon Teal:* rare; lacks white "cheek" and blue bill. *Other diving ducks* (pp. 29–31): females lack long, stiff tail and dark facial stripe.
Best Sites: *Breeding:* Prairie Pothole Region; expanding breeding range southward. *In migration:* found statewide on any significant body of water.

RING-NECKED PHEASANT

Phasianus colchicus

A native of Asia, the spectacular Ring-necked Pheasant was introduced to Iowa in 1900 when a number of them escaped from game farms and hunting preserves. Cold snowy winters can be a problem for the pheasant but the availability of grain and corn crops, as well as hedgerows and sheltering woodlots, allows it to survive harsher temperatures. • Birders hear this bird more often than they see it, and the male's loud *ka-squawk* call is recognizable near farms, woodlots and brushy suburban parks. • Ring-necked Pheasants are not very strong long-distance fliers, but are swift runners and are able to fly in explosive bursts over small open areas to escape predators.

ID: large gamebird; unfeathered legs; long, barred tail. *Male:* green head; naked, red face patch; white "collar"; bronze underparts. *Female:* mottled brown overall; light underparts.

Size: *Male: L* 20–36 in; *W* 31 in (male is larger than female).

Status: introduced, abundant resident.

Habitat: *Breeding:* grasslands, grassy ditches, hayfields and fencelines, crop margins and woodland margins. *In fall and winter:* grain and corn fields, woodlands, cattail marshes and shrubby areas.

Nesting: on the ground, among grass or sparse vegetation or next to a log or other natural debris; in a slight depression lined with grass and leaves; female incubates 10–12 olive buff eggs for 23–28 days; male takes no part in parental duties.

Feeding: gleans the ground and vegetation for weed seeds, grains and insects in summer; eats mostly seeds, corn kernels and buds in winter.

Voice: *Male:* loud, raspy, roosterlike crowing: *ka-squawk;* whirring of wings, mostly just before sunrise.

Similar Species: male is distinctive. *Greater Prairie Chicken:* barred body; short, rounded tail. *Ruffed Grouse:* found in woodlands; smaller; rounded tail with dark terminal band.

Best Sites: rural areas statewide.

WILD TURKEY

Meleagris gallopavo

Wild Turkeys once occurred across Iowa, but habitat loss and overharvesting took a toll on these birds before they were extirpated in the early 1900s. Reintroduction of this species began in the 1960s and the Wild Turkey can again be found throughout the state. • Turkeys can run faster than 19 miles per hour and, although they prefer to feed on the ground and to travel by foot, they roost in trees at night and are able to fly short distances. • This charismatic bird is the only native North American animal that has been widely domesticated. The wild ancestors of chickens, pigs, cows, horses, sheep and most other domestic animals all came from Europe, Asia or Africa. In their natural habitat, Wild Turkeys are wary birds with acute senses and a highly developed social system.

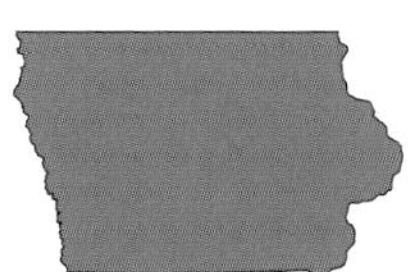

ID: naked, red blue head; dark, glossy, iridescent body plumage; barred, copper-colored tail; mostly unfeathered legs. *Male:* long, central breast tassel; colorful head and body; red wattles. *Female:* smaller; blue gray head; less iridescent body.
Size: *Male: L* 46 in; *W* 64 in. *Female: L* 37 in; *W* 50 in.
Status: common resident.
Habitat: deciduous, mixed and riparian woodlands; field edges; occasionally uses grain and corn crops in late fall and winter.
Nesting: in a depression on the ground under thick cover; nest is lined with grass and leaves; female incubates 10–12 speckled, pale buff eggs for up to 28 days.
Feeding: forages on the ground for seeds, fruits, bulbs and sedges; also eats insects, especially beetles and grasshoppers; may take small amphibians.
Voice: wide array of sounds; courting male gobbles loudly; alarm call is a loud *pert;* gathering call is a *cluck;* contact call is a loud *keouk-keouk-keouk*.
Similar Species: all other grouse and grouselike birds are much smaller. *Ring-necked Pheasant* (p. 36): feathered head and neck; long, narrow tail.
Best Sites: found statewide, especially in the northeast and in the south.

NORTHERN BOBWHITE

Colinus virginianus

Throughout fall and winter, Northern Bobwhites typically travel in large family groups called "coveys," collectively seeking out sources of food and huddling together during cold nights. When they huddle, members of the covey all face outward, enabling the group to detect danger from any direction. With the arrival of summer, breeding pairs break away from their coveys to perform elaborate courtship rituals in preparation for another nesting season. • The male's characteristic, whistled *bob-white* call, usually issued in spring, is often the only evidence of this bird's presence among the dense, tangled vegetation of its rural, woodland home. • Bobwhites benefit from habitat disturbance, using the early successional habitats created by fire, agriculture and forestry. Their population in Iowa fluctuates, based in part on the severity of winters. • The Northern Bobwhite is the only native quail in eastern North America.

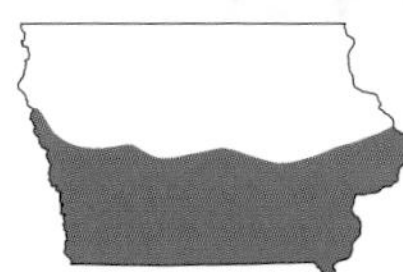

ID: mottled brown, buff and black upperparts; white crescents and spots edged in black on chestnut brown sides and upper breast; short tail. *Male:* white throat; broad, white "eyebrow." *Female:* buff throat and "eyebrow." *Immature:* smaller and duller overall; lacks black on underparts.

Size: *L* 10 in; *W* 13 in.

Status: locally common resident in the south; rare in the north.

Habitat: farmlands, open woodlands, woodland edges, grassy fencelines, roadside ditches and brushy, open country.

Nesting: in a shallow depression on the ground, often concealed by surrounding vegetation or a woven, partial dome; nest is lined with grass and leaves; pair incubates 12–16 white to pale buff eggs for 22–24 days.

Feeding: eats seasonally available seeds, berries, leaves, roots and nuts; also takes insects and other invertebrates.

Voice: whistled *hoy* is given year-round. *Male:* whistled, rising *bob-white* in spring and summer.

Similar Species: *Gray Partridge:* introduced; gray breast; chestnut on face. *Ring-necked Pheasant* (p. 36): much larger; females have pointed tails. *Greater Prairie Chicken:* larger; barred above and below.

Best Sites: Kellerton Grasslands; Medicine Creek; L. Rathbun.

COMMON LOON

Gavia immer

The quavering wail of the Common Loon pierces the stillness of quiet nights, its haunting call alerting cottagers that summer has begun. Loons float very low on the water, disappearing behind swells, then reappearing like ethereal guardians of the lakes. • Common Loons are well adapted to their aquatic lifestyle. These divers have nearly solid bones that make them less buoyant (most birds have hollow bones), and their feet are placed close to the back of their bodies for efficient underwater propulsion. Small bass, perch, sunfish, pike and whitefish are all fair game for these excellent underwater hunters. On land, however, their rear-placed legs make walking seem difficult, and with heavy bodies and small wings, they require a lengthy sprint along the water's surface before taking off. • It is thought that "loon" is derived from the Scandinavian word *lom*, meaning "clumsy person," in reference to this bird's awkward, clumsy appearance on land.

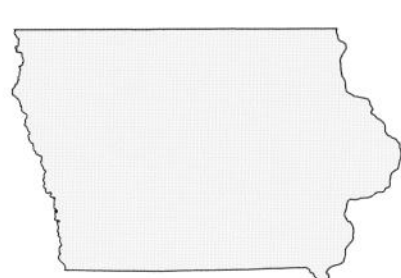

ID: *Breeding:* green black head; stout, thick, black bill; white "necklace"; black-and-white "checkerboard" upperparts; white breast and underparts; red eyes. *Nonbreeding:* much duller plumage; sandy brown back; light underparts. *In flight:* long wings beat constantly; hunchbacked appearance; legs trail behind tail.

Size: *L* 28–35 in; *W* 4–5 ft.

Status: common migrant, primarily in April and October to November; nonbreeders occasionally spend the summer; very rare in early winter.

Habitat: large lakes and reservoirs with open water.

Nesting: does not nest in Iowa.

Feeding: pursues small fish underwater to depths of 180 ft; occasionally eats large, aquatic invertebrates and larval and adult amphibians.

Voice: alarm call is a quavering tremolo, often called "loon laughter"; contact call is a long note *where aaare you?;* breeding notes are soft, short hoots; male territorial call is an undulating, complex yodel.

Similar Species: *Red-throated Loon:* smaller; slender bill; red throat in breeding plumage; defined white face and white-spotted back in nonbreeding plumage. *Pacific Loon:* smaller; dusty gray head often looks silver; dark "cap" extends down over eye and is lighter than back in nonbreeding plumage. *Double-crested Cormorant* (p. 43): uniformly blackish color with pale or orange throat patch; hooked bill usually held slightly upturned.

Best Sites: Spirit L.; Saylorville; Red Rock; Coralville; L. Rathbun.

PIED-BILLED GREBE

Podilymbus podiceps

The odd, exuberant chortle of the Pied-billed Grebe fits right in with the boisterous cacophony of our state's wetland communities. Heard more frequently than seen, the Pied-billed Grebe is the smallest, shyest and least colorful of our grebes. • It is an extremely wary bird and is far more common than encounters would lead you to believe. It swims inconspicuously in shallow waters of quiet bays and rivers, and can submerge its head so that only its nostrils and eyes remain above water. The floating nests of Pied-billed Grebes are placed among sparse vegetation so that predators can be seen approaching from far away. When frightened by an intruder, these birds cover their eggs and slide underwater, leaving behind a nest that looks like nothing more than a mat of debris. • The scientific name *podiceps,* which means "rump foot," refers to the way the bird's feet are located near the back of its body.

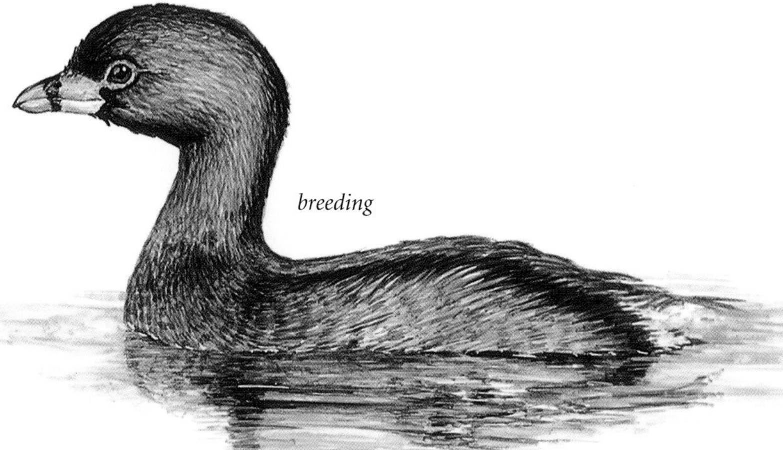

breeding

ID: *Breeding:* all-brown body; pale eye ring; black ring on pale bill; laterally compressed "chicken bill"; black throat; very short tail; white undertail coverts; pale belly. *Nonbreeding:* yellow eye ring; all-yellow bill; white "chin" and throat; brownish crown.

Size: *L* 12–15 in; *W* 16 in.

Status: common migrant from mid-March to mid-May and from mid-September to mid-November; fairly common summer resident; very rare in winter near open water.

Habitat: ponds, marshes, sheltered bays and backwaters with sparse emergent vegetation.

Nesting: floating platform nest, made of wet and decaying plants, is anchored to or placed among emergent vegetation; pair incubates 4–5 white to buff eggs for about 23 days and raises the striped young together.

Feeding: makes shallow dives and gleans the water's surface for aquatic invertebrates, small fish and adult and larval amphibians; occasionally eats aquatic plants.

Voice: loud, whooping call begins quickly, then slows down: *kuk-kuk-kuk cow cow cow cowp cowp cowp.*

Similar Species: *Eared Grebe:* red eyes; black-and-white head; golden "ear" tufts and chestnut flanks in breeding plumage; seldom seen in summer, but has breeding records. *Horned Grebe:* very rare in summer; red eyes; black-and-white head; golden "ear" tufts and red neck in breeding plumage. *American Coot* (p. 60): all-black body; pale bill extends onto forehead.

Best Sites: found statewide in appropriate habitat.

WESTERN GREBE

Aechmophorus occidentalis

The courtship displays of the Western Grebe are among the most elaborate and beautiful rituals seen in the bird world. During the "weed dance," the male and female swim with their torsos and heads held high, caressing each other with aquatic vegetation held in their bills. The "rushing" display, which Western Grebes are most famous for, involves two or more individuals exploding into a paddling sprint side by side across the water's surface. The grebes stand high, feet paddling furiously, with their wings stretched back and heads and necks held rigid, until the race ends with the pair breaking the water's surface in a graceful, headfirst dive. • Like most grebes, the eggs of this bird hatch at regular intervals. Parental duties are often divided, with each parent feeding half the fledged young. • Unlike its red-necked relative, the Western Grebe seems unable to adjust to the disturbances created by cottagers and recreationalists. Many lakes that once supported nesting colonies have been turned into vacation resorts.

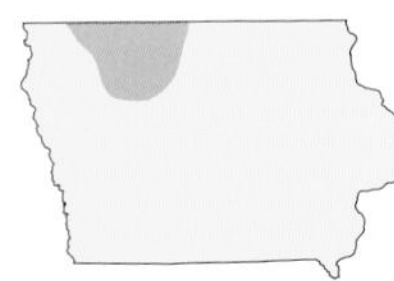

ID: long, thin, yellow bill; white "cheek"; black on face extends below red eyes; long, slender neck; black upperparts from base of bill to tail; white underparts from "chin" to belly.

Size: *L* 20–24 in; *W* 24 in.

Status: rare in migration from late April to mid-May and from mid-October to late November; very rare in summer, but has bred in northern Iowa.

Habitat: marshes with emergent vegetation.

Nesting: usually in colonies; floating nest of fresh and decaying vegetation is anchored or placed among emergent vegetation; pair incubates 2–7 bluish green to buffy eggs, often stained brown, for about 23 days.

Feeding: gleans the water's surface and dives for small fish, some amphibians and aquatic invertebrates.

Voice: high-pitched, double-note *crreeet-crreeet;* call sounds like a squeaky wheel when repeated in series.

Similar Species: *Clark's Grebe:* very similar; white of face extends above eyes; orange yellow bill; single-note call. *Double-crested Cormorant* (p. 43): immature has thicker neck, longer tail and yellow orange throat patch. *Red-necked Grebe:* shorter, stockier neck; dark eyes; darker sides and neck in nonbreeding plumage. *Loons* (p. 39): larger; shorter, thicker neck; heavier bill.

Best Sites: *Breeding:* Prairie Pothole Region. *In migration:* found statewide on large lakes.

AMERICAN WHITE PELICAN

Pelecanus erythrorhynchos

Pelicans are a majestic wetland presence with a wingspan only a foot shy of the height of a basketball hoop. Groups of foraging pelicans deliberately herd fish into schools, then dip their bills and scoop up their prey. Their porous, bucketlike bills are dramatically adapted for feeding. As the pelican lifts its bill from the water, the fish are held inside its flexible pouch while the water drains out. In a single scoop, a pelican can hold over 3 gallons of water and fish, which is about two to three times as much as its stomach can hold. American White Pelicans eat about 4 pounds of fish per day, but because they prefer nongame fish they do not pose a threat to the potential catches of fishermen. • The American White Pelican is the only large, white bird with black wing tips in the state that flies with its neck pulled back toward its wings.

nonbreeding

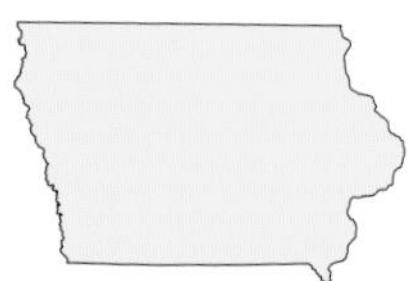

ID: very large, stocky, white bird; long, orange bill and throat pouch; black primary and secondary wing feathers; short tail; naked, orange skin patch around eye. *Breeding:* small, keeled plate develops on upper mandible; pale yellow crest on back of head. *Nonbreeding* and *immature:* white plumage is tinged brown.

Size: *L* 4½–6 ft; *W* 9 ft.

Status: common migrant, especially in March and September; a few nonbreeders spend the summer and a few are found on Christmas bird counts in December.

Habitat: large lakes or rivers.

Nesting: does not nest in Iowa.

Feeding: surface dips for small fish and amphibians; small groups of pelicans often feed cooperatively by herding fish.

Voice: generally quiet; adults rarely issue piglike grunts.

Similar Species: no other large, white bird has a long bill with a pouch. *Whooping Crane:* rare vagrant; long legs and neck extend in flight.

Best Sites: Saylorville; Red Rock; Coralville.

DOUBLE-CRESTED CORMORANT

Phalacrocorax auritus

The Double-crested Cormorant's beauty can take longer to appreciate than that of other birds. This slick-feathered bird often appears disheveled, and extra-close encounters typically reveal the foul stench of fish oil. Nevertheless, the Double-crested Cormorant's mastery of its aquatic environment is virtually unsurpassed. It is without oil glands, and therefore, lacks waterproof feathers. This adaptation helps the bird during underwater dives by decreasing its buoyancy. Instead of floating on the water after a bout of diving, the Double-crested Cormorant is often seen perched in a tree with its wings partially spread in an attempt to dry its feathers. The cormorant's long, rudderlike tail, excellent underwater vision and sealed nostrils also contribute to the success of its aquatic lifestyle. • Double-crested Cormorants are often found in the company of American White Pelicans during migration, and among colonies of terns and gulls during nesting.

juvenile

breeding

ID: all-black body; long, crooked neck; thin bill, hooked at tip; blue eyes. *Breeding:* throat pouch becomes intense orange yellow; fine, black plumes trail from "eyebrows." *Immature:* buff throat and breast; yellowish throat patch; brown upperparts. *In flight:* rapid wingbeats; kinked neck.

Size: *L* 26–32 in; *W* 4½ ft.

Status: common migrant in April and May and from mid-September through mid-November; rare summer resident; very rare in winter.

Habitat: large lakes and meandering rivers.

Nesting: colonial; on the ground on a low-lying island or high in a tree; nest platform is made of sticks, aquatic vegetation and guano; pair incubates 3–6 bluish white eggs for 25–33 days; young are fed by regurgitation.

Feeding: dives to depths of 30 ft or more when chasing small schooling fish or, rarely, amphibians and invertebrates.

Voice: generally quiet; may issue piglike grunts or croaks, especially near nesting colonies.

Similar Species: *Canada Goose* (p. 21): white "cheek"; brown overall. *Loons* (p. 39): straight bill; thicker neck; lacks throat patch.

Best Sites: *Breeding:* Mississippi R.; Coralville. *In migration:* found statewide. *Winter:* Mississippi R.

AMERICAN BITTERN

Botaurus lentiginosus

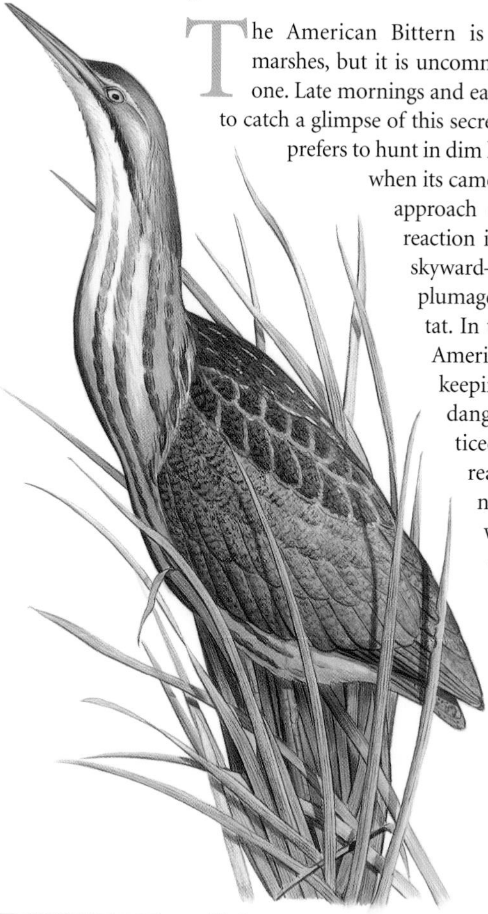

The American Bittern is common around productive marshes, but it is uncommon or even rare to actually see one. Late mornings and early afternoons are the best times to catch a glimpse of this secretive bird. The American Bittern prefers to hunt in dim light situations, at dawn or dusk, when its camouflage is most effective. • At the approach of an intruder, a bittern's first reaction is to freeze with its bill pointed skyward—its vertically streaked, brown plumage blends perfectly with its habitat. In the presence of an intruder, the American Bittern always moves slowly, keeping its camouflaged breast facing danger. Most times it will go unnoticed, but sometimes this defensive reaction can result in an unfortunate comical turn for the bittern when it tries to mimic a reed, even in an entirely open field.

nonbreeding

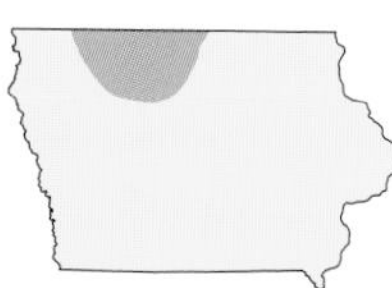

ID: brown upperparts; brown streaking from "chin" through breast; black streaks from bill down neck to shoulder; straight, stout bill; yellow legs and feet; black outer wings; short tail.

Size: *L* 23–27 in; *W* 3½ ft.

Status: uncommon migrant and breeder from April through November.

Habitat: marshes, wetlands and lake edges with tall, dense grass, sedges, bulrushes and cattails.

Nesting: singly; above the waterline in dense vegetation; nest platform is made of grass, sedges and dead reeds; nest often has separate entrance and exit paths; female incubates 3–5 pale olive or buff eggs for 24–28 days.

Feeding: patient stand-and-wait predator; strikes at small fish, crayfish, amphibians, reptiles, mammals and insects.

Voice: deep, slow, resonant, repetitive *pomp-er-lunk* or *onk-a-BLONK;* most often heard in the evening or at night.

Similar Species: *Black-crowned Night-Heron* (p. 48) and *Yellow-crowned Night-Heron:* immatures lack dark streak from bill to shoulder and have white-flecked upperparts. *Least Bittern:* much smaller; pale wing patch.

Best Sites: found statewide, but more common in Prairie Pothole Region.

GREAT BLUE HERON

Ardea herodias

The sight of an elegant Great Blue Heron is always memorable, whether you are observing its stealthy, patient hunting strategy or tracking its graceful wingbeats. The Great Blue Heron nests in large treetop colonies, known as rookeries, which are sensitive to human disturbance, so it is best to observe this bird's behavior from a distance. • This heron is often mistaken for a crane, but instead of holding its neck outstretched in flight, the Great Blue folds its neck back over its shoulders in an S-shape. • Though mostly a fish eater, this bird may also be found stalking fields and meadows in search of rodents.

breeding

ID: large, blue gray bird; long, curving neck; long, dark legs; blue gray back and wing coverts; straight, yellow bill; chestnut brown thighs. *Breeding:* richer colors; plumes streak from crown and throat. *In flight:* neck folds back over shoulders; legs trail behind body; slow, steady wingbeats.

Size: *L* 4–4½ ft; *W* 6 ft.

Status: common migrant and breeder, primarily from mid-March through mid-October; rare in winter.

Habitat: forages along edges of rivers, lakes, marshes, fields and wet meadows.

Nesting: colonial; usually in a tree, but occasionally on the ground; stick-and-twig platform nest is added to over years; can be up to 4 ft in diameter; pair incubates 4–7 pale blue eggs for about 28 days.

Feeding: patient stand-and-wait predator; strikes at small fish, amphibians, small mammals, aquatic invertebrates and reptiles; rarely scavenges.

Voice: usually quiet away from the nest; occasionally a deep, harsh *frahnk frahnk frahnk,* usually during takeoff.

Similar Species: *Green Heron, Black-crowned Night-Heron* (p. 48) and *Yellow-crowned Night-Heron:* much smaller; shorter legs. *Great* (p. 46), *Snowy* and *Cattle egrets:* all are predominantly white. *Sandhill Crane* (p. 61): red "cap"; flies with neck outstretched. *Little Blue Heron:* smaller; dark with purplish head; lacks yellow on bill. *Tricolored Heron:* smaller; darker upperparts; white underparts.

Best Sites: found statewide in appropriate habitat.

GREAT EGRET

Ardea alba

The plumes of the Great Egret and Snowy Egret were highly sought after in the early 20th century, used to decorate hats. An ounce of egret feathers cost as much as $32—more than an ounce of gold at that time—and, as a result, egret populations began to disappear. Some of the first conservation legislation in North America was enacted to outlaw the hunting of Great Egrets. • Egrets are actually herons, but were given their name for their impressive breeding plumes, referred to as "aigrettes." • The Great Egret is the symbol for the National Audubon Society, one of the oldest conservation organizations in the United States.

nonbreeding

breeding

ID: all-white plumage; yellow bill; black legs. *Breeding:* green skin patch between eyes and base of bill; white plumes trail from throat and rump. *In flight:* neck folds back over shoulders; legs extend backward.

Size: *L* 3–3½ ft; *W* 4 ft.

Status: uncommon to common migrant and occasional breeder from early April to October; most common in post-breeding stage from July through September.

Habitat: marshes, open riverbanks, irrigation canals, shallow waters of large reservoirs and lakeshores.

Nesting: colonial, but may nest in isolated pairs; in a tree or tall shrub; pair builds a platform of sticks and incubates 3–5 pale blue green eggs for 23–26 days.

Feeding: patient stand-and-wait predator; occasionally stalks; stabs at frogs, lizards, snakes and small mammals.

Voice: rapid, low-pitched, loud *cuk-cuk-cuk*.

Similar Species: *Snowy Egret:* rare; smaller; black bill; yellow feet. *Cattle Egret:* rare; smaller; stockier; orange bill and legs. *Whooping Crane:* rare vagrant; much larger; red crown; black-and-red "mask"; black primaries. *Little Blue Heron:* immature has 2-tone bill and greenish legs.

Best Sites: found statewide in appropriate habitat. *Breeding*: Mississippi R.

GREEN HERON

Butorides virescens

This crow-sized heron is far less conspicuous than its Great Blue cousin. The Green Heron eats primarily small fish and prefers to hunt in shallow, weedy wetlands, where it often perches just above the water's surface. Occasionally, while hunting, it will craftily drop small debris, including twigs, vegetation and feathers, onto the water as a form of bait, attracting fish into striking range. • If the light is just right, you may catch a glimmer of green reflect off the back and outer wings of this bird. • Unlike most herons, Green Herons generally nest singly rather than communally, though they can sometimes be found in loose colonies. • The scientific name *virescens* is Latin for "growing or becoming green," and refers to this bird's transition from a streaky, brown juvenile to a greenish adult.

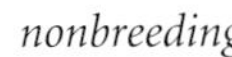

nonbreeding

ID: stocky; green black crown; chestnut brown face and neck; bill is dark above and greenish below; white foreneck and belly; iridescent, green and blue gray back and wings; relatively short, yellow green legs; short tail. *Breeding male:* bright orange legs. *Immature:* heavy streaking along neck and underparts; dark brown upperparts.

Size: *L* 15–22 in; *W* 26 in.

Status: uncommon, but regular migrant and breeder from early May to September.

Habitat: freshwater marshes, lakes and streams with dense shoreline or emergent vegetation.

Nesting: nests singly or in small, loose groups; male begins and female completes construction of a stick platform in a tree or shrub, usually very close to water; pair incubates 3–5 pale blue green to green eggs for 19–21 days; young are fed by regurgitation.

Feeding: stand-and-wait or stalking predator; stabs prey with its bill; eats small fish, frogs, tadpoles, crayfish, aquatic and terrestrial insects, small rodents, snakes, snails and worms.

Voice: alarm and flight call are a loud *kowp, kyow* or *skow;* aggression call is a harsh *raah;* frequently silent until startled.

Similar Species: *Black-crowned Night-Heron* (p. 48): larger; white "cheek"; pale gray and white neck; 2 long, white plumes trail down from crown; immature has streaked face and white flecking on upperparts. *Least Bittern:* smaller; buffy yellow shoulder patches, sides and flanks. *American Bittern* (p. 44): larger; more brown overall; black streak from bill to shoulder.

Best Sites: found statewide in appropriate habitat.

BLACK-CROWNED NIGHT-HERON

Nycticorax nycticorax

When the setting sun has sent most wetland waders to their nightly roosts, Black-crowned Night-Herons are just arriving to hunt the marshy waters and voice their hoarse squawks. These herons patrol the shallows for prey, which can be spotted in the dim light with their large, light-sensitive eyes. They remain alongside water until morning, and then flap off to treetop roosts. • During the breeding season or in cloudy weather, the Black-crowned Night-Heron sometimes forages during the day. A popular hunting strategy for day-active birds is to sit motionless atop a few bent cattails to wait for any passing prey, including ducklings, small shorebirds and young muskrats. • Young night-herons are commonly seen around large cattail marshes in fall, but because of their heavily streaked underparts, they are easily confused with other immature herons and American Bitterns. • *Nycticorax*, meaning "night raven," refers to this bird's distinctive nighttime calls.

immature

breeding

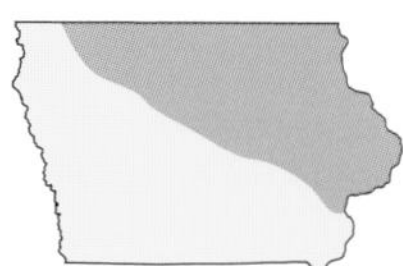

ID: black "cap" and back; white "cheek," foreneck and underparts; gray neck and wings; dull yellow legs; stout, black bill; large, red eyes. *Breeding:* 2 white plumes trail down from crown. *Immature:* lightly streaked underparts; brown upperparts with white flecking.

Size: *L* 23–26 in; *W* 3½ ft.

Status: uncommon migrant from mid-April through mid-May; rare breeder, departing by October; occasionally found during Christmas bird counts.

Habitat: shallow cattail and bulrush marshes, lakeshores and along slow rivers.

Nesting: colonial, often with Great Blue Herons and Great Egrets; in a tree or shrub; male gathers the nest material; female builds a loose nest platform of twigs and sticks and lines it with finer materials; pair incubates 3–4 pale green eggs for 21–26 days.

Feeding: often at dusk; patient stand-and-wait predator; stabs for small fish, amphibians, aquatic invertebrates, reptiles, young birds and small mammals.

Voice: deep, guttural *quark* or *wok,* often heard as the bird takes flight.

Similar Species: *Yellow-crowned Night-Heron:* rare; white plumes; white crown and "cheek" patch on otherwise black head; gray back; immature is very similar to Black-crowned immature. *American Bittern* (p. 44): similar to immature Black-crowned Night-Heron, but bittern has black streak from bill to shoulder and is lighter brown overall. *Green Heron* (p. 47): chestnut brown face and neck; iridescent, green and blue gray back; immature has heavily streaked underparts. *Great Blue Heron* (p. 45): much larger; longer legs and neck.

Best Sites: marshes in the Prairie Pothole Region.

TURKEY VULTURE

Cathartes aura

Turkey Vultures are unmatched in their ability to use updrafts and thermals to patrol the skies. • The Turkey Vulture eats carrion almost exclusively—its bill and feet are not nearly as powerful as those of eagles, hawks and falcons, which kill live prey. Its red, featherless head may appear grotesque, but this adaptation allows it to remain relatively clean while feeding on messy carcasses. • Vultures seem to have mastered the art of regurgitation. This seemingly vulgar habit enables parents to transport food over long distances to their young and also helps engorged birds to repulse an attacker or "lighten up" for an emergency takeoff. • Recent studies have shown that vultures are most closely related to storks, not to hawks and falcons as was previously thought. Molecular similarities with storks, and the shared tendency to defecate on their own legs to cool down, strongly support this taxonomic reclassification.

ID: all black; bare, red head. *Immature:* gray head. *In flight:* head appears small; wings 2-tone with silver gray flight feathers; black wing linings; wings are held in a shallow "V"; rocks from side-to-side when soaring.

Size: *L* 26–32 in; *W* 5½–6 ft.

Status: common migrant and breeder from mid-March to mid-October.

Habitat: usually seen flying over open country, shorelines or roads; rarely seen over forested areas.

Nesting: in a cave crevice or among boulders; sometimes in a hollow stump or log; no nest material is used; female lays 2 dull white eggs, spotted with reddish brown, on bare ground; pair incubates the eggs for up to 41 days; young are fed by regurgitation.

Feeding: carrion.

Voice: generally silent; occasionally produces a hiss or grunt if threatened.

Similar Species: *Golden Eagle* and *Bald Eagle* (p. 51): lack silvery gray wing linings; wings are held flat in flight; do not rock when soaring; head is more visible in flight. *Black Vulture*: rare vagrant; gray head; black wings with white or silvery patches near tip.

Best Sites: found statewide.

OSPREY

Pandion haliaetus

The Osprey is the only species in its family found on every continent except Antarctica. • Most fish-eating birds land on water and dive for their food like cormorants, or enter the water headfirst like gannets. The Osprey takes the middle ground—it hovers above the water, then folds its wings and hurls itself in a perilous headfirst dive toward a flash of silver or a slowly moving shadow. An instant before striking, the Osprey rights itself and thrusts its feet forward to grasp its prey, sometimes disappearing beneath the surface. • The Osprey's feet are specialized to prevent its squirming catch from making an escape. Two toes face forward and two face backward, all equipped with spines to help the Osprey clamp tightly onto the most slippery of fish.

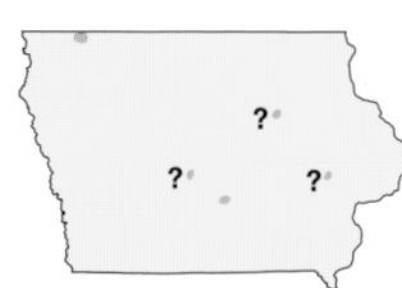

ID: dark brown upperparts; white underparts; dark eye line; light crown; yellow eyes. *Male:* all-white throat. *Female:* fine, dark "necklace." *In flight:* long wings are held in shallow "M"; dark "wrist" patches; brown-and-white banded tail.

Size: *L* 22–25 in; *W* 4½–6 ft.

Status: fairly common migrant from mid-April to mid-May and in September and October; a few remain in summer; Iowa DNR has been releasing Ospreys in an attempt to establish a breeding population.

Habitat: lakes, large reservoirs and slow-flowing rivers and streams.

Nesting: on a treetop, usually near water; may also use a specially made platform, utility pole or tower up to 100 ft high; massive stick nest is reused over many years; pair incubates 2–4 yellowish eggs, spotted with reddish brown, for about 38 days; both adults feed the young, but the male hunts more.

Feeding: dives for fish.

Voice: series of melodious ascending whistles: *chewk-chewk-chewk;* also a frequent *kip-kip-kip*.

Similar Species: *Bald Eagle* (p. 51): larger; holds its wings straighter while soaring; larger bill with yellow base; yellow legs; clean white head and tail on otherwise dark body; lacks white underparts and dark "wrist" patches. *Rough-legged Hawk* (p. 56): winter visitor; smaller; hovers with wings in an open "V"; light phase has whitish wing linings and light tail band.

Best Sites: releases near Waterloo, Spirit L., Saylorville, Red Rock and Coralville.

BALD EAGLE

Haliaeetus leucocephalus

The Bald Eagle is a source of inspiration and wonder for anyone longing for a wilderness experience. Though it cannot compete with the image of the Golden Eagle, or its talon strength, legends endow the Bald Eagle with a mystical quality. • Bald Eagles feed mostly on fish and scavenged carrion. Sometimes an eagle will steal food from an Osprey, resulting in a spectacular aerial chase. • Pairs perform dramatic displays, flying to great heights, locking talons and tumbling perilously toward the ground. • Bald Eagles do not mature until their fourth or fifth year, only then receiving their characteristic white head and tail plumage. • These raptors generally mate for life. They renew their pair bonds each year by adding new sticks and branches to their massive nests, the largest of any North American bird.

immature

ID: dark brown body; white head and tail; yellow bill and feet; broad wings are held flat in flight. *1st-year:* dark overall; dark bill; some white in underwings. *2nd-year:* dark "bib"; white in underwings. *3rd-year:* mostly white plumage; yellow at base of bill; yellow eyes. *4th-year:* variably light and dark plumage; light head with dark facial streak; yellow bill; paler eyes. *In flight:* broad wings are held flat.

Size: *L* 30–43 in; *W* 5½–8 ft.

Status: endangered; locally common to abundant migrant and winter resident; rare breeder, mainly in the eastern half of the state.

Habitat: large lakes and rivers.

Nesting: usually in a tree bordering a lake or large river, but may be far from water; huge stick nest, up to 15 ft across, is often reused for many years; pair incubates 1–3 white eggs for 34–36 days; pair feeds the young.

Feeding: eats waterbirds, small mammals and fish captured at water's surface; frequently feeds on carrion; sometimes pirates from Ospreys.

Voice: thin, weak squeal or gull-like cackle: *kleek-kik-kik-kik* or *kah-kah-kah.*

Similar Species: adult is distinctive. *Osprey* (p. 50): like a 4th-year Bald Eagle, but has dark "wrist" patches, dark bill, and M-shaped wings in flight. *Golden Eagle:* dark overall, except for golden nape; tail may appear faintly banded with white; immature has prominent white patch on wings and at base of tail.

Best Sites: *Breeding:* mainly in the eastern half of the state. *Winter:* Mississippi R.; Red Rock; Saylorville; Desoto NWR.

NORTHERN HARRIER

Circus cyaneus

The Northern Harrier may be the easiest raptor to identify on the wing because no other midsized hawk routinely flies so close to the ground. It cruises low over fields, meadows and marshes, grazing the tops of long grasses and cattails, relying on sudden surprise attacks to capture its prey. Its owl-like, parabolic facial disc also helps it to hunt by reflecting sound. • The Northern Harrier was once known as the "Marsh Hawk" in North America, and it is still called "Hen Harrier" in Europe. Britain's Royal Air Force was so impressed by this bird's maneuverability that it named its Harrier aircraft after this bird. • The courtship flight of the Northern Harrier is a spring event worth seeing. The pale-colored male climbs almost vertically into the sky and then stalls, sending himself into a reckless dive toward solid ground. At the last second he catches himself and heads skyward again. • This bird has declined in numbers, owing to a loss of habitat, and is an endangered breeder in Iowa.

♀

♂

ID: white rump; black wing tips; long wings and tail. *Male:* blue gray to silver gray upperparts; white underparts; indistinct tail bands, except for 1 dark subterminal band. *Female:* dark brown upperparts; streaky brown-and-buff underparts. *Immature:* rich reddish brown plumage; streaked breast, sides and flanks; dark tail bands.

Size: *L* 16–24 in; *W* 3½–4 ft.

Status: endangered; fairly common migrant from mid-March to mid-April and from mid-September through October; occasionally breeds; a few are present in winter.

Habitat: open country, including fields, wet meadows, cattail marshes, bogs and croplands.

Nesting: on the ground, often slightly raised on a mound; usually in grass, cattails or tall vegetation; shallow depression or platform nest is lined with grass, sticks and cattails; female incubates 4–6 bluish white eggs for 30–32 days.

Feeding: hunts in low, rising and falling flights; eats small mammals, birds, amphibians, reptiles and some invertebrates.

Voice: most vocal near the nest and during courtship, but generally quiet; high-pitched *ke-ke-ke-ke-ke-ke* near the nest.

Similar Species: *Rough-legged Hawk* (p. 56): broader wings; dark "wrist" patches; black tail with wide, white base; dark belly. *Red-tailed Hawk* (p. 55): lacks white rump and long, narrow tail. *Short-eared Owl:* same habitat; broad, rounded wings; mothlike flight.

Best Sites: Medicine Creek; Union Hills BCA; Kellerton BCA.

COOPER'S HAWK

Accipiter cooperii

The Cooper's Hawk glides silently along forest clearings, using surprise and speed to snatch its prey from midair. Females have the size and build of male Goshawks and can seize and decapitate birds as large as Ruffed Grouse, which they sometimes pursue on the ground like overweight roadrunners. • It is a challenge distinguishing the Cooper's Hawk from the smaller Sharp-shinned Hawk, which is a rare nester and common migrant in Iowa. The Cooper's has a shallower, stiffer-winged flight and the Sharpie has deeper strokes with more bend in the wings. Also, Sharp-shins have a square tail and the Cooper's is more rounded. • This forest hawk bears the name of William Cooper, one of the many hunters who supplied English and American ornithologists with bird specimens for museum collections during the early 19th century.

immature

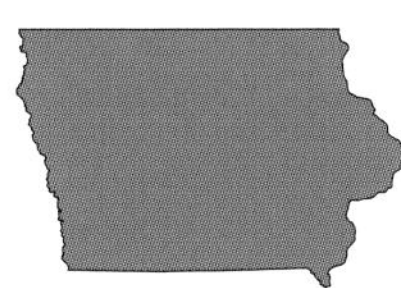

ID: squarish head; red eyes; blue gray back; red horizontal barring on underparts; short, rounded wings; long, straight, heavily barred, rounded tail; dark barring on pale undertail and underwings; white terminal tail band. *Immature:* brown overall; dark eyes; vertical brown streaks on breast and belly. *In flight:* flap-and-glide flier.

Size: *Male: L* 15–17 in; *W* 27–32 in. *Female: L* 17–19 in; *W* 32–37 in.

Status: year-round resident; more common in migration from late March through early May and in September and October; increasingly common breeder.

Habitat: mixed woodlands, riparian woodlands and woodlots; visits feeders.

Nesting: nest of sticks and twigs is built in the crotch of a deciduous or coniferous tree, often near a stream or pond; might reuse an abandoned crow's nest; female incubates 3–5 bluish white eggs for 34–36 days; male feeds the female during incubation.

Feeding: pursues prey in flight; eats mostly songbirds, squirrels and chipmunks; uses plucking post.

Voice: fast, woodpecker-like *cac-cac-cac-cac.*

Similar Species: *Sharp-shinned Hawk:* smaller; tail often square; thinner terminal tail band. *Goshawk:* rare winter visitor; larger; pearly gray plumage. *American Kestrel* (p. 57): smaller; 1 dark "tear streak"; 1 dark "sideburn"; long, pointed wings; open country habitat.

Best Sites: found statewide in appropriate habitat.

BROAD-WINGED HAWK

Buteo platypterus

The generally shy and secretive Broad-winged Hawk prefers different habitat than most other buteos. It shuns the open fields and forest clearings favored by the Red-tailed Hawk, secluding itself instead in dense, often wet forests. Its short, broad wings and highly flexible tail help it to maneuver in heavy growth. • Most hunting is done from a high perch with a good view. The Broad-winged Hawk may be so attached to its perch that it will return to it after being flushed and resume its vigilant search for a meal. • At the end of the nesting season, "kettles" of buteos and other hawks spiral upward from their forest retreats, testing thermals for the opportunity to head south. Broad-winged Hawks are often the most numerous species in these flocks. When cool temperatures, moderate winds and sunny skies prevail, large concentrations of these birds, numbering in the tens of thousands, can sometimes be seen, especially in the eastern half of the state.

light morph

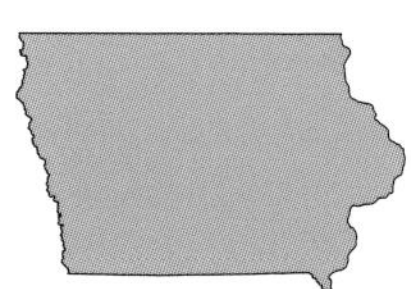

ID: heavily barred, rufous brown breast; dark brown upperparts; broad, black-and-white tail bands; broad wings with pointed tips. *Immature:* dark brown streaks on white breast, belly and sides; buff and dark brown tail bands. *In flight:* pale underwings are outlined with dark brown.

Size: *L* 14–19 in; *W* 32–39 in.

Status: high conservation priority; common migrant from mid-April to early May and in September.

Habitat: *Breeding:* dense mixed and deciduous forests and large woodlands. *In migration:* escarpments and shorelines; riparian and deciduous forests and woodland edges.

Nesting: usually in a deciduous tree, often near water; bulky stick nest is built 20–40 ft above the ground; usually builds a new nest each year; mostly the female incubates 2–4 brown-spotted, whitish eggs for 28–31 days; both adults raise the young.

Feeding: swoops from a perch for small mammals, amphibians, insects and young birds; often seen hunting from roadside telephone poles.

Voice: high-pitched, whistled *peeeo-wee-ee;* generally silent during migration.

Similar Species: *Red-shouldered Hawk:* dark bands on tail wider than light bands; reddish "shoulder" patch hard to see. *Other buteos* (pp. 54–56): lack multiple bands on tail and dark-edged wings. *Accipiters* (p. 53): long, narrow tails with less distinct banding.

Best Sites: *Breeding:* Effigy Mounds/Yellow River Forest; Ledges SP; Stephen's SF. *In migration:* Effigy Mounds; Grammer Grove and Hitchcock NA hawk watches.

RED-TAILED HAWK

Buteo jamaicensis

dark morph

immature

The Red-tailed Hawk is the most commonly seen hawk in many areas of North America. It is conspicuous year-round, particularly near agricultural lands. An afternoon drive through the country will reveal resident Red-tails perching on exposed tree limbs, fence posts or utility poles overlooking open fields and roadsides. • During their spring courtship, excited Red-tailed Hawks dive at each other, sometimes locking talons and tumbling through the air together before breaking away to avoid crashing to the ground. • The Red-tailed Hawk's impressive piercing call is often paired with the image of an eagle in TV commercials and movies. • This hawk's tail does not obtain its brick red coloration until the bird matures into a breeding adult. • Several subspecies occur in Iowa in winter, including the very dark "Harlan's" Hawk, which may have a whitish tail and the pale-colored "Krider's."

ID: dark upperparts with some white highlights; dark brown band of streaks across belly; red tail. *Immature:* extremely variable, generally darker; band of streaks on belly; lacks red tail. *In flight:* fan-shaped tail; white or occasionally tawny brown underside and underwing linings; dark leading edge on underside of wing; light underwing flight feathers with faint barring.

Size: *Male: L* 18–23 in; *W* 4–5 ft. *Female: L* 20–25 in; *W* 4–5 ft.

Status: common year-round; more common in migration in March and from late September through October.

Habitat: open country with some trees; also roadsides, interstate medians, fields, woodlots, hedgerows, mixed forests and moist woodlands.

Nesting: in woodlands adjacent to open habitat; usually in a deciduous tree; rarely on a cliff or in a conifer; bulky stick nest is usually added to each year; pair incubates 2–4 brown-blotched, whitish eggs for 28–35 days; male feeds female and young.

Feeding: scans for food while perched or soaring; rarely stalks prey on foot; eats voles, mice, rabbits, chipmunks, birds, amphibians and reptiles; rarely takes large insects.

Voice: powerful, descending scream: *keeearrrr*.

Similar Species: *Rough-legged Hawk* (p. 56): dark "wrist" patches on underwings; white tail base; broad, dark, terminal tail band. *Broad-winged Hawk* (p. 54) and *Red-shouldered Hawk:* smaller; banded tails. *Swainson's Hawk:* all-dark back; more pointed wing tips; dark flight feathers and pale wing linings in flight; holds wings in shallow "V."

Best Sites: found statewide in appropriate habitat.

ROUGH-LEGGED HAWK

Buteo lagopus

The number of Rough-legged Hawks found in our state varies with the rising and falling population densities of voles and northern lemmings. When vole and lemming numbers are high, Rough-legs can produce up to seven young, but in lean years a pair is fortunate to raise a single chick. • During a hunt, the Rough-legged Hawk often "wind-hovers" while scanning the ground below, only occasionally flapping to maintain a stationary position while facing upwind. • In the far north where it breeds, this hawk usually requires an elevated nest site on a high cliff ledge, crevice or boulder pile, but will often settle on a tower or an abandoned radar station. • The name *lagopus*, meaning "hare's foot," refers to this bird's distinctive feathered legs, which are an adaptation for survival in cold climates.

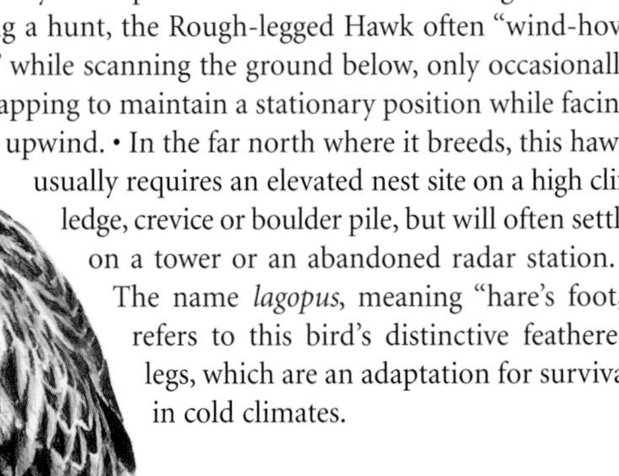

♀

light morph

♂

dark morph

ID: dark brown upperparts; light flight feathers; legs are feathered to the toes; white tail base with a wide, dark subterminal band. *Light morph:* wide, dark abdominal "belt"; darkly streaked breast and head; dark "wrist" patches; light underwing linings. *Dark morph:* dark wing linings, head and underparts. *Immature:* lighter streaking on breast; bold belly band; buff leg feathers. *In flight:* dark "wrist" patches; frequently hovers.

Size: *L* 19–24 in; *W* 4–4¾ ft.

Status: uncommon, regular winter resident from October to late March.

Habitat: *Breeding:* coastal tundra; requires an elevated natural or artificial ledge for nesting. *In migration* and *winter:* tundra, fields, meadows, open bogs and agricultural croplands.

Nesting: does not nest in Iowa.

Feeding: soars and hovers while searching for prey; primarily eats small rodents; occasionally eats birds, amphibians and large insects.

Voice: alarm call is a catlike *kee-eer,* usually dropping at the end.

Similar Species: *Other buteos* (pp. 54–56): adults lack dark "wrist" patches and white base on tail. *Northern Harrier* (p. 52): facial disc; lacks dark "wrist" patches and dark belly band; longer, thinner tail lacks broad, dark subterminal band. *Osprey* (p. 50): summer visitor; usually hovers over water.

Best Sites: found statewide, but especially in the north.

AMERICAN KESTREL

Falco sparverius

The American Kestrel is the smallest and most common of our falcons. It hunts from telephone wire and fence post perches, and is a familiar sight in Iowa. • Studies have shown that the Eurasian Kestrel can detect ultraviolet reflections from rodent urine on the ground. It is unknown if the American Kestrel has this same ability, but it is frequently seen hovering above the ground while looking for small, ground-dwelling prey. • The American Kestrel repeatedly lifts its tail while perched, a helpful identification tip when viewing this bird from afar. • This bird was formerly named the "Sparrow Hawk"—its scientific name *sparverius* means "pertaining to a sparrow."

ID: 2 distinctive facial stripes. *Male:* rusty back; blue gray wings; blue gray crown with rusty "cap"; lightly spotted underparts. *Female:* rusty back, wings and breast streaking. *In flight:* frequently hovers; long, rusty tail; buoyant, indirect flight style.

Size: *L* 7½–8 in; *W* 20–24 in.

Status: common year-round; abundant in migration from mid-March to early April and from mid-September to early October; common breeder.

Habitat: open fields, riparian woodlands, woodlots, forest edges, bogs, roadside ditches, grassy highway medians, grasslands and croplands; nest boxes along highways.

Nesting: in a tree cavity or abandoned woodpecker or flicker cavity; may use a nest box; mostly the female incubates 4–6 white to pale brown eggs, spotted with brown and gray, for 29–30 days; both adults raise the young.

Feeding: swoops from a perch (a tree, fenceline, post, road sign or powerline) or from hovering flight; eats mostly insects and some small rodents, birds, reptiles and amphibians.

Voice: loud, often repeated, shrill *killy-killy-killy* when excited; female's voice is lower pitched.

Similar Species: *Merlin:* 1 facial stripe; less colorful; does not hover; flight is more powerful and direct. *Sharp-shinned Hawk:* reddish barring on underparts; short, rounded wings; lacks facial stripes; flap-and-glide flight. *Mourning Dove* (p. 77): brown overall; small head; pointed tail.

Best Sites: found statewide in appropriate habitat.

PEREGRINE FALCON

Falco peregrinus

No bird elicits more admiration than a hunting Peregrine Falcon in full flight, and nothing causes more panic in a tightly packed flock of ducks or shorebirds. Every twist and turn of the group is matched by the falcon until it finds a weaker or less-experienced bird. Diving at speeds of up to 220 miles per hour, the Peregrine clenches its feet and then strikes its prey with a lethal blow that often sends both falcon and prey tumbling. • The Peregrine Falcon's awesome speed and hunting skills were, however, little defense against the pesticide, DDT. Contaminated birds lay eggs with thin shells that were easily broken during incubation, and this bird was extirpated in Iowa by the late 1960s. DDT was banned in North America in 1972 and, in the late 1980s, the Midwest Peregrine Falcon Restoration program introduced Peregrine Falcons into cities throughout the Midwest, including Des Moines and Cedar Rapids. • Historically, Peregrine Falcons nested along the Mississippi River bluffs in Iowa, and they have been found nesting on every continent except Antarctica.

ID: prominent, dark "helmet"; blue gray back; light underparts with fine, dark spotting and flecking. *Immature:* brown back; heavier breast streaks; gray feet and cere. *In flight:* pointed wings; long, narrow, dark-banded tail.

Size: *Male: L* 15–17 in; *W* 3–3½ ft. *Female: L* 17–19 in; *W* 3½–4 ft.

Status: endangered; reintroduced, rare resident; more common in migration.

Habitat: lakeshores, river valleys, river mouths, urban areas and open fields. *In migration:* wetlands.

Nesting: rocky cliffs or outcroppings, building ledges or rooftops; nest consists of prey remains, leaves and grass; nest site is often reused; mostly the female incubates 3–4 creamy to buff eggs, heavily blotched with reddish brown, for 32–34 days.

Feeding: high-speed, diving stoops; strikes birds with clenched feet in midair; eats primarily pigeons, waterfowl, shorebirds, flickers and larger songbirds; rarely eats small mammals or carrion; prey is consumed on a nearby perch.

Voice: loud, harsh, continuous *cack-cack-cack-cack-cack* near the nest site.

Similar Species: *Gyrfalcon:* larger; longer tail; lacks dark "helmet." *Merlin:* smaller; heavily streaked breast and belly; lacks prominent, dark "helmet." *Prairie Falcon:* rare vagrant; light brown; dark "armpits."

Best Sites: downtown areas of cities, such as Council Bluffs, Des Moines, Cedar Rapids and Davenport.

SORA

Porzana carolina

The secretive Sora, like most rails, is seldom seen, even though it is the most common and widespread rail in North America. Its elusive habits and preference for dense marshlands force most birders to settle for only a glimpse at this small bird. On occasion, the Sora has been known to search open shallows for food, unconcerned with onlookers. • The Sora has two main calls: a clear, whistled *coo-wee* that is easy to imitate and a strange, descending whinny. • Although its feet are not webbed or lobed, the Sora swims quite well over short distances. It appears to be a weak and reluctant flyer, but the Sora migrates hundreds of miles each year between its breeding and wintering wetlands. • The Sora is also known as the "Carolina Rail," likely pertaining to its scientific name, meaning "of Carolina."

breeding

ID: short, yellow bill; black face, throat and foreneck; gray neck and breast; long wings and tail; long, greenish legs. *Immature:* no black on face; greener bill; buffier with paler underparts.

Size: *L* 8–10 in; *W* 14 in.

Status: common migrant with peaks in May and September; uncommon breeder.

Habitat: wetlands with abundant emergent cattails, bulrushes, sedges and grasses.

Nesting: usually over water, but occasionally in a wet meadow under concealing vegetation; well-built basket nest is made of grass and aquatic vegetation; pair incubates 10–12 buff or olive buff, darkly speckled eggs for 18–20 days.

Feeding: gleans and probes for seeds, plants, aquatic insects and mollusks.

Voice: usual call is a clear, 2-note *coo-wee;* alarm call is a sharp *keek;* courtship song begins *or-Ah or-Ah,* descending quickly in a series of maniacal *weee-weee-weee* notes.

Similar Species: *Virginia Rail* and *King Rail:* long, downcurved bill; chestnut brown wing patch; rufous breast; King Rail much larger. *Yellow Rail:* smaller; streaked back; tawny upperparts; white throat; white trailing edges of wings are seen in flight.

Best Sites: Ruthven WA; Dunbar Slough; Snake Creek Marsh. *Breeding:* Prairie Pothole Region.

AMERICAN COOT

Fulica americana

The American Coot is truly an all-terrain bird: in its quest for a meal, it dives and dabbles like a duck, swims about skillfully with lobed feet or grazes confidently on land. • American Coots squabble constantly during the breeding season, not just among themselves, but also with any waterbird that has the audacity to intrude upon their waterfront property. These odd birds can often be seen scooting across the surface of a pond, charging rivals with flailing, splashing wings. • Outside the breeding season, coots gather amicably together in large groups. During spring and fall, thousands congregate at select staging sites in the state, and are are easy to spot because of their pendulous head movements while swimming. • The American Coot is colloquially known as "Mud Hen," and many people mistakenly believe that the American Coot is a species of duck.

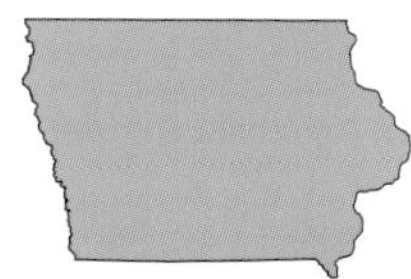

ID: gray black overall; white, chickenlike bill with dark ring around tip; reddish spot on white forehead shield; long, greenish yellow legs; lobed toes; red eyes. *Immature:* lighter body color; darker bill and legs; lacks prominent forehead shield.

Size: *L* 13–16 in; *W* 24 in.

Status: abundant migrant, especially in April and October; common breeder; a few may overwinter.

Habitat: shallow marshes, ponds and wetlands with open water and emergent vegetation; also sewage lagoons.

Nesting: in emergent vegetation; pair builds a floating nest of cattails and grass; pair incubates 6–11 brown-spotted, buffy white eggs for 21–25 days.

Feeding: gleans the water's surface, dives or tips up and grazes on land; eats aquatic vegetation, insects, snails, crayfish, worms, tadpoles and fish; may steal food from ducks.

Voice: calls frequently in summer, day and night: *kuk-kuk-kuk-kuk-kuk;* also grunts.

Similar Species: *Common Moorhen:* reddish forehead shield; yellow-tipped bill; white streak on flanks. *Ducks* (pp. 23–35): all lack chickenlike, white bill and uniformly black body. *Grebes* (pp. 40–41): lack white forehead shield and all-dark plumage.

Best Sites: found statewide. *Breeding:* more common in the north; Prairie Pothole Region. *Winter:* open water.

SANDHILL CRANE

Grus canadensis

Deep, resonant, rattling calls announce the approach of a flock of migrating Sandhill Cranes long before they pass overhead. Their coiled tracheas allow them to call louder and farther. At first glance, the large, V-shaped flocks look very similar to those of Canada Geese, but cranes circle upwards on thermal rises, then slowly soar downwards until they find another rise, continuing this pattern all the way to their nesting sites. • Migrating flocks of Sandhills consist mainly of mated pairs and close family members. Cranes mate for life, reinforcing pair bonds each spring with an elaborate courtship dance. It has often been equated with human dancing—a seemingly strange comparison until you see the ritual firsthand. • Sandhill Cranes are sensitive to disturbance while nesting, so they prefer to raise their young in isolated areas.

nonbreeding

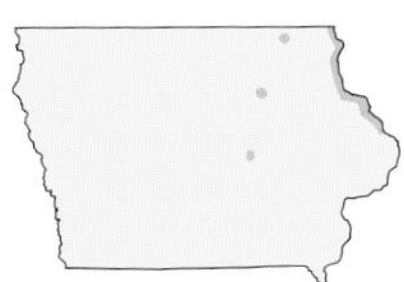

ID: very large, gray bird with long neck and legs; naked, red crown; long, straight bill; plumage is often stained rusty red from iron oxides in water. *Immature:* reddish brown plumage may appear patchy; lacks red crown. *In flight:* extends neck and legs; often glides, soars and circles.

Size: *L* 3½–4 ft; *W* 6–7 ft.

Status: rare migrant and breeder; number of nesting sites is increasing.

Habitat: *In migration:* agricultural fields and shorelines. *Breeding:* open marshes.

Nesting: on a large mound of aquatic vegetation in water or along a shoreline; pair incubates 2 brown-splotched, olive buff eggs for 29–32 days; egg hatching is staggered; young fly at about 50 days.

Feeding: probes and gleans the ground for insects, soft-bodied invertebrates, waste grain, shoots and tubers; frequently eats small vertebrates.

Voice: loud, resonant rattling *gu-rrroo gu-rrroo gurrroo*.

Similar Species: *Great Blue Heron* (p. 45): neck is folded back over shoulders in flight; lacks red forehead patch. *Whooping Crane:* all-white plumage; black flight feathers.

Best Sites: Upper Mississippi River NWR; Sweet Marsh; Otter Creek Marsh; Cardinal Marsh.

KILLDEER

Charadrius vociferus

The ubiquitous Killdeer is often the first shorebird a birder learns to identify. Its boisterous calls rarely fail to catch the attention of people passing through its diverse nesting environments. The Killdeer's preference for open fields, gravel driveways, beach edges, golf courses and abandoned industrial areas has allowed it to thrive throughout our rural and suburban landscapes. • If you happen to wander too close to a Killdeer nest, the parent will try to lure you away by issuing loud alarm calls and feigning a broken wing. Most predators take the bait and, once they have been led far enough away, the parent suddenly recovers from its "injury" and flies off, sounding its piercing calls. Similar distraction displays are widespread phenomena in the bird world, but in our region, the Killdeer's broken wing act is by far the most impressive. • The scientific name *vociferus* aptly describes this vocal bird, but double-check all calls in spring—the Killdeer is often imitated by a European Starling.

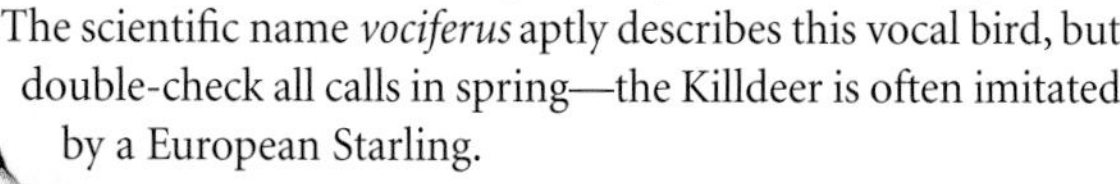

ID: brown head; white "eyebrow"; white face patch above bill; black forehead band; white upperparts with 2 black breast bands; brown back; white underparts; rufous rump; long, dark yellow legs; tail projects beyond wing tips. *Immature:* downy; 1 breast band.

Size: *L* 9–11 in; *W* 24 in.

Status: common migrant and breeder from mid-March to mid-November; a few may remain in mild winters.

Habitat: open ground, fields, lakeshores, sandy beaches, mudflats, gravel streambeds, wet meadows and grasslands.

Nesting: on open ground, often on paths or parking lots; in a shallow, usually unlined, depression; pair incubates 4 darkly spotted, pale buff eggs for 24–28 days; occasionally raises 2 broods.

Feeding: run-and-stop foraging technique; eats mostly insects; also takes spiders, snails, earthworms and crayfish.

Voice: loud, distinctive *kill-dee kill-dee kill-deer* and variations, including *deer-deer.*

Similar Species: *Semipalmated Plover:* smaller; only 1 breast band. *Piping Plover:* smaller; lighter upperparts; 1 breast band.

Best Sites: widespread.

LESSER YELLOWLEGS

Tringa flavipes

With a series of continuous, rapid-fire *tew-tew* calls, Lesser Yellowlegs streak across the surface of wetlands and lakeshores. Though Yellowlegs visit for only a short time in spring, the fall migration period is longer from mid-July to mid-October. • Many birders find it a challenge to separate Lesser Yellowlegs and Greater Yellowlegs in the field. With practice, you will notice that the Lesser's bill is finer, straighter and not noticeably longer than the width of its head. The Lesser appears to have longer legs and wings, making it seem slimmer and taller than the Greater, and it is also more commonly seen in flocks. If the identifying characteristics of this bird prove inadequate, listen for its call: the Lesser Yellowlegs usually gives a pair of peeps, while the Greater generally gives three or more. • The scientific name *flavipes* is derived from Latin words meaning "yellow foot."

breeding

nonbreeding

ID: all-dark bill is not noticeably longer than width of head; subtle, dark eye line; light lores; fine, dense, dark streaking on head, neck and breast; brown black back and upperwing; bright yellow legs.
Size: *L* 10–11 in; *W* 24 in.
Status: common migrant from mid-March to late May and from mid-July to mid-October, with some lingering into November; north-and southbound birds nearly overlap in June.
Habitat: shorelines of lakes, rivers, marshes and ponds.
Nesting: does not nest in Iowa.
Feeding: snatches prey from the water's surface; frequently wades in shallow water; primarily eats aquatic invertebrates, but also takes small fish and tadpoles.
Voice: typically, a high-pitched pair of *tew* notes.
Similar Species: *Greater Yellowlegs:* larger; bill slightly upturned and noticeably longer than width of head; *tew* call is usually given in a series of 3 notes. *Solitary Sandpiper:* white eye ring; greenish legs. *Willet:* much bulkier; heavier bill; dark, greenish legs; black-and-white wings.
Best Sites: found statewide in appropriate habitat.

SPOTTED SANDPIPER

Actitis macularius

The Spotted Sandpiper is a widespread breeder in Iowa, and during the summer is the most frequently encountered sandpiper throughout most of our region. It is usually encountered individually or in small flocks of less than 10 birds. • The Spotted Sandpiper practices polyandry, an uncommon breeding method that occurs in about one percent of all bird species. The female defends her territory and mates with several males in a single breeding season, leaving each one to tend to the nest and incubate the eggs. • Although its breast spots are not noticeable from a distance, the Spotted Sandpiper's tendency to burst into flight from the shore and its stiff-winged, quivering flight pattern are easily recognizable. Also look for this bird's habit to continuously teeter when it forages. • The scientific name *macularius* is Latin for "spot," referring to the spots on this bird's underparts in breeding plumage.

breeding

nonbreeding

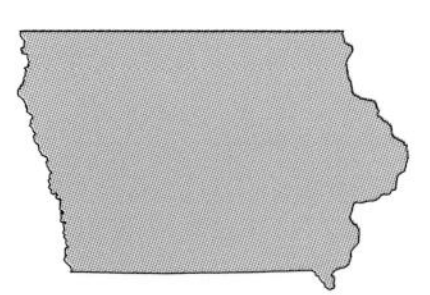

ID: *Breeding:* black-tipped, orange bill; white "eyebrow"; white underparts are heavily spotted with black; yellow orange legs. *Nonbreeding* and *immature:* unspotted, white breast, foreneck and throat; brown bill; dull yellow legs. *In flight:* white upperwing stripe; flies close to the water's surface with very rapid, shallow wingbeats.

Size: *L* 7–8 in; *W* 15 in.

Status: regularly common migrant and breeder from mid-March to mid-November, with some remaining in mild winters.

Habitat: shorelines, gravel beaches, ponds, marshes, alluvial wetlands, rivers, streams, swamps and sewage lagoons; occasionally seen in cultivated fields.

Nesting: usually near water; often under vegetation among logs or under bushes; in a shallow depression lined with grass; the male, almost exclusively, incubates 4 creamy buff, heavily blotched eggs for 19–22 days and raises the young.

Feeding: picks and gleans along shorelines for terrestrial and aquatic invertebrates; also snatches flying insects from the air.

Voice: sharp, crisp *eat-wheat, eat-wheat, wheat-wheat-wheat-wheat.*

Similar Species: *Solitary Sandpiper:* taller; complete eye ring; lacks spotting on breast. *Other sandpipers* (pp. 63–66): mostly black bills and legs; lack spotting on breast.

Best Sites: widespread in appropriate habitat.

LEAST SANDPIPER

Calidris minutilla

The Least Sandpiper is the smallest North American shorebird, but its size does not deter it from performing migratory feats. Like most other "peeps," the Least Sandpiper migrates almost the entire length of the globe twice each year, from the Arctic to the southern tip of South America and back. • Arctic summers are incredibly short, so shorebirds must maximize their breeding efforts. Least Sandpipers lay large eggs relative to those of other sandpipers, with entire clutches sometimes weighing over half the weight of the female! The young hatch in an advanced state of development and are able to get a head start on fall migration. Some begin moving south as early as the first week of July. • Although light-colored legs are a good field mark for the Least Sandpiper, bad lighting or mud can confuse matters. • The scientific name *minutilla* is Latin for "very small"—apt for the littlest sandpiper.

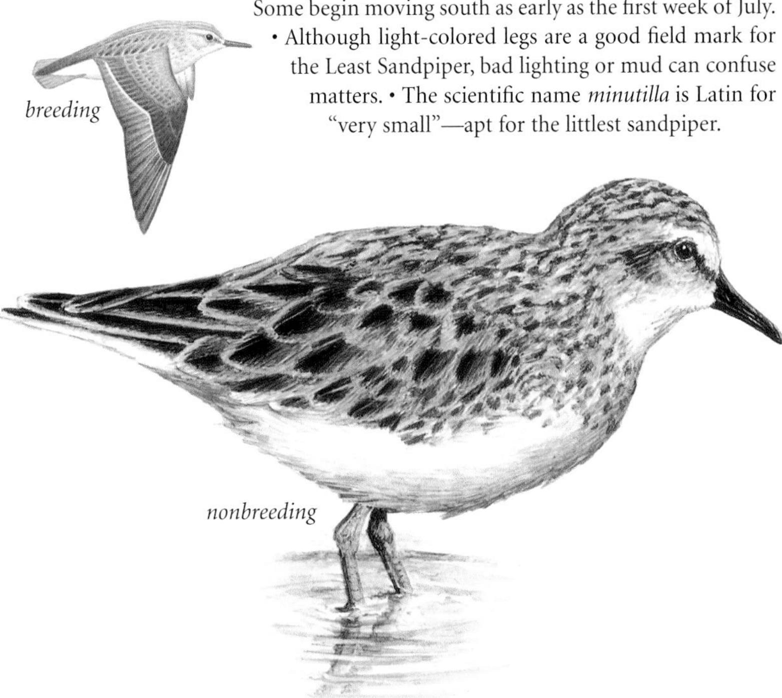

breeding

nonbreeding

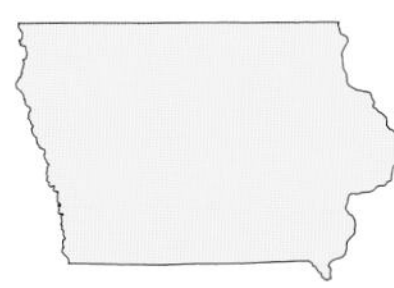

ID: black bill; dark, mottled back; yellowish legs. *Breeding:* buff brown breast, head and nape; light breast streaking; prominent white "V" on back. *Nonbreeding:* more gray brown overall. *Immature:* similar to adult, but with faintly streaked breast.

Size: *L* 5–6½ in; *W* 13 in.

Status: common to abundant migrant in April and May and from mid-July to mid-September.

Habitat: sandy beaches, lakeshores, ditches, sewage lagoons, mudflats and wetland edges.

Nesting: does not nest in Iowa.

Feeding: probes or pecks for insects, crustaceans, small mollusks and occasionally seeds.

Voice: high-pitched *kreee.*

Similar Species: *Semipalmated, Baird's, White-rumped* and *Western sandpipers:* all have black legs. *Pectoral Sandpiper* (p. 66): larger; heavier breast streaking.

Best Sites: found statewide in appropriate habitat.

PECTORAL SANDPIPER

Calidris melanotos

This widespread traveler can be found in every state and province in North America during its epic annual migrations. In spring and fall, Pectoral Sandpipers are conspicuous at mudflats and in wet, grassy fields, often appearing in large flocks of over 1000 birds. In our state, lingering spring migrants barely depart to the north before the first fall migrants start to appear. • Unlike most sandpipers, the Pectoral exhibits sexual dimorphism—the females are only two-thirds the size of the male. • When agitated, the male will inflate the air sacs in his neck, causing his feathers to rise. If threatened, flocks of Pectorals will suddenly launch into the air and converge into a single, swirling mass.

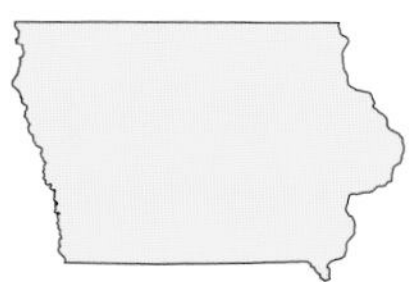

ID: black bill with slightly down-curved tip; may have a faintly rusty, dark crown and back; mottled upperparts; brown breast streaks end at edge of white belly; white undertail coverts; long, yellow legs; folded wings extend beyond the tail. *Juvenile:* less spotting on breast; broader, white feather edges on the back form 2 white "Vs."

Size: *L* 8¾ in; *W* 18 in (female is smaller).

Status: abundant migrant arriving in March, peaking in late April and early May and from mid-July into October.

Habitat: along lakeshores, marshes, mudflats and flooded fields.

Nesting: does not nest in Iowa.

Feeding: probes and pecks for small insects, including flies, beetles and grasshoppers; may also take small mollusks, amphipods, berries, seeds, moss, algae and some plant material.

Voice: sharp, short, low *krrick krrick*.

Similar Species: *Buff-breasted Sandpiper:* buffy color; small head and bill. *Other peeps* (p. 65): all lack the well-defined, dark "bib" and most have dark legs.

Best Sites: found statewide in appropriate habitat.

WILSON'S SNIPE

Gallinago delicata

The eerie, hollow, winnowing of a courting male Wilson's Snipe is a familiar sound heard in northern marshes. Wilson's Snipes can be heard displaying day or night during spring. Their specialized outer tail feathers vibrate rapidly in the air as they perform daring, headfirst dives high above their habitat. • Outside the courtship season, this well-camouflaged bird becomes shy and secretive, remaining concealed in vegetation. Only when an intruder approaches will a snipe flush from cover, performing a series of aerial zigzags—an evasive maneuver designed to confuse predators. Because of this habit, hunters who were skilled enough to shoot a snipe came to be known as "snipers," a term later adopted by the military. • The snipe's eyes are placed far back on its head, allowing the bird to see both forward and backward. • This bird used to be named "Common Snipe."

ID: long, sturdy, bicolored bill; dark eye stripe; heavily striped head, back, neck and breast; dark barring on sides and flanks; unmarked, white belly; relatively short legs. *In flight:* quick zigzags on takeoff.

Size: *L* 10½–11½ in; *W* 18 in.

Status: common migrant from March to early May and from late September to early November; rare breeder; a few may overwinter.

Habitat: cattail and bulrush marshes, sedge meadows, poorly drained floodplains, bogs, fens and willow and red osier dogwood tangles.

Nesting: usually in dry grass, often under vegetation; nest is made of grass, moss and leaves; female incubates 4 olive buff to brown eggs, marked with dark brown, for 18–20 days; both parents raise the young, often splitting the brood.

Feeding: probes soft substrates for larvae, earthworms and other soft-bodied invertebrates; also eats mollusks, crustaceans, spiders, small amphibians and some seeds.

Voice: eerie, accelerating courtship song is produced in flight: *woo-woo-woo-woo-woo-woo;* often sings *wheat wheat wheat* from an elevated perch; alarm call is a nasal *scaip*.

Similar Species: *Short-billed Dowitcher* and *Long-billed Dowitcher:* all-dark bills; longer legs; usually seen in flocks; lack heavy striping on head, back, neck and breast. *American Woodcock* (p. 68): yellowish bill; light-colored bars on black crown and nape; unmarked, buff underparts. *Marbled Godwit:* much larger; slightly upturned bill; much longer legs.

Best Sites: Prairie Pothole Region. *Breeding:* mainly in northern Iowa. *Winter:* near open water.

AMERICAN WOODCOCK

Scolopax minor

This denizen of moist woodlands and damp thickets usually goes about its business in a quiet and reclusive manner, but during courtship the male American Woodcock reveals his true character. Just before dawn or just after sunset, the male will strut provocatively in an open woodland clearing or a brushy, abandoned field, while calling out a series of loud *peeent* notes. With his cryptic and inconspicuous attire, he twitters through the air in a circular flight display, and then, with wings partly folded, he plummets to the ground in the zigzag pattern of a falling leaf. • Once extensively hunted to dangerously low numbers, the woodcock population has recovered in recent years and is now once again considered a game species.

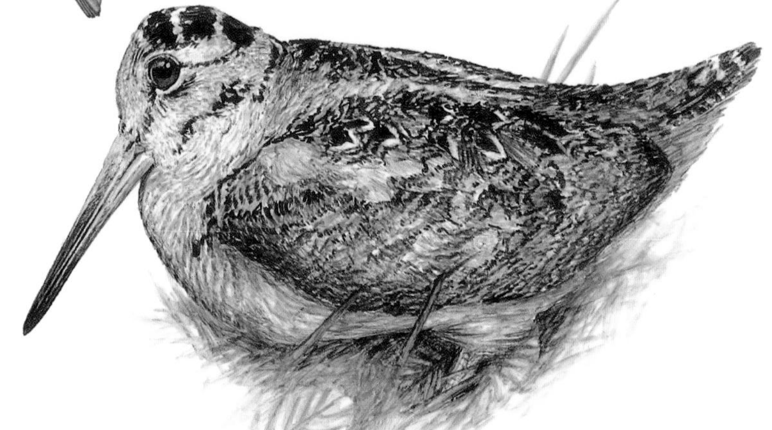

ID: very long, sturdy bill; large, dark eyes; light-colored bars on the black crown and hindneck; large head; short neck; chunky body; unmarked, buff underparts; very short legs. *In flight:* rounded wings.

Size: *L* 11 in; *W* 18 in.

Status: high conservation priority; common, early migrant and breeder from February through November; a few winter records.

Habitat: moist woodlands and brushy thickets adjacent to grassy clearings or abandoned fields.

Nesting: on the ground in woods or overgrown fields; female builds a scrape lined with dead leaves and other debris; female incubates 4 brown-and-gray blotched, pinkish buff eggs for 20–22 days; female tends the young.

Feeding: probes in soft, moist soil for earthworms and insect larvae; also takes spiders, snails, millipedes and some plant material, including seeds, sedges and grasses.

Voice: nasal *peeent;* high-pitched whistling during courtship dance; twitters when flushed.

Similar Species: *Wilson's Snipe* (p. 67): heavily striped head, back, neck and breast; dark barring on sides and flanks. *Dowitchers:* all-dark bills; longer legs; usually seen in flocks; lack light-colored barring on dark crown and hindneck.

Best Sites: widespread in appropriate habitat, but more common in eastern third of the state.

FRANKLIN'S GULL

Larus pipixcan

Franklin's Gulls are regularly seen in migration throughout Iowa. They are our most common small gull with flocks that are often joined by other, rarer species. • The Franklin's Gull is not a typical "seagull"—a large part of its life is spent inland. On its traditional nesting territory on the prairies, it is affectionately known as "Prairie Dove." It has a dovelike profile and often follows tractors across agricultural fields, snatching up insects from the tractor's path in much the same way its cousins follow fishing boats. • The majority of Franklin's Gulls winter along the Pacific coast of Peru and Chile, and they are one of the only two gull species that migrate long distances between breeding and wintering grounds. • This gull was named for Sir John Franklin, the British navigator and explorer who disappeared while searching for the Northwest Passage in the 19th century.

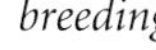

breeding

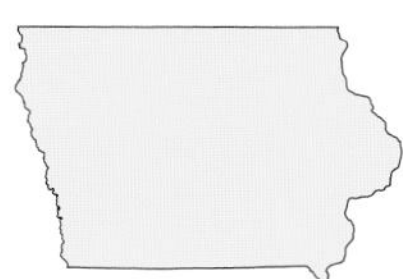

ID: dark gray mantle; broken, white eye ring; white underparts. *Breeding:* black head; orange red bill and legs; breast might have pinkish tinge. *Nonbreeding:* white head; dark patch on side of head. *In flight:* white border on wings; black crescent on wing tips; white underwings.

Size: *L* 13–15 in; *W* 3 ft.

Status: common to locally abundant migrant in April and May and from late August to early November with a few breeding and winter records.

Habitat: agricultural fields, marshlands, river and lake shorelines, rivermouths and landfills.

Nesting: does not regularly nest in Iowa.

Feeding: opportunistic; gleans agricultural fields and meadows for grasshoppers and insects; catches dragonflies, mayflies and other flying invertebrates in midair; also eats small fish and some crustaceans.

Voice: mewing, shrill *weeeh-ah weeeh-ah* while feeding and in migration.

Similar Species: *Bonaparte's Gull:* black bill; conspicuous white wedge on forewing. *Black-headed Gull:* rare, but regular in NW Iowa; paler mantle; conspicuous white wedge on forewing; breeding has much more white on back of head; nonbreeding lacks black face "mask." *Sabine's Gull:* vagrant; large, black, white and gray triangles on upperwing; dark, yellow-tipped bill. *Laughing Gull:* vagrant; larger; longer, heavier bill; black legs; nonbreeding lacks black "hood." *Little Gull:* rare vagrant; much smaller; paler mantle; lacks black crescent on wing tips; breeding lacks broken white eye ring and white nape; nonbreeding lacks black "hood."

Best Sites: found statewide, but most common in western and central Iowa.

RING-BILLED GULL

Larus delawarensis

The Ring-billed Gull's numbers have greatly increased in recent years, and its tolerance for humans has made it a part of our everyday lives, which often involves them scavenging our litter or fouling the windshields of our automobiles! • It is most common in migration at large reservoirs and lakes. Some remain in winter as long as there is open water. • Some people feel that Ring-billed Gulls have become pests—parks, beaches, golf courses and fast-food parking lots are often inundated with marauding gulls looking for food handouts. Few species, however, have fared as well as the Ring-billed Gull in the face of human development, which, in itself, is something to appreciate.

nonbreeding

breeding

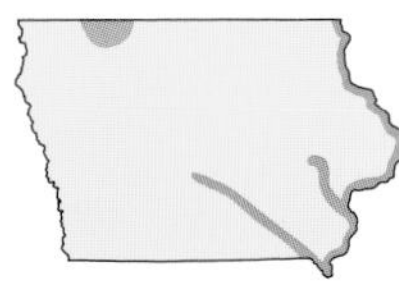

ID: white head; yellow eyes, bill and legs; black ring around bill tip; pale gray mantle; white underparts. *Immature:* gray back; brown wings and breast. *In flight:* black wing tips with a few white spots.

Size: *L* 18–20 in; *W* 4 ft.

Status: year-round resident and most common gull in Iowa; abundant in migration; has bred in extreme northern Iowa; a few may overwinter.

Habitat: *Breeding:* sparsely vegetated islands, open beaches, breakwaters and dredge-spoil areas. *In migration* and *winter:* lakes, rivers, landfills, golf courses, fields and parks.

Nesting: colonial; in a shallow scrape on the ground, lined with plants, debris, grass and sticks; pair incubates 2–4 brown-blotched, gray to olive eggs for 23–28 days.

Feeding: gleans the ground for human food waste, spiders, insects, rodents, earthworms, grubs and some waste grain; scavenges for carrion; surface-tips for aquatic invertebrates and fish.

Voice: high-pitched *kakakaka-akakaka;* also a low, laughing *yook-yook-yook.*

Similar Species: most larger gulls lack the clean-cut black ring on bill. *Herring Gull* (p. 71): larger; usually has red spot on bill; pinkish legs. *California Gull* and *Lesser Black-backed Gull:* larger; darker mantles.

Best Sites: found statewide in appropriate habitat. *In migration:* Saylorville; Red Rock.

HERRING GULL

Larus argentatus

Although Herring Gulls are as adept as their smaller Ring-billed relatives at scrounging handouts on the beach, they are more likely to be found in wilderness areas than urban settings. Settling on lakes and large rivers where Ring-billed Gulls would never be found, Herring Gulls choose to either nest comfortably in large colonies, or in a secluded pair, miles from other gulls. • Herring Gulls are skilled hunters, but are also opportunistic and can be found scavenging on human litter. • In some areas, increasing Herring Gull populations has resulted in decreasing tern numbers owing to this gull's fondness for tern eggs and nestlings. • Like many gulls, Herring Gulls have a small red spot on the lower mandible that serves as a target for nestling young. When a downy chick pecks at the lower mandible, the parent recognizes the cue and regurgitates its meal.

nonbreeding

breeding

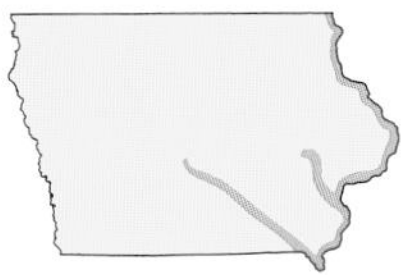

ID: large; yellow bill; light eyes; red spot on lower mandible; light gray mantle; pink legs. *Breeding:* white head; white underparts. *Nonbreeding:* white head and nape are washed with brown. *Immature:* mottled brown overall. *In flight:* white-spotted, black wing tips.

Size: *L* 23–26 in; *W* 4 ft.

Status: common migrant from mid-February to early April and from November to mid-December; some remain in winter.

Habitat: large lakes, wetlands, rivers, landfills and urban areas. *Winter:* Mississippi R.; reservoirs.

Nesting: does not nest in Iowa.

Feeding: surface-tips for aquatic invertebrates and fish; gleans the ground for insects and worms; scavenges dead fish and human food waste; eats other birds' eggs and young.

Voice: loud, buglelike *kleew-kleew;* also an alarmed *kak-kak-kak*.

Similar Species: *Ring-billed Gull* (p. 70): smaller; black bill ring; yellow legs. *Thayer's, Glaucous* and *Iceland gulls:* paler mantle; little or no black on wings. *Lesser Black-backed Gull* and *Slaty-backed Gull:* much darker mantle. *California Gull:* smaller; dark eyes; black-and-red spot on lower mandible; yellowish legs.

Best Sites: Pool 19; Saylorville; Red Rock. *Winter:* open water along the Mississippi R. and Missouri R.

CASPIAN TERN

Sterna caspia

In size and habit, the mighty Caspian Tern bridges the gap between the smaller terns and the larger, raucous gulls. It is the largest tern in North America, with slower wingbeats and a more gull-like flight than most other terns. The Caspian is often mistaken for a type of gull, until its raucous call gives it away. This tern's distinctive, heavy, red orange bill and slightly forked tail also help to reveal its true identity. • Caspian Terns are often seen together with gulls on shoreline sandbars and mudflats in migration or during the breeding season, when they nest in colonies on exposed islands and protected beaches. • The sight of a Caspian Tern foraging for small, schooling fish is impressive. Flying high over open waters, it hovers, then suddenly folds its wings and plunges headfirst toward its target. • The Caspian Tern is strictly a migrant and breeder in our region, retreating to the Gulf of Mexico in winter. • This species was first collected from the Caspian Sea, hence its name. Caspian Terns are found nesting all over the world, in Eurasia, Africa and even Australia.

breeding

ID: *Breeding:* black "cap"; heavy, red orange bill has faint black tip; light gray mantle; black legs; shallowly forked tail; white underparts; long, frosty, pointed wings; dark gray on underside of outer primaries. *Nonbreeding:* black "cap" streaked with white.

Size: *L* 19–23 in; *W* 4–4½ ft.

Status: uncommon migrant from mid-April to mid-May and throughout September; a few nonbreeders occasionally spend the summer.

Habitat: wetlands and shorelines of large lakes and rivers.

Nesting: does not nest in Iowa.

Feeding: hovers over water and plunges headfirst after small fish, tadpoles and aquatic invertebrates; also feeds by swimming and gleaning at the water's surface.

Voice: low, harsh *ca-arr;* loud *kraa-uh;* juveniles answer with a high-pitched whistle.

Similar Species: *Other terns* (pp. 73–74): much smaller; daintier bills; primaries mostly pale on underside. *Ring-billed Gull* (p. 70): yellow bill with black ring; rounded tail; black wing tips.

Best Sites: widespread in appropriate habitat.

FORSTER'S TERN

Sterna forsteri

The Common Tern so closely resembles the Forster's Tern that the two often seem indistinguishable. Nearly every small white tern you see in Iowa, however, will be a Forster's. • Most terns are known for their extraordinary ability to catch fish in dramatic headfirst dives, but the Forster's excels at gracefully snatching flying insects in midair. • The Forster's Tern has an exclusively North American breeding distribution, but it bears the name of a man who never visited this continent: German naturalist Johann Reinhold Forster. Forster, who lived and worked in England and accompanied Captain Cook on his 1772 voyage around the world, examined tern specimens sent from Hudson Bay, Canada, and was the first to recognize this bird as a distinct species. In 1832, Thomas Nuttall was the first taxonomist to name this species "Forster's Tern" in his *Manual of Ornithology.*

nonbreeding

breeding

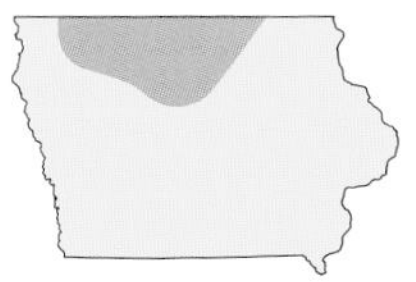

ID: *Breeding:* black "cap" and nape; thin, orange, black-tipped bill; light gray mantle; pure white underparts; white rump; orange legs; gray tail with white outer edges. *Nonbreeding:* black band through eyes; lacks black "cap." *In flight:* forked gray tail; long, pointed wings.

Size: *L* 14–16 in; *W* 31 in.

Status: high conservation priority; uncommon migrant from mid-April through May and from July through September; locally rare breeder.

Habitat: *Breeding:* cattail marshes. *In migration:* lakes and marshes.

Nesting: colonial; in a cattail marsh on floating vegetation; occasionally on a muskrat lodge or in an old grebe nest; pair incubates 3 brown-marked, buff to olive eggs for 23–25 days.

Feeding: hovers above the water and plunges headfirst after small fish and aquatic invertebrates; catches flying insects and snatches prey from the water's surface.

Voice: flight call is a nasal, short *keer keer;* also a grating *tzaap.*

Similar Species: *Common Tern:* darker red bill and legs; mostly white tail; gray wash on underparts; dark wedge near tip of primaries. *Caspian Tern* (p. 72): much larger overall; much heavier, red orange bill. *Arctic Tern:* rare vagrant; gray underparts; short, red legs; white tail with gray outer edges; lacks black-tipped bill. *Least Tern:* smaller; yellow bill; white forehead.

Best Sites: Prairie Pothole Region.

BLACK TERN

Chlidonias niger

Black Terns fly like acrobats, slicing through the sky with grace, even in a stiff wind. When these terns leave our region in August and September, they head for the warmer climates of Central and South America. • Black Terns are finicky nesters and refuse to return to sites that show even slight changes in water level or in the density of emergent vegetation. This selectiveness, coupled with the degradation of marshes across North America, has contributed to a significant decline in populations of this bird over recent decades. Commitment to restoring and protecting valuable wetland habitats will eventually help the Black Tern to reclaim its once prominent place in the bird kingdom. • In order to spell this tern's genus name correctly, one must misspell *chelidonias*, the Greek word for "swallow." The Black Tern is named for its swallowlike, darting flight when it pursues insects.

nonbreeding

breeding

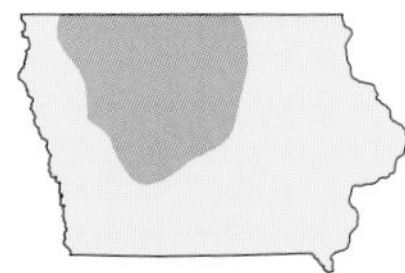

ID: *Breeding:* black bill; black head and underparts; gray back, tail and wings; white undertail coverts; reddish black legs. *Nonbreeding:* white underparts and forehead; molting fall birds may be mottled with brown. *In flight:* long, pointed wings; shallowly forked tail.

Size: *L* 9–10 in; *W* 24 in.

Status: high conservation priority; fairly common spring migrant from mid- to late May; less common in fall; local breeder in the north.

Habitat: shallow, freshwater cattail marshes, wetlands, lake edges and sewage ponds with emergent vegetation.

Nesting: loosely colonial; flimsy nest of dead plant material is built on floating vegetation, a muddy mound or a muskrat house; pair incubates 3 darkly blotched, olive to pale buff eggs for 21–22 days.

Feeding: snatches insects from the air, tall grasses and the water's surface; also eats small fish.

Voice: greeting call is a shrill, metallic *kik-kik-kik-kik-kik;* typical alarm call is *kreea*.

Similar Species: *Other terns* (pp. 72–73): all are light in color; nonbreeding Black Tern is similar, but shows some dark smudging on back and shoulder.

Best Sites: found statewide, mostly in spring. *Breeding:* Prairie Pothole Region.

ROCK PIGEON

Columba livia

Introduced to North America in the early 17th century, Rock Pigeons have always settled wherever cities, towns and farms can be found. Most birds seem content to nest on buildings or farmhouses, but "wilder" members of this species can occasionally be seen nesting on tall cliffs, usually along lakeshores. • It is believed that Rock Pigeons were domesticated from Eurasian birds as a source of meat in about 4500 BC. Since their domestication, Rock Pigeons have been used as message couriers (both Caesar and Napoleon used them), scientific subjects and even as pets. Much of our understanding of bird migration, endocrinology and sensory perception derives from experiments involving Rock Pigeons. • All members of the pigeon family, including doves, feed their young "milk." Because birds lack mammary glands, it is not true milk, but a nutritious liquid produced by glands in the bird's crop. The chicks insert their bills down the adult's throat to eat the thick, protein-rich fluid. • This bird's variable coloration is a result of semi-domestication and extensive inbreeding over time. Until recently, the Rock Pigeon was known as the "Rock Dove."

ID: color is highly variable (iridescent blue gray, red, white or tan); usually has white rump and orange feet; dark-tipped tail. *In flight:* holds wings in deep "V" while gliding.

Size: *L* 12–13 in; *W* 28 in.

Status: common resident.

Habitat: urban areas, around buildings, railroad yards, agricultural areas and high cliffs.

Nesting: on a ledge in a barn or on a cliff, bridge, building or tower; flimsy nest is built from sticks, grass and assorted vegetation; pair incubates 2 white eggs for 16–19 days; pair feeds the young "pigeon milk"; may raise broods year-round.

Feeding: gleans the ground for waste grain, seeds and fruits; occasionally eats insects.

Voice: soft, cooing *coorrr-coorrr-coorrr.*

Similar Species: *Mourning Dove* (p. 77): smaller; slimmer; pale brown plumage; long tail and wings. *Eurasian Collared-Dove* (p. 76): no white rump. *Merlin:* not as heavy bodied; longer tail; does not hold wings in a "V"; wings do not clap on takeoff.

Best Sites: widespread in appropriate habitat.

EURASIAN COLLARED-DOVE

Streptopelia decaocto

If it hasn't already, the Eurasian Collared-Dove will be coming to a suburb near you very soon. Originally from the Middle East, this species expanded through Europe along with the human population in the 20th century. Fifty birds were released in the Bahamas in 1974, and in only a few years, some of these doves had made their way to mainland Florida. By 2003, they could be found in Montana. • In warmer climates the Eurasian Collared-Dove can breed six times a year. Its young disperse long distances and its love of suburban areas and ease around humans seems to be encouraging the dispersal of this bird throughout much of North America.

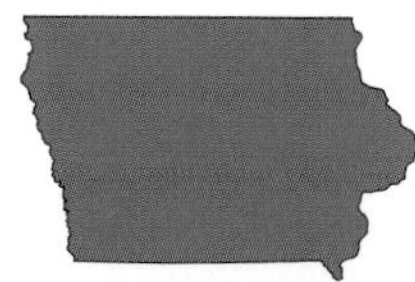

ID: pale gray overall; white outlined, dark "collar" across back of neck; white outer tail; gray band across wing coverts.
Size: *L* 12–13 in; *W* 18–20 in.
Status: rare resident, but spreading rapidly throughout the state.
Habitat: suburbs, farmlands, parks with both open ground and tree cover.
Nesting: flimsy stick platform is built in a tree, shrub or on a building; pair alternates incubation of 1–4 white or pale buff eggs for 14–19 days.
Feeding: mainly forages on the ground; eats mostly seeds with some berries and fruits; young are fed "pigeon milk."
Voice: a soft, repeated, *coo-COO-coo.*
Similar Species: *Mourning Dove* (p. 77): pointed tail; lacks black "collar." *Rock Pigeon* (p. 75): stockier; usually has a white rump and black tail band.
Best Sites: grain storage facilities; expanding population statewide.

MOURNING DOVE

Zenaida macroura

The soft cooing of the Mourning Dove that filters through our broken woodlands, farmlands and suburban parks and gardens is often confused with the muted sounds of a hooting owl. • The Mourning Dove is one of the most abundant and widespread native birds in North America and a very popular game bird. It has benefited from human-induced changes to the landscape, and its numbers and distribution have increased since the continent was settled. It is encountered in both rural and urban habitats but avoids heavily forested areas. • Despite its fragile look, the Mourning Dove is a swift, direct flier whose wings often whistle as the bird cuts through the air at high speed. Listen for the clap of its wings when it bursts into flight. • This bird's common name reflects its sad, cooing song. The scientific name *Zenaida* honors Zenaïde, Princess of Naples and the wife of naturalist Charles-Lucien Bonaparte, nephew of the French emperor.

ID: small head; dark bill; sleek body; buffy, gray brown plumage; dark, shiny patch below ear; pale rosy underparts; dull red legs; black spots on upperwing; long, white-trimmed, tapering tail.

Size: *L* 11–13 in; *W* 18 in.

Status: abundant resident; less common in winter.

Habitat: open and riparian woodlands, woodlots, forest edges, agricultural and suburban areas and open parks.

Nesting: in the fork of a shrub or tree, occasionally on the ground; female builds a shallow platform nest from twigs supplied by the male; pair incubates 2 white eggs for 14 days; young are fed "pigeon milk."

Feeding: gleans the ground and vegetation for seeds; visits feeders.

Voice: mournful *oh-HOO-woo-woo,* usually higher pitched in the middle.

Similar Species: *Rock Pigeon* (p. 75): stockier; iridescent neck; white rump; shorter tail. *Eurasian Collared-Dove* (p. 76): black "collar"; rounded tail with white corners. *American Kestrel* (p. 57): more colorful; broader tail; narrower wings. *Great Horned Owl* (p. 80): lower pitched, resonant *hoo-hoo-hooooo hoo-hoo.*

Best Sites: widespread.

YELLOW-BILLED CUCKOO

Coccyzus americanus

Most of the time, the Yellow-billed Cuckoo skillfully negotiates its tangled home within impenetrable, deciduous undergrowth in silence, relying on obscurity for survival. But for a short period during nesting, the male cuckoo tempts fate by issuing a barrage of loud, rhythmic courtship calls. Among farmers it is believed that the calling cuckoo predicts rain, hence its nickname, "Rain Crow." • Though some Yellow-billed Cuckoos may lay eggs in the unattended nests of neighboring Black-billed Cuckoos, neither of these birds are considered to be "brood parasites" as the Old World cuckoos are. • Some Yellow-billed Cuckoos migrate as far south as Argentina for winter.

ID: yellow eye ring; downcurved bill with black upper mandible and yellow lower mandible; olive brown upperparts; white underparts; long tail with large, white spots on underside; rufous tinge on primaries.

Size: *L* 11–13 in; *W* 18 in.

Status: uncommon migrant and breeder from mid-May to late September.

Habitat: semi-open deciduous habitats; dense tangles and thickets at the edges of orchards, urban parks, agricultural fields and roadways; sometimes woodlots.

Nesting: on a horizontal branch in a deciduous shrub or small tree, within 7 ft of the ground; builds a flimsy platform of twigs lined with roots and grass; pair incubates 3–4 pale bluish green eggs for 9–11 days.

Feeding: gleans insect larvae, especially hairy caterpillars; also eats beetles, grasshoppers, cicadas, berries, small fruits, small amphibians and occasionally the eggs of small birds.

Voice: deep, hollow *kuk-kuk-kuk-kuk kuk kop kow kowlp kowlp,* slowing near the end.

Similar Sp¶ecies: *Black-billed Cuckoo:* all-black bill; red eye ring; less prominent, white undertail spots; lacks rufous tinge on primaries; juveniles have buff eye ring and may have buff wash on throat and undertail coverts. *Mourning Dove* (p. 77): short, straight bill; buffy gray brown plumage; black spots on upperwing; pointed, triangular tail.

Best Sites: found statewide in appropriate habitat.

EASTERN SCREECH-OWL

Megascops asio

The diminutive Eastern Screech-Owl is a year-round resident of deciduous woodlands, but its presence is rarely detected. Most screech-owls sleep away the daylight hours snuggled safely inside a tree cavity or an artificial nest box. • The noise of mobbing chickadees or squawking gangs of Blue Jays may alert you to an owl's presence, but the Eastern Screech-Owl can still be hard to find, huddled, motionless in a tangled brush. More commonly, you will find this owl by listening for its eerie, "horse-whinny" courtship calls and loud, spooky trills at night. • Despite its small size, the Eastern Screech-Owl is an adaptable hunter. It has a varied diet that ranges from insects, small rodents, earthworms and fish to birds larger than itself. • Unique among the owls found in our region, Eastern Screech-Owls are polychromatic: they have both red and gray color morphs. A breeding pair may be of the same color or mixed.

gray morph

red morph

ID: short "ear" tufts; reddish or grayish overall; dark breast streaking; yellow eyes; pale grayish bill.

Size: *L* 8–9 in; *W* 20–22 in.

Status: common resident.

Habitat: mature deciduous forests, open deciduous and riparian woodlands, orchards and shade trees with natural cavities.

Nesting: in a natural cavity or artificial nest box; no lining is added; female incubates 4–5 white eggs for about 26 days; male brings food to the female during incubation.

Feeding: feeds from dusk until dawn; takes small mammals, earthworms, fish, birds and insects, including moths in flight.

Voice: horselike, falling "whinny"; also a low, slow trill, easily imitated.

Similar Species: *Northern Saw-whet Owl:* long, reddish streaks on white underparts; lacks "ear" tufts. *Long-eared Owl:* much longer, slimmer body; longer, closer-set "ear" tufts; rusty facial disc; grayish, brown and white body. *Great Horned Owl* (p. 80): much larger; lacks vertical breast streaks.

Best Sites: found statewide in appropriate habitat.

GREAT HORNED OWL

Bubo virginianus

The familiar *hoo-hoo-hoooo hoo-hoo* that resounds through campgrounds, suburban parks and farmyards is the call of the adaptable and superbly camouflaged Great Horned Owl. This formidable, primarily nocturnal, hunter uses its acute hearing and powerful vision to hunt a wide variety of prey. Almost any small creature that moves is fair game for the Great Horned Owl. This bird apparently has a poorly developed sense of smell, being that it is the only consistent predator of skunks. • Great Horned Owls often begin their courtship as early as January, at which time their hooting calls make them quite conspicuous. In February and March, females have started to incubate their eggs, and by the time the last migratory birds have moved into our region, Great Horned owlets have already fledged. • The large eyes of an owl are fixed in place, so to look up, down or to the side, the bird must move its entire head. As an adaptation to this situation, an owl can swivel its neck 180 degrees to either side and 90 degrees up and down!

ID: overall plumage is light gray to dark brown; yellow eyes; tall "ear" tufts set wide apart; white "chin"; fine, horizontal barring on breast; facial disc is outlined in black and often rusty orange; heavily mottled gray, brown and black upperparts.

Size: *L* 18–25 in; *W* 3–5 ft.

Status: common resident.

Habitat: fragmented forests, agricultural areas, woodlots, meadows, riparian woodlands, wooded suburban parks and the wooded edges of landfills and town dumps.

Nesting: in the abandoned stick nest of another bird; may also nest on a cliff; adds little or no material to the nest; mostly the female incubates 2–3 dull whitish eggs for 28–35 days.

Feeding: mostly nocturnal, but also hunts at dusk or by day in winter; usually swoops from a perch; eats small mammals, birds, snakes, amphibians and fish.

Voice: call during the breeding season is 4–6 deep hoots: *hoo-hoo-hoooo hoo-hoo* or *Who's awake? Me too;* male also gives higher-pitched hoots.

Similar Species: *Long-eared Owl:* smaller; thinner; vertical breast streaks; "ear" tufts are closer together. *Eastern Screech-Owl* (p. 79): much smaller; vertical breast streaks. *Other owls* (pp. 79–81): lack "ear" tufts. *Mourning Dove* (p. 77): less resonant hoots usually rise and fall.

Best Sites: widespread in appropriate habitat.

BARRED OWL

Strix varia

Each spring, the memorable sound of courting Barred Owls echoes through our forests: *Who cooks for you? Who cooks for you all?* Escalating laughs, hoots and gargling howls reinforce the bond between pairs. At the height of courtship and when raising young, a pair of Barred Owls may continue their calls well into daylight hours, and may even answer the noon whistle or a locomotive. They also tend to be more vocal when the moon is full and the air is calm. • Barred Owls are usually most active between midnight and 4 AM, when the forest floor rustles with the movements of mice, voles and shrews. These owls have relatively weak talons, so they prey on smaller animals. • Barred Owls were once inhabitants of the moist, deciduous woodlands and swamps that covered our region, but their numbers have declined with the destruction of these habitats. In the absence of suitable tree hollows, their preferred nesting sites, Barred Owls may resort to abandoned stick nests or may even nest on the ground. • This bird is often referred to as the "Old-Eight-Hooter."

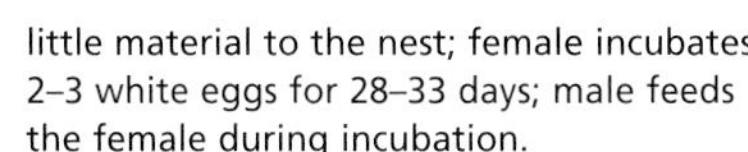

ID: mottled, dark gray brown plumage; pale bill; dark eyes; horizontal barring around neck and upper breast; vertical streaking on belly.

Size: *L* 17–24 in; *W* 3½–4 ft.

Status: common resident of river valleys in the southeast; less frequent towards the northwest.

Habitat: mature deciduous and mixed wood forests, especially in dense stands near swamps, streams and lakes.

Nesting: in a natural tree cavity, broken treetop or abandoned stick nest; adds very little material to the nest; female incubates 2–3 white eggs for 28–33 days; male feeds the female during incubation.

Feeding: nocturnal; swoops down on prey from a perch; eats mostly mice, voles and squirrels; also takes amphibians and small birds.

Voice: loud, hooting, rhythmic, laughing call is heard mostly in spring: *Who cooks for you? Who cooks for you all?*

Similar Species: *Great Horned Owl* (p. 80): "ear" tufts; light-colored eyes. *Short-eared Owl:* yellow eyes; lacks horizontal barring on upper breast. *Great Gray Owl:* winter vagrant; larger; yellow eyes; well-defined, ringed facial disc; black "chin" patch; lacks horizontal barring on upper breast.

Best Sites: found statewide in appropriate habitat.

COMMON NIGHTHAWK

Chordeiles minor

Each May and June, the male Common Nighthawk flies high above forest clearings and lakeshores, gaining elevation in preparation for the climax of his noisy aerial dance. From a great height, the male swiftly dives, then thrusts his wings forward in a final braking action to pull out of it. This quick motion of the wings produces a deep, hollow *vroom* that attracts female nighthawks. • Like other members of the nightjar family, the Common Nighthawk is adapted for catching insects in midair: its gaping mouth is surrounded by feather shafts that funnel insects into its mouth. • Nighthawks tend not to be as nocturnal as other nightjars, but they still spend most of the daylight hours resting on a tree limb or on the ground. These birds have very short legs and small feet, and they sit along the length of a tree branch, rather than across it like most other perching birds.

ID: cryptic, mottled plumage; barred underparts. *Male:* white throat. *Female:* buff throat. *In flight:* bold, white "wrist" patches on long, pointed wings; shallowly forked, barred tail; erratic flight.

Size: *L* 8½–10 in; *W* 24 in.

Status: common migrant and breeder from mid-May through mid-September; often form small flocks as they move south.

Habitat: *Breeding:* in forest openings, on gravel rooftops and in fields with sparse cover or bare patches. *In migration:* anywhere large numbers of flying insects can be found; usually roosts in trees, often near water.

Nesting: on bare ground or gravel rooftops; no nest is built; female incubates 2 well-camouflaged eggs for about 19 days; both adults feed the young.

Feeding: primarily at dawn and dusk; catches insects in flight; eats mosquitoes, blackflies, midges, beetles, flying ants and moths.

Voice: frequently repeated, nasal *peent peent;* also makes a deep, hollow *vroom* with its wings during courtship flight.

Similar Species: *Whip-poor-will* (p. 83) and *Chuck-will's-widow:* less common; found in forests; shorter, rounder wings; rounded tails; lack white "wrist" patches. *Swallows* (pp. 107–111) and *Chimney Swift* (p. 84): much smaller.

Best Sites: found statewide, especially around street lights in summer.

WHIP-POOR-WILL

Caprimulgus vociferus

This nocturnal hunter fills the late evening with repeated calls of its own name: *whip-poor-will.* Although the Whip-poor-will is heard throughout many open woodlands, this cryptic bird is rarely seen. Because of its camouflaged plumage, sleepy daytime habits and secretive nesting behavior, a hopeful observer must literally stumble upon a Whip-poor-will to see it. Only occasionally is this bird seen roosting on an exposed tree branch or alongside a quiet road. • The Whip-poor-will is one of three members of the nightjar, or "goatsucker," family found in the state. Birds in this family were named "Goatsuckers" during the days of Aristotle because of a widely believed superstition that they would suck milk from the udders of female goats. • Within days of hatching, young Whip-poor-wills scurry away from their nest in search of protective cover. For the first 20 days after hatching, the parents feed them regurgitated insects.

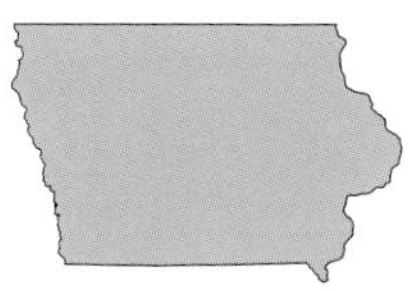

ID: mottled, brown gray overall with black flecking; reddish tinge on rounded wings; black throat; long, rounded tail. *Male:* white "necklace"; white outer tail feathers. *Female:* buff "necklace."

Size: *L* 9–10 in; *W* 16–20 in.

Status: uncommon migrant and breeder from May through August.

Habitat: open deciduous and pine woodlands; often along forest edges.

Nesting: often along the edge of a clearing under herbaceous plant growth; on the ground in leaf or pine needle litter; no nest is built; female incubates 2 whitish eggs, blotched with brown and gray, for 19–20 days; both adults raise the young.

Feeding: catches insects in flight; eats mostly moths, beetles and mosquitoes; some grasshoppers are taken and swallowed whole.

Voice: loud, whistled *whip-poor-will*, with emphasis on the *will*.

Similar Species: *Chuck-will's-widow:* larger; darker breast; much less white on male's tail. *Common Nighthawk* (p. 82): long, pointed wings; shallowly forked, barred tail; white patches on wings; much more conspicuous behavior.

Best Sites: found statewide, but more common in the east.

CHIMNEY SWIFT

Chaetura pelagica

Chimney Swifts spend more time in the sky than most aircraft—they feed, drink, bathe, collect nesting material and even mate while in flight! They spend much of their time scooping up flying insects high above urban neighborhoods, and only the business of nesting or resting keeps these birds off their wings. Chimney Swifts are most conspicuous when they forage on warm summer evenings and during fall migration, when huge flocks migrate south with large numbers of Common Nighthawks. • Declining Chimney Swift populations may be the result of a decrease in available tree cavities for nesting. They acquired their name from their frequent choice of nest site, and with some luck and a keen eye, you may see a group of swifts plunge into an unused chimney. • The legs of a Chimney Swift are so weak and small that if one were to land on the ground, it may not be able to gain flight again. Strong claws, instead, allow it to cling to vertical surfaces.

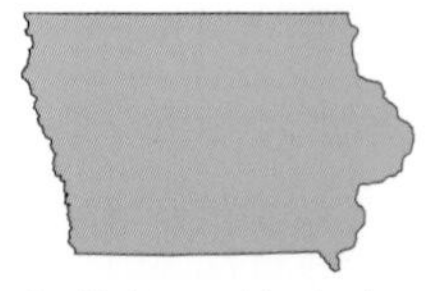

ID: brown overall; slim body and long, thin, pointed, crescent-shaped wings; squared tail.
In flight: rapid wingbeats; boomerang-shaped profile; erratic flight pattern.
Size: *L* 4½–5½ in; *W* 12–13 in.
Status: common migrant and breeder from early May to mid-October, with huge concentrations in September.

Habitat: roosts and nests in chimneys; may nest in tree cavities in more remote areas.
Nesting: often colonial; nests deep in the interior of a chimney or tree cavity, or in the attic of an abandoned building; pair uses saliva to attach a half-saucer nest of short, dead twigs to a vertical wall; pair incubates 4–5 white eggs for 19–21 days; both adults feed the young.
Feeding: flying insects are swallowed whole during continuous flight.
Voice: rapid, chattering call is given in flight: *chitter-chitter-chitter;* also gives a rapid series of *chip* notes.
Similar Species: *Swallows* (pp. 107–111): broader, shorter wings; smoother flight pattern; most have forked or notched tail.
Best Sites: found statewide in appropriate habitat.

RUBY-THROATED HUMMINGBIRD

Archilochus colubris

Ruby-throated Hummingbirds span the ecological gap between birds and bees—they feed on the sweet, energy-rich nectar that flowers provide, and pollinate the flowers in the process. Many avid gardeners and birders cultivate nectar-producing plants in their yards to attract these delightful birds. Even nongardeners can attract hummingbirds by maintaining a clean sugarwater feeder in a safe location. • Weighing about as much as a nickel, a hummingbird is capable of briefly achieving speeds of up to 62 miles per hour. It is also among the few birds that are able to fly vertically and in reverse. In straight-ahead flight, hummingbirds beat their wings up to 80 times per second, and their hearts can beat up to 1200 times per minute! • Each year, Ruby-throated Hummingbirds migrate across the Gulf of Mexico, an incredible, nonstop journey of more than 500 miles. In order to accomplish this, these little birds double their body mass by fattening up on insects and nectar before departing.

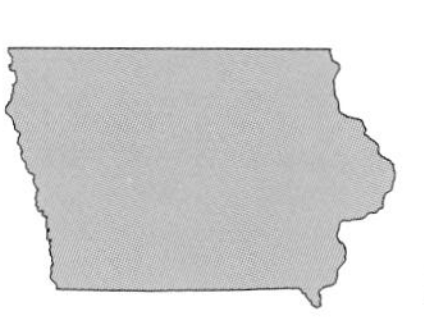

ID: tiny; long bill; iridescent, green back; light underparts; dark tail. *Male:* ruby red throat. *Female* and *immature:* fine, dark throat streaking.
Size: *L* 3½–4 in; *W* 4½ in.
Status: fairly common migrant and uncommon breeder from May through September.
Habitat: open, mixed woodlands, wetlands, orchards, tree-lined meadows, flower gardens and backyards with trees and feeders.
Nesting: on a horizontal tree limb; tiny, deep cup nest of plant down and fibers is held together with spider silk; lichens and leaves are pasted on the exterior wall of the nest; female incubates 2 white eggs for 13–16 days; female feeds the young.
Feeding: sucks nectar from blooming flowers and sugar-sweetened water from feeders; also eats small insects and spiders.
Voice: produces a loud *chick* and other high squeaks; soft buzzing of the wings while in flight.
Similar Species: *Rufous Hummingbird:* rare vagrant; male has bright, reddish orange on flanks and back; female has red-spotted throat and reddish flanks.
Best Sites: *Breeding:* more common in the east. *In migration:* found statewide.

BELTED KINGFISHER

Ceryle alcyon

The boisterous Belted Kingfisher closely monitors many of our lakes, rivers, streams, marshes and beaver ponds, and can often be spotted uttering its distinctive, rattling call while perched on a bare branch that extends out over a productive pool. With a precise headfirst dive, the kingfisher can catch fish at depths of up to 23 inches, or snag a frog immersed in only a few inches of water. The kingfisher has even been observed diving into water to elude avian predators. • During the breeding season, a pair of kingfishers typically takes turns excavating the nest burrow. They use their bills to chip away at an exposed sandbank and then kick loose material out of the tunnel with their feet. The female kingfisher has the traditional female reproductive role for birds, but, interestingly, is more colorful than her mate with a red band across her belly. • In Greek mythology, Alcyon (Halcyone), the daughter of the wind god, grieved so deeply for her drowned husband that the gods transformed them both into kingfishers.

ID: white "collar"; long, straight bill; small, white patch near eye; shaggy crest; blue gray breast band; short legs; white underwings. *Male:* no belt. *Female:* rust-colored belt (may be incomplete).

Size: *L* 11–14 in; *W* 20 in.

Status: uncommon resident.

Habitat: rivers, large streams, lakes, marshes and beaver ponds, especially near exposed soil banks, gravel pits or bluffs.

Nesting: in a cavity at the end of an earth burrow dug by the pair, often up to 6 ft long; pair incubates 6–7 white eggs for 22–24 days; both adults feed the young.

Feeding: dives headfirst into water, either from a perch or from hovering flight; eats mostly small fish, aquatic invertebrates and tadpoles.

Voice: fast, repetitive, cackling rattle, a little like a teacup shaking on a saucer.

Similar Species: *Blue Jay* (p. 104): more intense blue color; smaller bill and head; different behavior.

Best Sites: found statewide.

RED-HEADED WOODPECKER

Melanerpes erythrocephalus

Closely related to the western Acorn Woodpecker (*M. formicivorus*), this bird lives in the eastern United States, mostly in deciduous woodlands, in urban parks and in fields with open groves of large trees. Red-headed Woodpeckers were once common throughout their range, but their numbers have declined dramatically over the past century. The introduced European Starling has usurped many nesting cavities. Also, these birds are frequently struck by vehicles when they dart from their perches over roadways to catch flying insects. • When Alexander Wilson, the "father" of American ornithology, first arrived in North America, the Red-headed Woodpecker was one of the first birds to greet him. Inspired, Wilson wrote of this woodpecker: "His tricolored plumage, so striking...A gay and frolicsome disposition, diving and vociferating around the high dead limbs of some large tree, amusing the passenger with their gambols." • This bird's scientific name *erythrocephalus* means "red head" in Greek.

juvenile

ID: bright red head, throat and "bib"; black back, wings and tail; white breast, belly, rump, lower back and inner wing patches. *Juvenile:* brown head, back, wings and tail; slight brown streaking on white underparts.

Size: *L* 9–9½ in; *W* 17 in.

Status: common to abundant from mid-April through September; uncommon in winter.

Habitat: open deciduous woodlands, especially oak woodlands, urban parks, river edges and roadsides with groves of scattered trees.

Nesting: male excavates a nest cavity in a dead tree or limb; pair incubates 4–5 white eggs for 12–13 days; both adults feed the young.

Feeding: flycatches for insects; hammers dead and decaying wood for grubs; eats mostly insects, earthworms, spiders, nuts, berries, seeds and fruit; may also eat some young birds and eggs.

Voice: loud series of *kweer* or *kwrring* notes; occasionally a chattering *kerr-r-ruck;* also drums softly in short bursts.

Similar Species: adult is distinctive. *Red-bellied Woodpecker* (p. 88): whitish face and underparts; black-and-white barring on back. *Yellow-bellied Sapsucker* (p. 89): large, white wing patch.

Best Sites: found statewide. *Winter:* more common in the south.

RED-BELLIED WOODPECKER

Melanerpes carolinus

The Red-bellied Woodpecker is found year-round in southeastern North America, but its numbers fluctuate depending on the availability of habitat and winter conditions. In recent years, the Red-bellied Woodpecker has extended its range to the north, possibly because of mild winters or urban sprawl. • These birds often issue noisy rolling *churr* calls as they poke around wooded landscapes in search of a meal. Unlike most woodpeckers, Red-bellies consume large amounts of plant material, seldom excavating wood for insects. They also regularly visit feeders for seeds. • The Red-bellied Woodpecker's trademark belly is only a small reddish area that can be difficult to see in the field. • Studies of banded Red-bellied Woodpeckers have shown that these birds have a life span in the wild of more than 20 years.

♂

♀

ID: reddish tinge on belly; black-and-white barring on back; white patches on rump and base of primaries. *Male:* red nape extends to forehead. *Female:* red nape. *Juvenile:* dark gray crown; streaked breast.

Size: *L* 9–10½ in; *W* 16 in.

Status: common resident.

Habitat: mature deciduous woodlands; occasionally in wooded residential areas.

Nesting: in a natural cavity or the abandoned cavity of another woodpecker; female selects one of several nest sites excavated by the male; pair incubates 4–5 white eggs for 12–14 days; both adults raise the young.

Feeding: forages in trees, on the ground or occasionally on the wing; eats mostly insects, seeds, nuts and fruit; may also eat tree sap, some plant matter, small amphibians, bird eggs or small fish.

Voice: call is a soft, rolling *churr;* drums in second-long bursts.

Similar Species: no other Iowa woodpecker has a black-and-white-barred back. *Northern Flicker* (p. 92): black "bib"; brown back with dark barring; large, dark spots on underparts; longer tail; yellow underwings.

Best Sites: found statewide in appropriate habitat.

YELLOW-BELLIED SAPSUCKER

Sphyrapicus varius

Yes, there really is a Yellow-bellied Sapsucker, and finding one of these quiet birds is sure to be a highlight of an early spring birdwalk in Iowa. The drumming of sapsuckers—with their irregular rhythm reminiscent of Morse code—differs from that of other local woodpeckers. • Lines of parallel, freshly drilled "wells" in tree bark are a sure sign that sapsuckers are nearby. Even in migration, sapsuckers leave these trademark patterns in trees. The wells fill with sweet, sticky sap that attracts insects; the sapsuckers then make their rounds, eating both the trapped bugs and the pooled sap. Sapsuckers do not actually suck sap—they lap it up with a tongue that resembles a paintbrush. • Other species such as hummingbirds, kinglets, warblers and waxwings benefit from the wells made by Yellow-bellied Sapsuckers, especially early in the season when flying insects, fruits and nectar are rare.

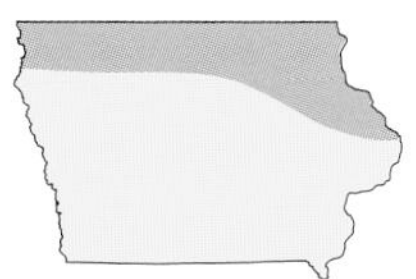

ID: black "bib"; red forecrown; black-and-white face, back, wings and tail; large, white wing patch; yellow wash on lower breast and belly. *Male:* red "chin." *Female:* white "chin." *Juvenile:* brownish overall, but with large, clearly defined wing patches.
Size: *L* 7–9 in; *W* 16 in.
Status: uncommon migrant in April and from mid-September through mid-October; rare summer and winter resident.
Habitat: deciduous and mixed forests, especially dry, 2nd-growth woodlands.
Nesting: in a cavity; usually in a poplar or birch tree with heart rot; often lines the cavity with wood chips; pair incubates 5–6 white eggs for 12–13 days.
Feeding: drills "wells" in trees to collect sap and trap insects; also flycatches and hammers trees for insects.
Voice: nasal, catlike meow; territorial and courtship hammering has an irregular rhythm.
Similar Species: *Downy Woodpecker* (p. 90) and *Hairy Woodpecker* (p. 91): white back; lack large, white wing patches and red forecrown.
Best Sites: *Breeding:* northeast area of Iowa. *In migration* and *winter:* found statewide.

DOWNY WOODPECKER

Picoides pubescens

A regular patron of backyard suet feeders, the small and common Downy Woodpecker is often the first woodpecker a novice birder will identify with confidence. It is generally more approachable and tolerant of human activities than are most birds, and its dainty appearance and brisk staccato calls soon render it familiar. But, these encounters are not always free of confusion—the closely related Hairy Woodpecker looks remarkably similar. • The Downy Woodpecker's small bill is ideal for poking at tiny crevices and extracting invertebrates and wood-boring grubs. • Like other members of the woodpecker family, the Downy has evolved a number of features that help to cushion the repeated shocks from a lifetime of hammering. These characteristics include a strong bill, strong neck muscles, a flexible, reinforced skull and a brain that is tightly packed in its protective cranium. Another feature that Downies share with other woodpeckers is feathered nostrils, which serve to filter out the sawdust it produces when hammering.

ID: short, stubby bill; black eye line and crown; clear white breast and back; mostly black tail; black-and-white wings; black-spotted, white outer tail feathers. *Male:* small, red patch on back of head. *Female:* no red patch.

Size: *L* 6–7 in; *W* 12 in.

Status: common resident.

Habitat: all wooded environments, especially deciduous and mixed forests and areas with tall, deciduous shrubs.

Nesting: pair excavates a cavity in a dying or decaying trunk or limb and lines it with wood chips; excavation takes more than 2 weeks; pair incubates 4–5 white eggs for 11–13 days; both adults feed the young.

Feeding: forages on and probes trunks and branches of saplings and shrubs; eats insect eggs, cocoons and adults and larvae of moths and butterflies; also eats nuts and seeds; visits suet feeders.

Voice: long, unbroken trill; calls are a sharp *pik* or *ki-ki-ki* or whiny *queek queek;* drums more than the Hairy Woodpecker and at a higher pitch, usually on smaller trees and dead branches.

Similar Species: *Hairy Woodpecker* (p. 91): larger; bill is as long as head; no spots on white outer tail feathers. *Yellow-bellied Sapsucker* (p. 89): large, white wing patch; red forecrown; lacks red nape and clean white back.

Best Sites: found statewide in appropriate habitat.

HAIRY WOODPECKER

Picoides villosus

A second or third look is often required to confirm the identity of the Hairy Woodpecker because it is so similar in appearance to its smaller cousin, the Downy Woodpecker. A convenient way to distinguish one bird from the other is by watching these woodpeckers at a backyard feeder. The Hairy Woodpecker is larger and more aggressive. • The secret to woodpeckers' feeding success is hidden in their skulls. Most woodpeckers have very long tongues—in some cases more than four times the length of the bill—made possible by twin structures that wrap around the perimeter of the skull. These structures store the tongue in much the same way that a measuring tape is stored in its case. Besides being long and maneuverable, the tip of the tongue is sticky with saliva and is finely barbed to help seize reluctant wood-boring insects. • Rather than singing during courtship, woodpeckers drum rhythmically on trees.

♀ ♂

ID: larger; black "cheek" and crown; bill is about as long as head; white breast and back; white-spotted, black wings; black tail with unspotted, white outer feathers. *Male:* small, red patch on back of head. *Female:* no red patch.

Size: *L* 8–9½ in; *W* 15 in.

Status: uncommon resident

Habitat: deciduous and mixed forests.

Nesting: pair excavates a nest site in a live or decaying tree trunk or limb; excavation takes more than 2 weeks; cavity is lined with wood chips; pair incubates 4–5 white eggs for 12–14 days; both adults feed the young.

Feeding: hammers, probes and forages on tree trunks and branches for insects and their eggs, cocoons and larvae; also eats nuts, fruit and seeds; visits suet feeders, especially in winter.

Voice: loud, sharp call: *peek peek;* long, unbroken trill: *keek-ik-ik-ik-ik-ik;* drums less regularly and at a lower pitch than the Downy Woodpecker, always on tree trunks and large branches.

Similar Species: *Downy Woodpecker* (p. 90): very similar; smaller; shorter bill; dark spots on white outer tail feathers. *Yellow-bellied Sapsucker* (p. 89): red forecrown; large, white wing patch lacks red nape and clean white back. *Black-backed Woodpecker:* rare vagrant; yellow forecrown; predominantly black head; black barring on sides.

Best Sites: found statewide in appropriate habitat.

NORTHERN FLICKER

Colaptes auratus

Unlike most woodpeckers, this species spends much of its time on the ground, feeding mostly on ants. It appears almost robinlike as it hops about in parks and cemeteries and along forest clearings in grassy meadows and fields. • Flickers are often seen bathing in dusty depressions. The dust particles absorb oils and bacteria that are harmful to the birds' feathers. To clean even more thoroughly, flickers will squish captured ants and then preen themselves with the remains; ants contain formic acid, which may kill small parasites on the flickers' skin and feathers. • Like many woodpeckers, the Northern Flicker has zygodactyl feet—each foot has two toes facing forward and two toes pointing backward—which allow the bird to move vertically up and down tree trunks. Stiff tail feathers also help to prop up this woodpecker's body while it scales trees and excavates cavities.

ID: black "bib"; long bill; brownish to buff face; gray crown; spotted, buff to whitish underparts; brown, barred back and wings; yellow underwings and undertail (may be salmon in vagrant "Red-Shafted" subspecies); white rump. *Male:* black "mustache" stripe; red nape crescent. *Female:* no "mustache."

Size: *L* 12½–13 in; *W* 20 in.

Status: common resident, especially in migration, from mid-March to mid-May and from mid-September to mid-October; uncommon in winter with decreasing numbers in the north.

Habitat: open deciduous, mixed and coniferous woodlands and forest edges, fields, meadows, beaver ponds, parks, cemeteries and suburbs.

Nesting: pair excavates a cavity in a dead or dying deciduous tree or may use a nest box; excavation takes about 2 weeks; cavity is lined with wood chips; pair incubates 5–8 white eggs for 11–16 days; both adults feed the young.

Feeding: forages on the ground for ants and other terrestrial insects; probes bark; also eats berries and nuts; occasionally flycatches.

Voice: loud, laughing, rapid *kick-kick-kick-kick-kick-kick; woika-woika-woika* issued during courtship.

Similar Species: *Red-bellied Woodpecker* (p. 88): more red on head; black-and-white pattern on back; wings with white flash; shorter tail.

Best Sites: widespread in appropriate habitat.

PILEATED WOODPECKER

Dryocopus pileatus

With its flaming red crest, swooping flight and maniacal call, this impressive, deep-forest dweller can stop hikers in their tracks. Using its powerful, dagger-shaped bill with stubborn determination, the Pileated Woodpecker chisels out uniquely shaped rectangular cavities in its unending search for grubs and ants. These cavities are often the first indication that a breeding pair is resident in an area. • Because they require large home territories, these magnificent birds are not encountered frequently. A pair of breeding Pileated Woodpeckers generally needs more than 100 acres of mature forest in which to settle. • As a primary cavity nester, the Pileated Woodpecker plays an important role in forest ecosystems. Other birds and even mammals depend on the activities of this woodpecker—ducks, small falcons, owls and even flying squirrels are frequent nesters in abandoned Pileated Woodpecker cavities. • Not surprisingly, a woodpecker's bill becomes shorter as the bird ages. In his historic painting of the Pileated Woodpecker, John J. Audubon correctly depicted the bills of the juveniles as slightly longer than those of the adults.

♂

♀

ID: predominantly black; yellow eyes; white "chin"; stout, dark bill; white stripe runs from bill to shoulder; flaming red crest; white wing linings. *Male:* red "mustache"; red crest extends from bill to nape. *Female:* no "mustache"; gray brown forehead.

Size: *L* 16–19 in; *W* 29 in.

Status: high conservation priority; uncommon resident in the east and northeast; local resident elsewhere.

Habitat: extensive tracts of mature deciduous, mixed or coniferous forests; along major rivers; some occur in riparian woodlands or woodlots in suburban and agricultural areas.

Nesting: pair excavates a cavity in a dead or dying tree trunk; excavation takes 3–6 weeks; cavity is lined with wood chips; pair incubates 4 white eggs for 15–18 days; both adults feed the young.

Feeding: hammers the base of rotting trees, creating fist-sized or larger, rectangular holes; eats carpenter ants, wood-boring beetle larvae, berries and nuts.

Voice: loud, fast, laughing, rolling *woika-woika-woika-woika;* long series of *kuk* notes; loud, resonant drumming.

Similar Species: *Other woodpeckers* (pp. 87–92): much smaller. *American Crow* (p. 105): lacks white underwings and flaming red crest.

Best Sites: Upper Mississippi; Effigy Mounds/Yellow River Forest; Mines of Spain; Ledges; Stephen's SF.

EASTERN WOOD-PEWEE

Contopus virens

Perched on an exposed tree branch in a suburban park, woodlot edge or neighborhood yard, the male Eastern Wood-Pewee whistles his plaintive *pee-ah-wee* all day long throughout summer. Some of the keenest suitors will even sing late into the evening, long after most birds have silenced their weary courtship songs. • Like other flycatchers, the Eastern Wood-Pewee makes aerial sallies from exposed perches to snatch flying insects in midair, a technique referred to as "hawking." • Many insects have evolved defense mechanisms to avert potential predators such as the Eastern Wood-Pewee and its flycatching relatives. • Wood-Pewees winter in Central and South America.

ID: dark upper mandible; dull yellow orange base on lower mandible; whitish throat; olive gray to olive brown upperparts; gray breast and sides; whitish or pale yellow belly, flanks and undertail coverts; 2 narrow, white wing bars.
Size: *L* 6–6½ in; *W* 10 in.
Status: common migrant and breeder from mid-May to mid-September.
Habitat: open, mixed and deciduous woodlands and woodland edges with a sparse understory; rarely in open, coniferous woodlands.
Nesting: on the fork of a horizontal deciduous branch, well away from the trunk; open cup nest of grass, plant fibers and lichen is bound with spider silk; female incubates 3 whitish eggs, with dark blotches concentrated at the larger end, for 12–13 days.
Feeding: flycatches insects from a perch or gleans foliage while hovering.
Voice: *Male:* song is a clear, slow, plaintive *pee-ah-wee,* with a lower 2nd note, sometimes followed by a down-slurred *pee-oh,* with or without pauses; also a *chip* call.
Similar Species: *Eastern Phoebe* (p. 96): all-dark bill; often pumps its tail; lacks conspicuous white wing bars. *Eastern Kingbird* (p. 99): larger; all-dark bill; brighter white underparts; white-tipped tail. Empidonax *flycatchers* (p. 95): smaller; eye rings; more conspicuous wing bars. *Olive-sided Flycatcher:* larger; white rump tufts; olive gray "vest"; lacks conspicuous white wing bars.
Best Sites: found statewide in appropriate habitat.

WILLOW FLYCATCHER

Empidonax traillii

Upon arriving in a suitable shrubby area with thick willows and tangled shrubbery, male Willow Flycatchers sing energetically from carefully chosen perches. They utter their sneezing *fitz-bew* call and battle vocally over preferred territories. During spring migration these birds can only be distinguished from Alder Flycatchers (*E. alnorum*) by their different song. • Once territories have been established and the business of nesting begins, Willow Flycatchers become shy, inconspicuous birds that opt to remain out of sight. Only when an avian intruder violates an established boundary does the resident Willow Flycatcher aggressively reveal itself. After raising their young and fattening themselves on insects in late summer and early fall, Willow Flycatchers begin their migratory journey to Central and South America.

ID: faint or absent eye ring; white throat; yellowish belly; pale olive breast; olive brown upperparts; 2 white wing bars.

Size: *L* 5½–6 in; *W* 8½ in.

Status: locally uncommon, but regular migrant and breeder from mid-May to mid-August.

Habitat: hawthorn or apple shrubs, red-osier dogwood, willow or other low growth on abandoned farmlands, in riparian corridors and wetlands.

Nesting: in a fork or on a branch in a dense shrub, usually 3–7 ft above the ground; female builds an open cup nest with grass, bark strips and plant fibers, lined with down; female incubates 3–4 whitish to pale buff eggs, with brown spots concentrated toward the larger end, for 12–15 days.

Feeding: flycatches insects; also hovers and gleans insects from vegetation.

Voice: song is a quick, sneezy *fitz-bew* that drops off at the end and is repeated up to 30 times a minute; call is a quick *whit.*

Similar Species: *Eastern Wood-Pewee* (p. 94): larger; lacks eye ring and conspicuous wing bars. *Alder Flycatcher:* song is *fee-bee-o;* usually found in wetter areas. *Least Flycatcher:* song is a clear *che-bek;* bolder, white eye ring; greener upperparts; pale, gray white underparts. *Acadian Flycatcher:* song is a forceful *peet-sa;* yellowish eye ring; greener upperparts; yellower underparts. *Yellow-bellied Flycatcher:* song is a liquid *che-lek;* yellowish eye ring; greener upperparts; yellower underparts.

Best Sites: found statewide in appropriate habitat.

EASTERN PHOEBE

Sayornis phoebe

Whether you are poking around your summer cottage, a campground picnic shelter or your backyard shed, there is a very good chance you will stumble upon an Eastern Phoebe family and their marvelous nest. Arriving earlier than most summer residents, the Eastern Phoebe's nest building and territorial defense strategy is normally well underway by the time most other songbirds arrive in Iowa in May. Once limited to nesting on natural cliffs and fallen riparian trees, this adaptive flycatcher has gradually found success in nesting on buildings and bridges, with a preference for sites near water. • Eastern Phoebes sometimes reuse their nest sites for many years, and they should be left undisturbed if found. Some people have caught on to the benefits of having phoebe tenants—these birds can be effective in controlling pesky insects. • Some other birds wag their tails while perched, but few species can match the enthusiasm of the Eastern Phoebe's pumping tail.

breeding

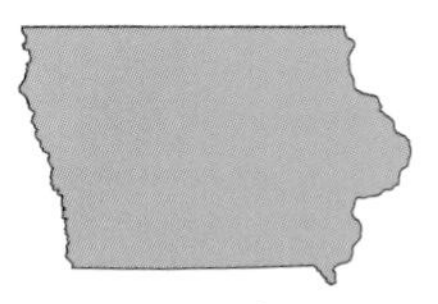

ID: all-dark bill; gray brown upperparts; belly may be washed with yellow in fall; white underparts with gray wash on breast and sides; no obvious wing bars; dark legs; frequently pumps its tail.

Size: *L* 6½–7 in; *W* 10½ in.

Status: uncommon to fairly common migrant and breeder from March through October; rarely lingers into late fall and winter.

Habitat: open deciduous woodlands, forest edges and clearings; usually near water.

Nesting: under the ledge of a building, picnic shelter, culvert, bridge, cliff or well; cup-shaped mud nest is lined with moss, grass, fur and feathers; female incubates 4–5 white eggs, often with a few reddish brown spots, for about 16 days; both adults feed the young.

Feeding: flycatches beetles, flies, wasps, grasshoppers, mayflies and other insects; occasionally plucks aquatic invertebrates and small fish from the water's surface.

Voice: *Male:* song is a hearty, snappy, frequent *fee-bee;* call is a sharp *chip.*

Similar Species: *Eastern Wood-Pewee* (p. 94): smaller; bicolored bill; wing bars; does not pump its tail. *Olive-sided Flycatcher:* dark "vest"; white, fluffy patches often visible above wings. Empidonax *flycatchers* (p. 95): most have eye rings and conspicuous wing bars. *Eastern Kingbird* (p. 99): white-tipped tail; black upperparts.

Best Sites: found statewide in appropriate habitat.

GREAT CRESTED FLYCATCHER

Myiarchus crinitus

The Great Crested Flycatcher's nesting habits are unusual for a flycatcher: it is a cavity nester, and although it prefers to nest in a natural tree cavity or abandoned woodpecker nest, it occasionally uses a nest box intended for a bluebird. Once in a while, the Great Crested Flycatcher decorates the entrance of its nest with a shed snakeskin. The purpose of this practice is not fully understood, but it might make any would-be predators think twice! In some instances, this versatile bird has even been known to substitute translucent plastic wrap for genuine snakeskin. • The Great Crested Flycatcher prefers open or semi-open hardwood forests and is a common summer resident in Iowa. • Songbirds such as the Great Crested Flycatcher are often thought of as birds that fly south for the winter. In reality, it would be more correct to say that they fly north for the summer. This flycatcher, as well as many other migrants, are subtropical or tropical birds of Central and South America that visit our country only briefly to raise their young before returning home.

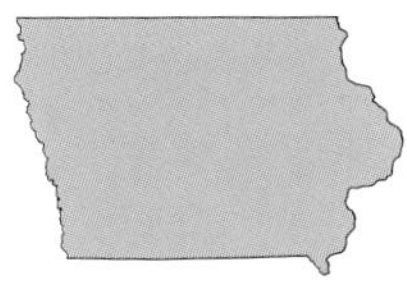

ID: heavy, black bill; peaked, "crested" head; dark olive brown upperparts; gray throat and upper breast; bright yellow belly and undertail coverts; reddish brown tail.

Size: *L* 8–9 in; *W* 13 in.

Status: common migrant and breeder from May to mid-September.

Habitat: deciduous and mixed woodlands and forests, usually near openings or edges.

Nesting: in a tree cavity, nest box or other artificial cavity; nest is lined with grass, bark strips and feathers; may hang a shed snakeskin or plastic wrap from the entrance; female incubates 5 creamy white to pale buff eggs, marked with lavender, olive and brown, for 13–15 days.

Feeding: often in the upper branches of deciduous trees; flycatches for insects; may also glean caterpillars and occasionally fruit.

Voice: loud, whistled *wheep!* and a rolling *prrrrreet!*

Similar Species: *Western Kingbird* (p. 98): all-gray head, neck and breast; darker tail with white outer margins; lacks head crest. *Yellow-bellied Flycatcher:* much smaller; yellow throat; lacks reddish brown tail and large, all-black bill.

Best Sites: found statewide, but more common in the heavier southern and eastern woodlands.

WESTERN KINGBIRD

Tyrannus verticalis

More typical of the western prairies, the Western Kingbird is an uncommon to rare visitor in our state. • Western Kingbirds are commonly observed while surveying for prey from fence posts, power lines and utility poles. When a kingbird spots an insect, it may chase it for up to 50 feet before a capturing it. • Once you have witnessed the kingbird's brave attacks against much larger birds, such as crows and hawks, it is easy to understand why this brawler was awarded the name "kingbird." • Its scientific name *verticalis* refers to the bird's hidden, red crown patch, which flares during courtship displays and while in combat with rivals. The red patch, however, is not a good identifying mark because it is rarely visible. • The tumbling, aerial courtship display of the Western Kingbird is a good indication that this bird might be breeding. The male twists and turns, rising to heights of 50 feet or more above the ground, then stalls, tumbles and flips while plummeting back to earth.

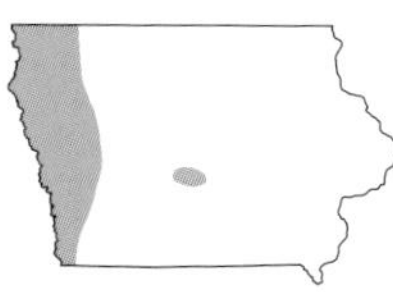

ID: faint, dark gray "mask"; thin, orange red crown (rarely seen); white "chin"; black bill and tail; gray head and breast; ashy gray upperparts; yellow belly and undertail coverts; white edge on outer tail feathers.

Size: *L* 8–9 in; *W* 15½ in.

Status: rare migrant and breeder from May to mid-September.

Habitat: open scrubland areas with scattered patches of brush or hedgerows; along the edges of open fields.

Nesting: in a deciduous tree near the trunk; bulky cup nest of grass, weeds and twigs is lined with fur, plant down and feathers; female incubates 3–5 whitish, heavily blotched eggs for 18–19 days.

Feeding: flycatches aerial insects, including bees, wasps, butterflies, moths, grasshoppers and flies; occasionally eats berries.

Voice: chatty, twittering *whit-ker-whit;* also a short *kit* or extended *kit-kit-keetle-dot*.

Similar Species: *Eastern Kingbird* (p. 99): black upperparts; white underparts; white-tipped tail. *Great Crested Flycatcher* (p. 97): slightly crested head; brownish upperparts; reddish brown tail; yellowish wing bars; lacks white edges on outer tail feathers.

Best Sites: Missouri river valley. *Breeding:* state capitol complex in Des Moines and western portions of the state. *In migration:* eastern Iowa.

EASTERN KINGBIRD

Tyrannus tyrannus

When you think of a tyrant, images of an oppressive dictator or a large carnivorous dinosaur are much more likely to come to mind than images of a little bird. True as that might be, no one familiar with the pugnacity of the Eastern Kingbird would refute its scientific name, *Tyrannus tyrannus*. This bird is a brawler, and it will fearlessly attack crows, hawks and even humans that pass through its territory. Intruders are often vigorously pursued, pecked and plucked for some distance until the kingbird is satisfied that there is no further threat. In contrast, its butterfly-like courtship flight, which is characterized by short, quivering wingbeats, reveals a gentler side of this bird. • Eastern Kingbirds are common and widespread, so during a drive in the country it is likely you will spot at least one of these birds sitting on a fenceline or utility wire along a roadside. • Eastern Kingbirds rarely walk or hop on the ground—they prefer to fly, even for very short distances.

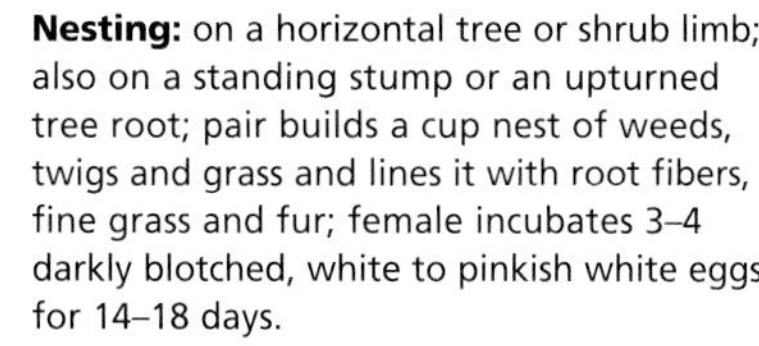

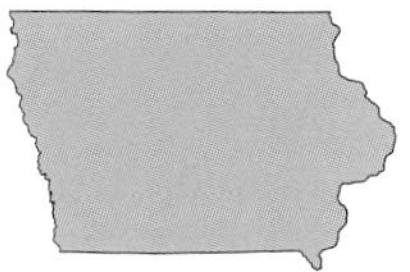

ID: black bill; small head crest; thin, orange red crown (rarely seen); dark gray to black upperparts; white underparts; black legs; white-tipped tail.

Size: *L* 8½ in; *W* 15 in.

Status: common migrant and breeder from late April or early May through September.

Habitat: rural fields with scattered trees or hedgerows, clearings in fragmented forests, open roadsides, burned areas and close to human settlements.

Nesting: on a horizontal tree or shrub limb; also on a standing stump or an upturned tree root; pair builds a cup nest of weeds, twigs and grass and lines it with root fibers, fine grass and fur; female incubates 3–4 darkly blotched, white to pinkish white eggs for 14–18 days.

Feeding: flycatches insects; infrequently eats berries.

Voice: call is a quick, loud, chattering *kit-kit-kitter-kitter;* also a buzzy *dzee-dzee-dzee*.

Similar Species: *Other flycatchers* (pp. 95–97): none have white underparts and a white-tipped tail. *Tree Swallow* (p. 108): smaller bill; iridescent, dark blue back; more streamlined body; lacks white-tipped tail.

Best Sites: found statewide in appropriate habitat.

LOGGERHEAD SHRIKE

Lanius ludovicianus

A shrike resembles a Northern Mockingbird in body shape and color, but the Loggerhead's method of hunting is very different. This predatory songbird has very acute vision. It often perches atop trees and on wires to scan for small prey. • Males display their hunting prowess by impaling prey on thorns or barbed wire. This behavior may also serve as a means of storing excess food during times of plenty. In spring, you may see a variety of skewered creatures baking in the sun. • Loggerhead Shrike populations have severely declined in many parts of this bird's North American range, earning it endangered species status in some states. Habitat destruction is thought to be the main reason for the population decline. Loggerheads are frequent victims in highway traffic fatalities and, in Iowa, their numbers have rapidly declined where fencerows have been cleared.

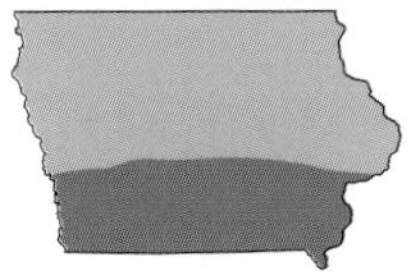

ID: black "mask" extends above hooked bill onto forehead; gray crown and back; white underparts; black tail and wings. *In flight:* white wing patches; white-edged tail. *Juvenile:* brownish gray, barred upperparts.

Size: *L* 9 in; *W* 12 in.

Status: species of concern; rare to uncommon migrant and breeder; more common in the south in winter.

Habitat: grazed pastures and marginal and abandoned farmlands with scattered hawthorn shrubs, fence posts, barbed wire and nearby wetlands; untilled open country.

Nesting: low in the crotch of a shrub or small tree; thorny hawthorn shrubs are often preferred; bulky cup nest of twigs and grass is lined with animal hair, feathers, plant down and rootlets; female incubates 5–6 pale buff to grayish white eggs, with dark spots concentrated at the larger end, for 15–17 days.

Feeding: swoops down on prey from a perch or attacks in pursuit; takes mostly large insects; regularly eats small birds, rodents and shrews; also eats carrion, small snakes and amphibians.

Voice: *Male:* high-pitched, hiccupy *bird-ee bird-ee* in summer; a harsh, infrequent *shack-shack* year-round.

Similar Species: *Northern Shrike:* winter visitor; larger; black "mask" does not extend above hooked bill; fine barring on sides and breast; immature has unbarred, light brown upperparts and finely barred underparts. *Northern Mockingbird:* slim bill; no "mask"; slimmer overall.

Best Sites: found statewide in appropriate habitat, especially in southern Iowa. *Winter:* south of Interstate 80.

YELLOW-THROATED VIREO

Vireo flavifrons

The Yellow-throated Vireo is usually found in mature deciduous woodlands where there is no understory and particularly likes tall oaks and maples. Similar to its treetop neighbor the Cerulean Warbler, the Yellow-throated Vireo forages high above the forest floor, making it difficult to observe. • Unmated males sing tirelessly as they search for nest sites, often placing a few pieces of nest material in several locations. When a female appears, the male dazzles her with his displays and leads her on a tour of potential nest sites within his large territory. If a bond is established, they will mate and build an intricately woven, hanging nest in the forking branches of a deciduous tree. The male is a devoted helper, assisting the female to build the nest, incubate the eggs and rear the young. • The Yellow-throated is North America's most colorful vireo and the only one with a bright yellow throat and breast and white belly. The Latin name *flavifrons* means "yellow front."

ID: bright yellow spectacles, throat and breast; olive upperparts; gray rump; dark wings and tail; 2 white wing bars; white belly and undertail coverts.

Size: *L* 5½ in; *W* 9½ in.

Status: common migrant and breeder in the southeast from May through mid-September; uncommon elsewhere.

Habitat: mature deciduous woodlands with minimal understory.

Nesting: pair builds a hanging cup nest in the fork of a deciduous tree branch; pair incubates 4 creamy white to pinkish eggs, with dark spots toward the larger end, for 14–15 days; each parent takes on guardianship of half the fledged young.

Feeding: forages for mostly insects on branches and foliage in the upper canopy; also eats seasonally available berries.

Voice: song is a slowly repeated series of hoarse phrases with long pauses in between: *ahweeo, eeoway, away;* calls include a throaty *heh heh heh.*

Similar Species: *Pine Warbler:* faint spectacles; thinner bill; faint, darkish streaking along sides; yellow belly; olive yellow rump. *Warbling Vireo* (p. 102): eye line instead of spectacles; no wing bars. *Blue-headed Vireo:* white spectacles and throat; yellow highlights in wings and tail. *White-eyed Vireo:* white eyes; white "chin" and throat; grayer head and back.

Best Sites: found statewide in appropriate habitat, primarily in the southeast.

WARBLING VIREO

Vireo gilvus

The charming Warbling Vireo is a common summer resident of deciduous woodlands. By early May, its wondrous and familiar voice fills many local parks and backyards. • The Warbling Vireo lacks splashy field marks and is only readily observed when it moves from one leafy hideout to another. Searching treetops for this generally inconspicuous vireo may literally be a "pain in the neck," but the satisfaction of visually confirming its identity is rewarding. • Although hanging nests of vireos are usually well hidden, in winter, their whereabouts are revealed, swinging precariously from bare, deciduous branches. • Old maples and cottonwoods are the preferred foraging and nesting sites of this species, and so, the Warbling Vireo remains one of Iowa's most widespread vireos.

breeding

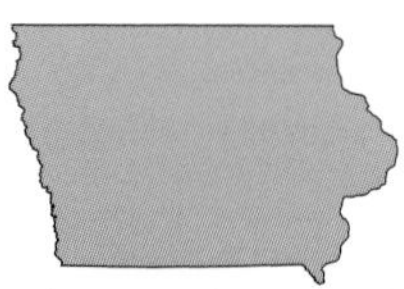

ID: partial, dark eye line borders white "eyebrow"; gray crown; olive gray upperparts; greenish flanks; white to pale gray underparts; bluish gray legs; no wing bars.

Size: *L* 5–5½ in; *W* 8½ in.

Status: common migrant and breeder from early May to early September.

Habitat: parks and gardens with deciduous trees, open deciduous woodlands.

Nesting: in a horizontal fork in a deciduous tree or shrub; hanging, basketlike cup nest is made of grass, roots, plant down, spider silk and a few feathers; pair incubates 4 darkly speckled, white eggs for 12–14 days.

Feeding: gleans foliage for insects; occasionally hovers.

Voice: *Male:* long, musical warble of slurred whistles.

Similar Species: *Philadelphia Vireo:* full, dark eye line borders white "eyebrow"; yellow breast, sides and flanks. *Red-eyed Vireo* (p. 103): black eye line extends to bill; blue gray crown; red eyes. *Tennessee Warbler:* blue gray "cap" and nape; slimmer bill; olive green back. *Orange-crowned Warbler:* more yellow overall; slimmer bill.

Best Sites: found statewide in appropriate habitat.

RED-EYED VIREO

Vireo olivaceus

The Red-eyed Vireo is the undisputed champion of vocal endurance in our region. In spring and early summer, males sing continuously through the day, usually five or six hours after sunrise, carrying on long after most songbirds have curtailed their courtship melodies. One particularly vigorous Red-eyed Vireo male holds the record for most songs delivered in a single day: approximately 22,000! • The Red-eyed Vireo has an unusual stance as it hops along branches, hunched over and diagonally facing its direction of travel. • There is no firm agreement about the reason for this vireo's red eye color. Red eyes are very unusual among songbirds and tend to be more prevalent in nonpasserines, such as hawks, grebes and some herons. • This adaptive bird has become part of many communities and is the most common vireo in our area. • Red-eyed Vireos sound a lot like American Robins, and new birders are often delighted to discover these nifty birds hiding behind a familiar song.

breeding

ID: dark eye line; red eyes; white "eyebrow"; black-bordered, blue gray crown; olive "cheek"; olive green upperparts; white to pale gray underparts; may have yellow wash on sides, flanks and undertail coverts, especially in fall; no wing bars.

Size: *L* 6 in; *W* 10 in.

Status: common to abundant migrant and breeder from mid-May to late September.

Habitat: deciduous woodlands with a shrubby understory.

Nesting: in a horizontal fork in a deciduous tree or shrub; hanging, basketlike cup nest is made of grass, roots, spider silk and cocoons; female incubates 4 white eggs, darkly spotted at the larger end, for 11–14 days.

Feeding: gleans foliage for insects, especially caterpillars; often hovers; also eats berries.

Voice: call is a short, scolding *neeah*. *Male:* song is a continuous, variable, robinlike run of quick, short phrases with distinct pauses in between: *Look-up, way-up, tree-top, see-me, here-I-am!*

Similar Species: *Philadelphia Vireo:* song is very similar, but slightly higher pitched; yellow breast; lacks black border on blue gray "cap." *Warbling Vireo* (p. 102): dusky eye line does not extend to bill; lacks black border on gray "cap." *Tennessee Warbler:* blue gray "cap" and nape; slimmer bill; olive green back.

Best Sites: found statewide in appropriate habitat, especially in the south and east.

BLUE JAY

Cyanocitta cristata

The large trees and bushy ornamental shrubs of our suburban neighborhoods and rural communities are perfect habitats for the adaptable Blue Jay. It is one of the most recognizable songbirds, and most common wherever there are fruit-bearing plants and well-maintained backyard feeding stations with sunflower seeds and peanuts. Blue Jays can appear a bit gluttonous at the feeder, but they are often storing the food in caches strategically placed around the neighborhood. • The Blue Jay embodies all the admirable traits and aggressive qualities of the corvid family, which also includes the magpie, crow and raven. Although beautiful, resourceful and vocally diverse, the Blue Jay is occasionally aggressive, raiding nests and bullying other feeder visitors. Whether on its own or gathered in a mob, the Blue Jay rarely hesitates to drive away smaller birds, squirrels or even cats when threatened. It seems there is no predator, not even the Great Horned Owl, that is too formidable for this bird to cajole or harass.

ID: blue crest; black "necklace"; black eye line and bill; blue upperparts; white underparts; white bar and flecking on wings; dark bars and white corners on blue tail.
Size: *L* 11–12½ in; *W* 16 in.
Status: common resident; flocks are seen in migration from mid-September through October; a few winter visitors.
Habitat: mixed deciduous forests, agricultural areas, scrubby fields and townsites.
Nesting: in the crotch of a tree or tall shrub; pair builds a bulky stick nest and incubates 4–5 greenish, buff or pale blue eggs, spotted with gray and brown, for 16–18 days.
Feeding: forages on the ground and among vegetation for nuts, berries, eggs, nestlings and seeds; also eats insects and carrion.
Voice: noisy, screaming *jay-jay-jay;* nasal *queedle queedle queedle-queedle* sounds like a muted trumpet; often mimics sounds.
Similar Species: none.
Best Sites: widespread throughout the state. *In fall migration:* Hitchcock WA hawk watch.

AMERICAN CROW

Corvus brachyrhynchos

American Crows are wary and intelligent birds that have flourished despite considerable human effort, over many generations, to reduce their numbers. These birds are ecological generalists, and much of their strength lies in their ability to adapt to a variety of habitats. • The American Crow is a common bird throughout much of our state in fall and winter, and may be seen roosting in flocks of hundreds or thousands on a chilly night. • Crows in captivity are impressive mimics, able to whine like a dog, cry like a child, squawk like a hen or laugh like a human. Some can even repeat simple spoken words. • The American Crow's cumbersome-sounding scientific name *Corvus brachyrhynchos* is Latin for "raven with the small nose."

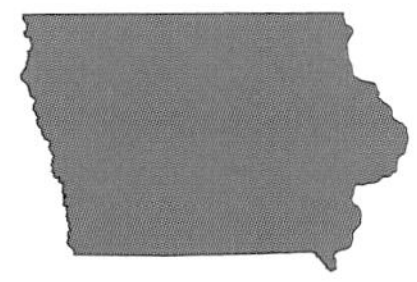

ID: all-black body; slim, sleek head and throat; black bill and legs; square-shaped tail.

Size: *L* 17–21 in; *W* 3 ft.

Status: abundant year-round resident; numbers increase in winter.

Habitat: urban areas, agricultural fields and other open areas with scattered woodlands.

Nesting: in a coniferous or deciduous tree or on a utility pole; large stick-and-branch nest is lined with fur and soft plant materials; female incubates 4–6 gray green to blue green eggs, blotched with brown and gray, for about 18 days.

Feeding: very opportunistic; feeds on carrion, small vertebrates, other birds' eggs and nestlings, berries, seeds, invertebrates and human food waste; also visits bird feeders.

Voice: distinctive, far-carrying, repetitive *caw-caw-caw.*

Similar Species: *Common Raven:* rare vagrant; larger; heavier bill; shaggy throat; wedge-shaped tail.

Best Sites: widespread throughout the state.

HORNED LARK

Eremophila alpestris

Horned Larks are among the earliest nesters in our region, settling on fields long before the snows are gone. They are present year-round and are one of the hardiest of our small birds. • The male Horned Lark performs an elaborate, song-flight courtship display. Flying and gliding in circles as high as 800 feet, the male issues his sweet, tinkling song before he closes his wings and plummets in a dramatic, high-speed dive that he aborts at the last second to avoid hitting the ground. • Horned Larks are commonly found along the shoulders of gravel roads, where they search for seeds. Although they can be conspicuous, these birds are often difficult to identify when they fly off into adjacent fields at the approach of a vehicle.

ID: *Male:* small, black "horns" (rarely raised); black line under eye extends from bill to "cheek"; light yellow to white face; pale throat; black breast band; dull brown upperparts; dark tail with white outer tail feathers. *Female:* less distinctively patterned; duller plumage overall.

Size: *L* 7 in; *W* 12 in.

Status: common resident, but abundant migrant in February, March and November; wintering and breeding birds are different subspecies.

Habitat: *Breeding:* open areas, including pastures, croplands, sparsely vegetated fields, weedy meadows and airports. *In migration* and *winter:* croplands, fields and roadside ditches.

Nesting: on the ground, in a shallow scrape lined with grass, plant fibers and roots; female chooses the nest site and incubates 3–4 pale gray to greenish white eggs, spotted with brown, for 10–12 days.

Feeding: gleans the ground for seeds; feeds insects to its young.

Voice: call is a tinkling *tsee-titi* or *zoot;* flight song is a long series of tinkling, twittered whistles.

Similar Species: *Sparrows* (pp. 137–49), *Lapland Longspur* (p. 148) and *American Pipit:* all lack distinctive facial pattern, "horns" and solid black breast band. *Sprague's Pipit:* spots rather than streaks on crown and back; young Horned Larks sometimes mistaken for spring migrant Sprague's.

Best Sites: found statewide in appropriate habitat, but most common in the north.

PURPLE MARTIN

Progne subis

Purple Martins once nested in natural tree hollows and cliff crevices, but with today's modern martin "condo" complexes, these birds have all but abandoned natural nest sites. Although the Purple Martin is our least common swallow, you may successfully attract it to your backyard with a well-placed complex, found near water and high on a pole. It is important that the condo be cleaned out and closed up each winter to avoid the luxurious dwellings being taken over by aggressive European Starlings and House Sparrows. If all goes well, a Purple Martin colony will return to your apartment complex each spring. The result is an endlessly entertaining summer spectacle of these spiraling birds in pursuit of flying insects and their young perched clumsily at the opening of their apartment cavities. • The scientific name *Progne* refers to Procne, the daughter of the king of Athens who, according to Greek mythology, was transformed into a swallow.

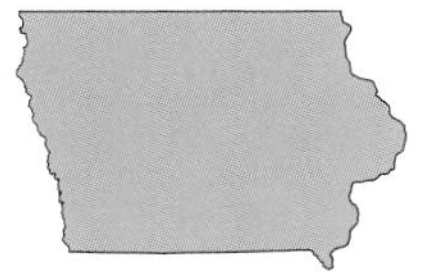

ID: glossy, dark blue body; small bill; slightly forked tail; pointed wings. *Male:* dark underparts. *Female:* sooty gray underparts.
Size: *L* 7–8 in; *W* 18 in.
Status: uncommon migrant and breeder; arrives in late March and most flocks disappear by mid-September.
Habitat: often near water in semi-open areas, urban lots, acreages and parks.
Nesting: communal; usually in a human-made, apartment-style birdhouse; also in a hollowed-out gourd; rarely in a tree cavity or cliff crevice; nest materials include feathers, grass, mud and vegetation; female incubates 4–5 white eggs for 15–18 days.
Feeding: mostly while in flight; usually eats flies, ants, bugs, dragonflies and mosquitoes; may also glean the ground for insects and rarely berries.
Voice: rich, fluty *pew-pew*, often heard in flight.
Similar Species: *European Starling* (p. 126): long bill (yellow in summer); lacks forked tail. *Barn Swallow* (p. 111): buff orange to reddish brown throat; whitish to cinnamon underparts; deeply forked tail. *Tree Swallow* (p. 108): white underparts.
Best Sites: widespread in appropriate habitat.

TREE SWALLOW

Tachycineta bicolor

Tree Swallows are often seen perched beside their fencepost nest boxes. When conditions are favorable, these busy birds are known to return to their young 10 to 20 times per hour, providing observers with numerous opportunities to watch and photograph them in action. • Tree Swallows prefer to nest in natural tree hollows or woodpecker cavities in standing snags, but where cavities are scarce, nest boxes may be used. They often occupy bluebird boxes, sometimes right next door to a bluebird family. Increasingly, landowners, park managers and forestry companies are realizing the value of dead trees and are choosing to leave them standing. • In bright spring sunshine, the iridescent backs of these birds appear dark blue; prior to fall migration, they appear green. Unlike other North American swallows, female Tree Swallows do not acquire their full adult plumage until their second or third year. • The scientific name *bicolor* is Latin for "two colors" and refers to the contrast between the bird's dark upperparts and white underparts.

ID: iridescent, dark blue or green head and upperparts; small bill; white underparts; dark rump; long, pointed wings; shallowly forked tail. *Female:* slightly duller. *Immature:* brown above; white below.

Size: *L* 5½ in; *W* 14½ in.

Status: abundant migrant and common breeder from mid-March to mid-October.

Habitat: ponds, marshes and lakes with snags or other cavities; also fencelines and open woodlands.

Nesting: in a tree cavity or nest box lined with weeds, grass and feathers; female incubates 4–6 white eggs for up to 19 days.

Feeding: catches flies, midges, mosquitoes, beetles and ants on the wing; also takes stoneflies, mayflies and caddisflies from the water's surface; may eat some berries and seeds.

Voice: alarm call is a metallic, buzzy *klweet*. *Male:* song is a liquid, chattering twitter.

Similar Species: *Purple Martin* (p. 107): male is dark blue overall; female has sooty gray underparts. *Eastern Kingbird* (p. 99): larger; longer bill; dark gray to blackish upperparts; white-tipped tail. *Bank Swallow* and *Northern Rough-winged Swallow* (p. 109): brown upperparts. *Barn Swallow* (p. 111): buff orange to reddish brown throat; deeply forked tail.

Best Sites: widespread in appropriate habitat.

NORTHERN ROUGH-WINGED SWALLOW

Stelgidopteryx serripennis

The inconspicuous Northern Rough-winged Swallow typically nests on sandy banks along rivers and streams, enjoying its own private piece of waterfront. It is most likely to be seen feeding over water, picking off insects on or near the surface. • Northern Rough-winged Swallows are usually seen in pairs, but they don't mind joining a crowd, and once in a while, a pair may nest among a large colony of similar-looking Bank Swallows. • Unlike other swallows, male Northern Rough-wings have curved barbs along the outer edge of their primary wing feathers. The purpose of this saw-toothed edge remains a mystery, but it may be used to produce sound during courtship displays. The ornithologist who initially named this bird must have been very impressed with its wings: *Stelgidopteryx* means "scraper wing" and *serripennis* means "saw feather."

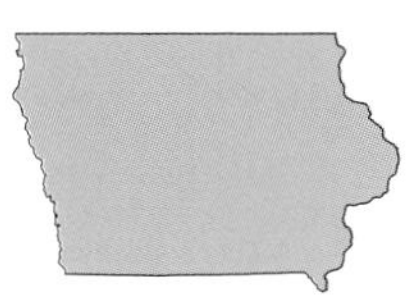

ID: small bill; dark "cheek"; pale throat; uniform brown upperparts; light, brownish gray underparts; dark rump. *In flight:* long, pointed wings; notched tail.

Size: *L* 5½ in; *W* 14 in.

Status: common migrant and breeder from mid- to late April to September.

Habitat: open and semi-open areas, including fields and open woodlands, usually near water; gravel pits.

Nesting: occasionally in small colonies; pair excavates a long burrow in a steep, earthen bank; sometimes reuses a kingfisher or rodent burrow; lines end of burrow with leaves and dry grass; generally the female incubates 4–8 white eggs for 12–16 days.

Feeding: catches flying insects on the wing; occasionally eats insects from the ground; drinks while flying.

Voice: often quiet; occasionally a quick, short, squeaky *brrrtt.*

Similar Species: *Bank Swallow:* dark breast band; pale back contrasts with darker wings. *Tree Swallow* (p. 108): dark, iridescent, bluish to greenish upperparts; clean white underparts. *Cliff Swallow* (p. 110): brown-and-blue upperparts; buff forehead and rump patch.

Best Sites: found statewide in appropriate habitat. *Breeding:* Ledges SP.

CLIFF SWALLOW

Petrochelidon pyrrhonota

The Cliff Swallow could appropriately be renamed "Bridge Swallow"—most colonies inhabit bridge crossings all over eastern North America. If you stop to inspect the underside of a bridge, you may see hundreds of their gourd-shaped mud nests stuck to the pillars and structural beams. Clouds of Cliff Swallows will often swirl up along either side of the roadway, dazzling passersby with their acrobatics and impressive numbers. • Master mud masons, Cliff Swallows roll mud into balls with their bills and press the pellets together to form their nests. Brooding parents peer out with their gleaming eyes watching the world go by, and their white forehead patch is a good indication to potential intruders that somebody is home. • Cliff Swallows are the last of their kind to arrive in Iowa in spring. • These swallows are brood parasites. Females often lay one or more eggs in the temporarily vacant nests of neighboring Cliff Swallows. The owners of parasitized nests accept the foreign eggs and care for them as if they were their own.

ID: buff forehead; rusty nape, "cheek" and throat; buff breast; white belly; blue gray head and wings; spotted undertail coverts; squarish tail.

Size: *L* 5½ in; *W* 13½ in.

Status: abundant migrant and breeder from mid-May to mid-September.

Habitat: steep banks, cliffs, bridges and buildings, often near watercourses.

Nesting: colonial; in open country under a bridge or on a cliff or building; often under the eaves of a barn; pair builds a gourd-shaped mud nest with a small opening near the bottom; pair incubates 4–5 brown-spotted, white to pinkish eggs for 14–16 days.

Feeding: forages over water, fields and marshes; catches flying insects on the wing; occasionally eats berries; drinks on the wing.

Voice: twittering chatter: *churrr-churrr;* also an alarm call: *nyew.*

Similar Species: *Barn Swallow* (p. 111): usually has rust-colored underparts and forehead; dark rump; deeply forked tail. *Other swallows* (pp. 107–110): lack buff forehead and rump patch.

Best Sites: widespread in appropriate habitat.

BARN SWALLOW

Hirundo rustica

Although Barn Swallows do not occur in mass colonies, they are as familiar to us as Cliff Swallows, often building their nests on human-made structures. Barn Swallows once nested on cliffs and in cave entrances, but their cup-shaped mud nests are now more often found under house eaves, in barns and boathouses, under bridges or on any other structure that provides shelter. • Unfortunately, not everyone appreciates nesting Barn Swallows—the young can be very messy—and people often scrape Barn Swallow nests off buildings just as the nesting season begins. However, these graceful birds are natural pest controllers, and their close association with urban areas and tolerance for human activity affords us the opportunity to observe and study the normally secretive reproductive cycle of birds. • This bird is the only one found in Iowa that exhibits the deeply forked "swallow tail." • *Hirundo* is Latin for "swallow," while *rustica* refers to this bird's preference for rural habitats.

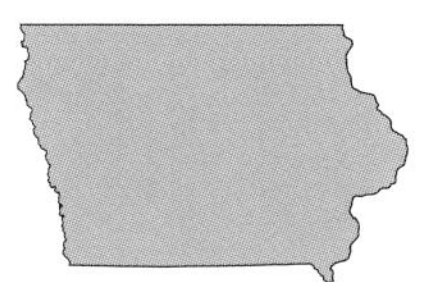

ID: rufous throat and forehead; blue black upperparts; rust- to buff-colored underparts; long, deeply forked tail; long, pointed wings.
Size: *L* 7 in; *W* 15 in.
Status: abundant migrant and breeder from April to mid-October; more common in the north central and northwest.
Habitat: open rural and urban areas where bridges, culverts and buildings are found near rivers, lakes, marshes or ponds.
Nesting: singly or in small, loose colonies; on a vertical or horizontal building structure under a suitable overhang, on a bridge or in a culvert; half or full cup nest is made of mud and grass or straw; pair incubates 4–7 white eggs, spotted with brown, for 13–17 days.
Feeding: catches flying insects on the wing.
Voice: continuous, twittering chatter: *zip-zip-zip;* also *kvick-kvick*.
Similar Species: *Cliff Swallow* (p. 110): buff rump and forehead; pale underparts; squared tail. *Purple Martin* (p. 107): shallowly forked tail; male is completely blue black; female has sooty gray underparts. *Tree Swallow* (p. 108): clean white underparts; notched tail.
Best Sites: found statewide in appropriate habitat, but more common in northern central and northwestern Iowa.

BLACK-CAPPED CHICKADEE

Poecile atricapillus

In winter, when most birds retreat into a slower mode of living or escape to warmer climes, the spunky Black-capped Chickadee remains in Iowa, never allowing the cold season to stifle its energy. Flocks of these energetic birds can be seen year-round as they flit from tree to tree, scouring branches and shriveled leaves for insects and sometimes hanging upside down to inspect every nook and cranny. All winter residents seem to fall into step with lively, active chickadees, and in spring and fall, migrants rely on the local knowledge of Black-caps to find the best foraging areas. • Most songbirds, including the Black-capped Chickadee, have both songs and calls. The chickadee's *swee-tee* song is heard primarily during spring courtship, and its *chick-a-dee-dee-dee* call keeps flocks together and maintains contact among flock members.

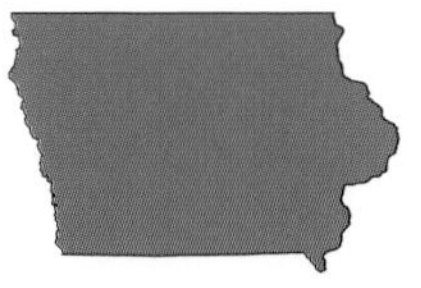

ID: black "cap" and "bib"; white "cheek"; white underparts; light buff sides and flanks; gray back and wings; dark legs; white edging on wing feathers.

Size: *L* 5–6 in; *W* 8 in.

Status: common resident.

Habitat: deciduous and mixed forests and woodlands, riparian woodlands, wooded urban parks; backyards with bird feeders in winter.

Nesting: excavates a cavity in a soft, rotting stump or tree or uses a woodpecker hole or nest box; cavity is lined with fur, feathers, moss, grass and cocoons; female incubates 6–8 white eggs with fine, reddish brown dots, for 12–13 days.

Feeding: gleans vegetation, branches and the ground for small insects and spiders; also eats conifer seeds and invertebrate eggs; visits backyard feeders.

Voice: call is a perky *chick-a-dee-dee-dee;* song is a slow, whistled *swee-tee* or *fee-bee.*

Similar Species: *Blackpoll Warbler:* breeding male has longer, paler bill, 2 white wing bars, dark streaking on white underparts and orangy legs.

Best Sites: found statewide in appropriate habitat.

TUFTED TITMOUSE

Baeolophus bicolor

This bird's amusing feeding antics and its insatiable appetite keep curious observers entertained at bird feeders. Grasping an acorn or sunflower seed with its tiny feet, the dexterous Tufted Titmouse repeatedly strikes its dainty bill against the hard outer coating to expose the inner core. • A breeding pair of Tufted Titmice will maintain their bond throughout the year, even when joining small, multi-species flocks for the cold winter months. The titmouse family bond is so strong that the young from one breeding season often stay with their parents long enough to help them with nesting and feeding duties the following year. In late winter, mating pairs break from their flocks to search for nesting cavities. If you are fortunate enough to have titmice living in your area, you might be able to attract a nesting pair by leaving out your own hair from a hairbrush in your yard—there is a good chance that these curious birds will gladly incorporate your offering into the construction of their nest.

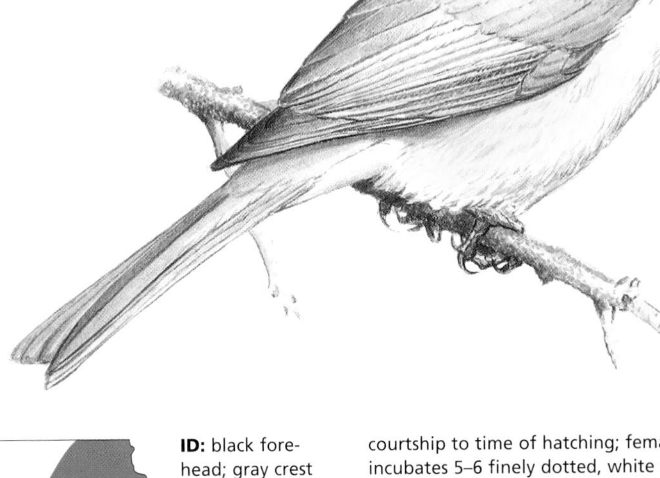

ID: black forehead; gray crest and upperparts; white underparts; buffy flanks.

Size: *L* 6–6½ in; *W* 10 in.

Status: common resident in the southeast; local in the northwest.

Habitat: deciduous woodlands, groves and suburban parks with large, mature trees.

Nesting: in a natural cavity or woodpecker cavity lined with soft vegetation and animal hair; female may be fed by the male from courtship to time of hatching; female incubates 5–6 finely dotted, white eggs for 12–14 days; both adults and occasionally a "helper" raise the young.

Feeding: forages on the ground and in trees; often hangs upside down; eats insects, seeds, nuts and fruits; visits feeders in winter for seeds and suet.

Voice: noisy, scolding calls like those of a chickadee; song is a whistled *peter peter* or *beedee beedee beedee.*

Similar Species: none.

Best Sites: widespread in appropriate habitat, especially in the southeast.

RED-BREASTED NUTHATCH

Sitta canadensis

The Red-breasted Nuthatch streaks toward a neighborhood bird feeder from the cover of a coniferous tree. It tosses a few empty shells and then selects its own meal before speeding off, seldom lingering long enough to be identified. • Red-breasted Nuthatches frequently join feeding flocks—groups of warblers, chickadees, kinglets, titmice and small woodpeckers often forage together through woodlands in winter or during migration. • The unusual body shape of nuthatches and their habit of moving headfirst down tree trunks sets them apart from other songbirds. Their nasal *yank-yank-yank* calls also often reveal their presence long before they are seen. • The Red-breasted Nuthatch smears the entrance of its nesting cavity with pitch from pine or spruce trees. The sticky doormat helps to keep the nest free of ants and other invertebrates that might enter and transmit fungal infections or parasitize nestlings.

ID: white "eyebrow"; black eye line and "cap"; straight bill; white "cheek"; gray blue upperparts; rusty underparts; short tail. *Male:* black crown; deeper rust on breast. *Female:* dark gray crown; light red wash on breast.

Size: *L* 4½ in; *W* 8½ in.

Status: irruptive migrant and winter visitor from late September through early May; 1 nesting record in Iowa.

Habitat: *Breeding* and *in migration:* evergreen plantations. *Winter:* conifer groves; mixed woodlands, especially those near bird feeders and cemeteries.

Nesting: excavates a cavity or uses an abandoned woodpecker nest; usually smears the entrance with pitch; nest is made of bark shreds, grass and fur; female incubates 5–6 white eggs, spotted with reddish brown, for about 12 days.

Feeding: forages down trees headfirst; probes for larval and adult invertebrates under loose bark; eats pine and spruce seeds in winter; often seen at feeders.

Voice: call is a slow, continually repeated, nasal *yank-yank-yank,* higher than the White-breasted Nuthatch; also a short *tsip.*

Similar Species: *White-breasted Nuthatch* (p. 115): larger; lacks black eye line and red underparts.

Best Sites: found statewide in appropriate habitat.

WHITE-BREASTED NUTHATCH

Sitta carolinensis

To a novice birder, seeing a White-breasted Nuthatch calling repeatedly while clinging to the underside of a branch is an odd sight. Moving headfirst down a tree trunk, the White-breasted Nuthatch forages for invertebrates, sometimes pausing to survey its surroundings and occasionally issuing a noisy call. Unlike woodpeckers and creepers, nuthatches do not use their tails to brace themselves against tree trunks—they grasp the tree using only the strength of their feet. • Nuthatches are presumably named for their habit of wedging seeds and nuts into crevices and hacking them open with their bills. • Although the White-breasted Nuthatch is a regular visitor to most backyard feeders, like its Red-breasted cousin, it only sticks around long enough to grab a seed and then dashes off. An offering of suet may persuade this tiny bird to stay a little while longer. • The scientific name *carolinensis* means "of Carolina"—the first White-breasted Nuthatch specimen was collected in South Carolina.

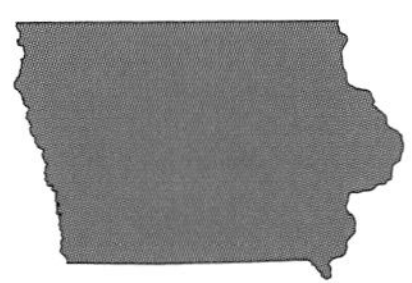

ID: white face; straight bill; white underparts; gray blue back; rusty undertail coverts; short tail; short legs. *Male:* black "cap." *Female:* dark gray "cap."

Size: *L* 5½–6 in; *W* 11 in.

Status: common resident.

Habitat: mixedwood forests, woodlots and backyards.

Nesting: in a natural cavity or an abandoned woodpecker nest in a large, deciduous tree; female lines the cavity with bark, grass, fur and feathers; female incubates 5–8 white eggs, spotted with reddish brown, for 12–14 days.

Feeding: forages down trees headfirst in search of larval and adult invertebrates; also eats nuts and seeds; regularly visits feeders.

Voice: song is a fast, nasal *yank-hank yank-hank,* less nasal than the Red-breasted Nuthatch; calls include *ha-ha-ha ha-ha-ha, ank ank* and *ip*.

Similar Species: *Red-breasted Nuthatch* (p. 114): black eye line; rusty underparts. *Black-capped Chickadee* (p. 112): black "bib."

Best Sites: found statewide in appropriate habitat.

BROWN CREEPER

Certhia americana

The cryptic Brown Creeper is never easy to find. Inhabiting old-growth forests for much of the year, it often goes unnoticed until a flake of bark suddenly takes the shape of a bird. If a creeper is frightened, it will freeze and flatten itself against a tree trunk, becoming even more difficult to see. • The Brown Creeper feeds by slowly spiraling up a tree trunk, searching for hidden invertebrates. When it reaches the upper branches, the creeper floats down to the base of a neighboring tree to begin another foraging ascent. Its long, stiff tail feathers prop it up against a tree trunk as it makes its way skyward. • Like the call of the Golden-crowned Kinglet, the thin whistled call of the Brown Creeper is so high pitched that many birders often fail to hear it. To increase the confusion, the creeper's song often takes on the boisterous quality of a wood-warbler's. • There are many species of creepers in Europe and Asia, but the Brown Creeper is the only member of its family found in North America.

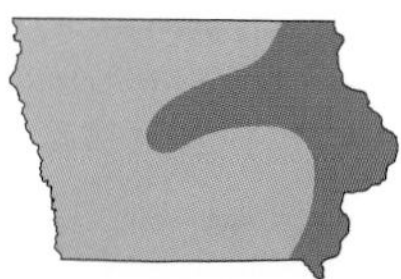

ID: white "eyebrow"; downcurved bill; brown back with buffy white streaks; white underparts; long, pointed tail feathers; rusty rump.

Size: *L* 5–5½ in; *W* 7½ in.

Status: uncommon migrant and wintering resident; rare breeder; most often seen from mid-April to early May and from late September to late October.

Habitat: mature, deciduous, coniferous and mixed forests and woodlands, especially in wet areas and floodplains with large, dead trees; also found near bogs.

Nesting: under loose bark; nest of grass and conifer needles is woven together with spider silk; female incubates 5–6 whitish eggs, dotted with reddish brown, for 14–17 days.

Feeding: hops up tree trunks and large limbs, probing loose bark for adult and larval invertebrates.

Voice: song is a surprisingly loud, very high-pitched *trees-trees-trees see the trees;* call is a high *tseee.*

Similar Species: *Red-breasted Nuthatch* (p. 114) and *White-breasted Nuthatch* (p. 115): gray blue back; straight or slightly upturned bill. *Woodpeckers* (pp. 87–93): larger; straight bills; lack brown back streaking.

Best Sites: found statewide in appropriate habitat. *Breeding:* mostly in Mississippi R. counties.

HOUSE WREN

Troglodytes aedon

The House Wren's bubbly song and energetic demeanor make it a welcome addition to any neighborhood. A small cavity in a standing dead tree or a custom-made nest box is usually all it takes to attract this joyful bird to most backyards. Sometimes even an empty flowerpot or vacant drainpipe is deemed a suitable nest site, provided there is a local abundance of insect prey. Occasionally, you may find that your nest site offering is packed full of twigs, but is left abandoned, without any nesting birds in sight. Male wrens often build numerous nests, which later serve as decoys or "dummy" nests. In such a case, you should just clean out the cavity and hope that another pair of wrens will find your real estate more appealing. • Frequently, wrens will raise a second or third brood, sometimes in the same nest hole. • In Greek mythology, Zeus transformed Aedon, the queen of Thebes, into a nightingale. The wonderfully warbled song of the House Wren is similar to that of a nightingale's. • This bird is sometimes called "Jenny Wren."

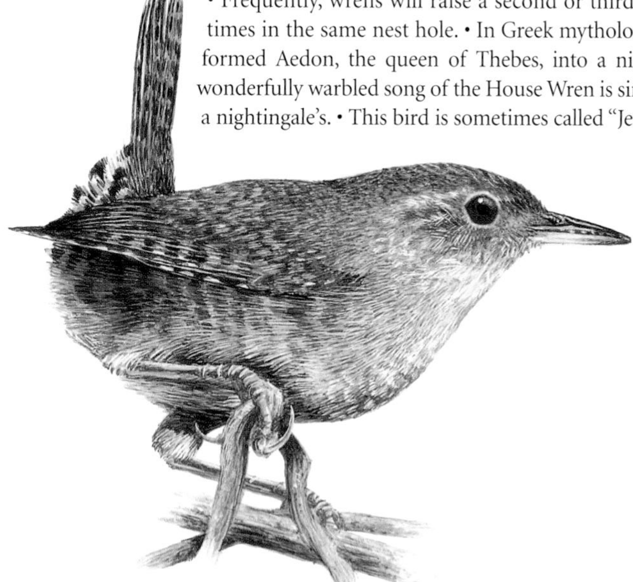

ID: faint, pale "eyebrow" and eye ring; whitish throat; brown upperparts; fine, dark barring on upper wings and lower back; short, upraised tail is finely barred with black; whitish to buff underparts; faintly barred flanks.

Size: *L* 4½–5 in; *W* 6 in.

Status: abundant migrant and breeder from late April to September.

Habitat: tangled thickets and shrubby openings in or at the edge of deciduous or mixed woodlands; often in shrubs and thickets near buildings.

Nesting: in a natural cavity or abandoned woodpecker nest; also in a nest box or other artificial cavity; nest of sticks and grass is lined with feathers, fur and other soft materials; female incubates 6–8 white eggs, heavily dotted with reddish brown, for 12–15 days.

Feeding: gleans the ground and vegetation for insects, especially beetles, caterpillars, grasshoppers and spiders.

Voice: song is a smooth, running, bubbly warble: *tsi-tsi-tsi-tsi oodle-oodle-oodle-oodle,* lasting about 2–3 seconds.

Similar Species: *Carolina Wren:* larger; rusty brown with a prominent "eyebrow." *Winter Wren:* smaller; darker overall; much shorter, prominent, dark barring on flanks; stubby tail. *Sedge Wren:* faint white streaking on dark crown and back.

Best Sites: found statewide in appropriate habitat.

MARSH WREN

Cistothorus palustris

Fueled by newly emerged aquatic insects, the Marsh Wren zips about in short bursts through tall stands of cattails and bulrushes. This expert hunter catches its prey with lightning speed, but don't expect to see the Marsh Wren in action—it is a reclusive bird that prefers to remain hidden deep within its dense marshland habitat. A patient observer might be rewarded with a brief glimpse of a Marsh Wren, but it is more likely that this bird's distinctive song, reminiscent of an old-fashioned treadle sewing machine, will inform you of its presence. • The Marsh Wren, formerly known as "Long-billed Marsh Wren," occasionally destroys the nests and eggs of other marsh-nesting songbirds, such as the Red-winged Blackbird. Victims are usually prevented from retaliating because the globe-shaped nest of the Marsh Wren keeps eggs well hidden, and several decoy nests help to divert predators. • The scientific name *palustris* is Latin for "marsh."

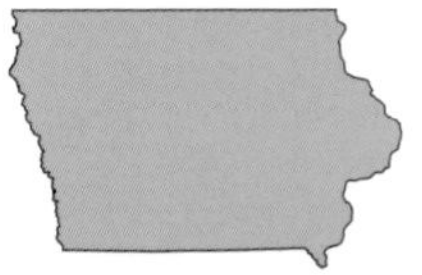

ID: bold, white "eyebrow"; unstreaked brown crown; long, thin, downcurved bill; white "chin" and belly; white to light brown upperparts; black triangle on upper back is streaked with white.

Size: *L* 5 in; *W* 6 in.

Status: uncommon migrant and breeder from May to early October; a few linger in winter.

Habitat: large cattail and bulrush marshes; occasionally in tall grass and sedge marshes.

Nesting: in a marsh among cattails or tall, emergent vegetation; globelike nest is woven from cattails, bulrushes, weeds and grass, lined with cattail down; female incubates 4–6 white to pale brown eggs, heavily dotted with dark brown, for 12–16 days.

Feeding: gleans vegetation and flycatches for adult aquatic invertebrates, especially dragonflies and damselflies.

Voice: *Male:* rapid, rattling, staccato warble sounds like an old-fashioned treadle sewing machine; call is a harsh *chek.*

Similar Species: *Sedge Wren:* smaller; streaked crown. *House Wren* (p. 117): faint "eyebrow"; back lacks black-and-white streaking. *Carolina Wren:* larger; buff underparts; back lacks streaking.

Best Sites: marshes of Prairie Pothole Region.

RUBY-CROWNED KINGLET

Regulus calendula

The loud, rolling song of the Ruby-crowned Kinglet is a familiar tune that echoes through Iowa during spring migration. The male kinglet erects his brilliant, red crown and sings to impress prospective mates, but once courting is finished and defending territory is no longer necessary, his crown remains hidden and cannot usually be seen, even with binoculars. • In migration, Ruby-crowned Kinglets are regularly seen flitting among treetops, intermingling with a colorful assortment of warblers and vireos. This bird might be mistaken for an *Empidonax* flycatcher, but the kinglet's frequent hovering and energetic wing-flicking behavior sets it apart from look-alikes. The wing flicking is thought to startle insects into movement, allowing the kinglet to spot them and pounce.

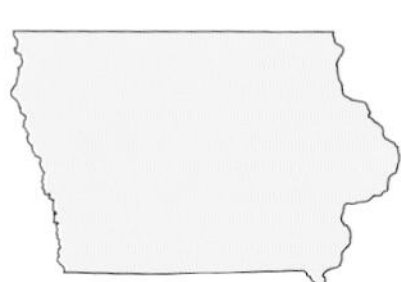

ID: bold, broken eye ring; olive green upperparts; whitish to yellowish underparts; dark wings; short, dark tail; 2 bold, white wing bars; flicks its wings. *Male:* small, red crown (usually hidden). *Female:* lacks red crown.

Size: *L* 4 in; *W* 7½ in.

Status: common migrant from mid-April to mid-May and from mid-September to late October; rarely found in winter.

Habitat: mixed woodlands; often found near moist forest openings and edges.

Nesting: does not nest in Iowa.

Feeding: gleans and hovers for insects and spiders; also eats seeds and berries.

Voice: *Male:* song is an accelerating and rising *tea-tea-tea-tew-tew-tew look-at-Me, look-at-Me, look-at-Me*.

Similar Species: *Golden-crowned Kinglet:* dark "cheek"; black border around orange or yellow crown; female has yellow crown. *Orange-crowned Warbler:* no eye ring or wing bars. Empidonax *flycatchers* (p. 95): complete eye ring or no eye ring at all; larger bill; longer tail; erect posture.

Best Sites: found statewide in appropriate habitat.

BLUE-GRAY GNATCATCHER

Polioptila caerulea

The fidgety Blue-gray Gnatcatcher is constantly on the move. This woodland inhabitant holds its tail upward like a wren and issues a soft *mew* as it flits restlessly from shrub to shrub, gleaning insects. • Gnatcatcher pairs remain close once a bond is established, and both parents share the responsibilities of nest building, incubation and raising the young. As soon as the young are ready to fly, they leave the nest for the cover of dense, shrubby tangles along woodland edges. Like most songbirds, Blue-gray Gnatcatchers mature quickly and will fly as far as South America within months of hatching. • Although this bird undoubtedly eats gnats, this food item is only a small part of its insectivorous diet. • The scientific name *Polioptila* means "gray feather," while *caerulea* means "blue."

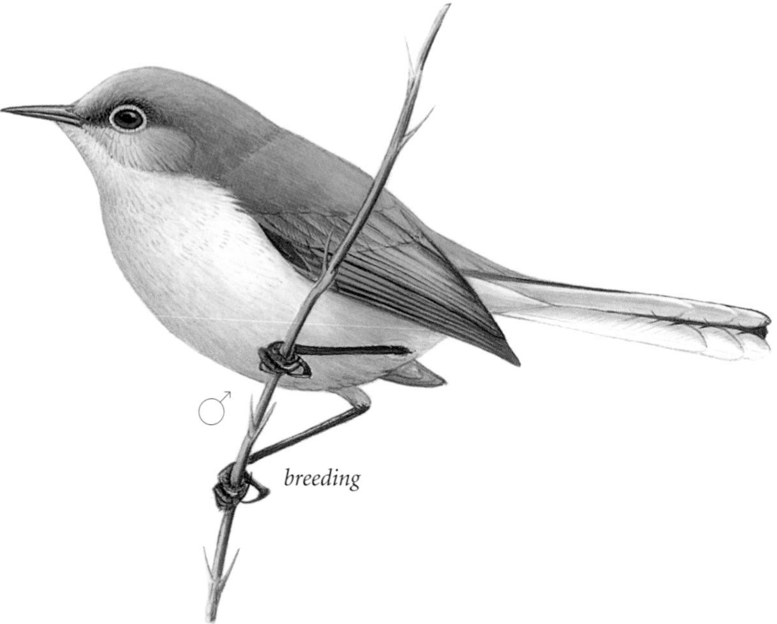

breeding

ID: white eye ring; blue gray upperparts; long tail; pale gray underparts; black uppertail with white outer tail feathers. *Breeding male:* darker upperparts; black border on side of forecrown.

Size: *L* 4½ in; *W* 6 in.

Status: common migrant and breeder from mid-April to mid-September.

Habitat: deciduous woodlands along streams, ponds, lakes and swamps; also in orchards, shrubby tangles along woodland edges and oak savannas.

Nesting: on a branch, usually halfway to the trunk; cup nest is made of plant fibers and bark chips, decorated with lichens and lined with fine vegetation, hair and feathers; female incubates 3–5 pale, bluish white eggs, dotted with reddish brown, for 11–15 days; male feeds female and young.

Feeding: gleans vegetation and flycatches for insects; also eats spiders and other invertebrates.

Voice: *Male:* song is a warbled series of whining notes; call is a soft *mew*.

Similar Species: *Golden-crowned Kinglet* and *Ruby-crowned Kinglet* (p. 119): olive green overall; short tail; wing bars.

Best Sites: Ledges SP; Shimek SF; eastern and central parts of the state.

EASTERN BLUEBIRD

Sialia sialis

Perhaps no other bird is as cherished and admired in rural areas as the lovely Eastern Bluebird. With the colors of the cool sky on its back and the warm setting sun on its breast, the male Eastern Bluebird looks like a piece of sky come to life. • When House Sparrows and European Starlings were introduced to North America, competition for nest sites increased and bluebird numbers began to decline. The creation of bluebird nest boxes has helped matters—the entrances to the boxes are perfect for a bluebird, but too small for the competing European Starling. The development of "bluebird trails" has also allowed bluebird populations to recover gradually throughout our region. Nest boxes are usually mounted on fence posts along highways and rural roads, providing these birds with convenient nesting places. • Eastern Bluebirds are fond of fields, uncultivated farmlands and mature woodland edges, but an elevated perch is necessary as a base from which to hunt insects.

♂

ID: chestnut red throat, breast and sides; white belly and undertail coverts; dark bill and legs. *Male:* deep blue upperparts. *Female:* thin, white eye ring; gray brown head and back are tinged with blue; paler chestnut on underparts; blue wings and tail.

Size: *L* 7 in; *W* 13 in.

Status: common migrant and breeder from mid-February through late November; rare winter visitor.

Habitat: cropland fencelines, meadows, fallow and abandoned fields, pastures, forest clearings and edges; also golf courses, orchards, large lawns and cemeteries.

Nesting: in an abandoned woodpecker cavity, natural cavity or nest box; female builds a cup nest of grass, weed stems and small twigs, lined with finer materials; mostly the female incubates 4–5 pale blue eggs for 13–16 days.

Feeding: swoops from a perch to pursue flying insects; also forages on the ground for invertebrates.

Voice: song is a rich, warbling *turr, turr-lee, turr-lee;* call is a chittering *pew.*

Similar Species: *Indigo Bunting* (p. 152): uniform blue coloration. *Tree Swallow* (p. 108): white breast.

Best Sites: found statewide in appropriate habitat. *Winter:* along major rivers in southern Iowa.

WOOD THRUSH

Hylocichla mustelina

The loud, warbled notes of the Wood Thrush once resounded through our woodlands, but forest fragmentation and urban sprawl have eliminated much of this bird's nesting habitat. Changed landscape has allowed for the invasion of common, open-area predators and parasites, such as raccoons, skunks, crows, jays and cowbirds, which traditionally had little access to nests that were insulated deep within vast stands of hardwood forest. Also, host families of American Robins have taken the place of the once prominent Wood Thrushes. • The Wood Thrush's wintering grounds extend from southeastern Mexico to Panama. It makes its way northward each spring, breeding primarily in the eastern U.S., from the Gulf Coast to southern Canada. • Naturalist and author Henry David Thoreau considered the Wood Thrush's song to be the most beautiful of avian sounds. Male Wood Thrushes can even sing two notes at once!

ID: plump body; bold, white eye ring; large, black spots on white breast, sides and flanks; rusty head and back; brown wings, rump and tail.
Size: *L* 8 in; *W* 13 in.
Status: uncommon and declining migrant and breeder from mid-May to September.
Habitat: moist, mature and preferably undisturbed deciduous woodlands and mixed forests.
Nesting: low in the fork of a deciduous tree; female builds a bulky cup nest of grass, twigs, moss, weeds, bark strips and mud, lined with softer materials; female incubates 3–4 pale, greenish blue eggs for 13–14 days.
Feeding: forages on the ground and gleans vegetation for insects and other invertebrates; also eats berries.
Voice: *Male:* bell-like phrases of 3–6 notes, followed by a trill; long pauses between phrases: *Will you live with me? Way up high in a tree, I'll come right down and seee!;* calls include a *pit pit* and *bweebee-beep*.
Similar Species: *Ovenbird* (p. 134): much smaller and browner; black-and-russet crown stripes; streaky spots on underparts. *Other thrushes* (pp. 121–123): smaller spots on underparts; most have colored wash on sides and flanks; all lack bold, white eye ring and rusty "cap" and back.
Best Sites: widespread in appropriate habitat.

AMERICAN ROBIN

Turdus migratorius

American Robins are the harbingers of spring, arriving in large numbers in our state every March. They are widespread in natural habitats, but are recognizable to most because of their tendency to inhabit our backyards and local parks. Some robins overwinter, but sightings are not as common. • A feeding robin tilts its head and may appear to be listening for prey, but it is actually looking for movements in the soil—it tilts its head because its eyes are placed on the sides of its head. • Robins are occasionally seen hunting with their bills stuffed with earthworms and grubs, a sign that hungry young robins are somewhere close at hand. The young are easily distinguished from their parents by their disheveled appearance and heavily spotted underparts. • The American Robin was named by English colonists after their beloved European Robin (*Erithacus rubecula*). Both birds have a red breast, even though they are only distantly related. The American Robin's closest European relative is, in fact, the Blackbird (*T. merula*), which is identical in all aspects except plumage.

ID: dark head; white throat streaked with black; black-tipped, yellow bill; incomplete, white eye ring; gray brown back; white undertail coverts. *Male:* black head; deep brick red breast. *Female:* dark gray head; light red orange breast. *Juvenile:* heavily spotted breast.

Size: *L* 10 in; *W* 17 in.

Status: abundant migrant and breeder from early March through late October; uncommon in winter.

Habitat: residential lawns and gardens, pastures, urban parks, broken forests, bogs and river shorelines.

Nesting: in a coniferous or deciduous tree or shrub; sturdy cup nest is built of grass, moss, loose bark and mud; female incubates 4 light blue eggs for 11–16 days; may raise up to 3 broods each year in some areas.

Feeding: forages on the ground and among vegetation for larval and adult insects, earthworms, other invertebrates and berries.

Voice: song is an evenly spaced warble: *cheerily cheer-up cheerio;* call is a rapid *tut-tut-tut.*

Similar Species: *Varied Thrush:* vagrant; black breast band; 2 orange wing bars.

Best Sites: widespread in appropriate habitat.

GRAY CATBIRD

Dumetella carolinensis

The Gray Catbird is common in summer, when nesting pairs build their loose cup nest deep within impenetrable tangles of shrubs, brambles and thorny thickets. The Gray Catbird vigorously defends its nesting territory with such effective defense tactics that the nesting success of its neighbors may increase as a result of this bird's constant vigilance. Although Brown-headed cowbirds attempt to parasitize these birds, female catbirds are very loyal to their nests and immediately eject foreign eggs. • True to its name, this bird's call sounds much like the scratchy mewing of a house cat. The Gray Catbird is a member of the mockingbird family, and its characteristic call and boisterous, mimicked phrases are often the only evidence of this bird's presence. • At dawn, Gray Catbirds can often be seen feeding on insects attracted to street lights.

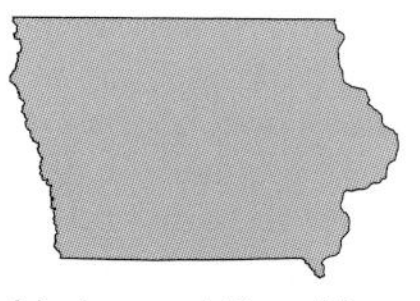

ID: dark gray overall; black "cap"; long tail may be dark gray to black; chestnut undertail coverts; black eyes, bill and legs.
Size: *L* 8½–9 in; *W* 11 in.
Status: common migrant and breeder from May through September.
Habitat: dense thickets, brambles, shrubby or brushy areas and hedgerows, often near water.
Nesting: in a dense shrub or thicket; bulky cup nest is loosely built with twigs, leaves and grass and is lined with fine material; female incubates 4 greenish blue eggs for 12–15 days.
Feeding: forages on the ground and in vegetation for a wide variety of ants, beetles, grasshoppers, caterpillars, moths and spiders; also eats berries and visits feeders.
Voice: calls include a catlike meow and a harsh *check-check;* song is a variety of warbles, squeaks and mimicked phrases, usually repeated once and often interspersed with a *mew* call.
Similar Species: *Brown Thrasher* (p. 125): rusty brown upperparts; streaked underparts; wing bars; repeats each song phrase twice. *Northern Mockingbird:* white wing patches; lacks black "cap" and chestnut undertail coverts. *Townsend's Solitaire:* winter vagrant; lacks black "cap" and chestnut undertail coverts.
Best Sites: found statewide in appropriate habitat; more common in northeastern and southern Iowa.

HER

les that rise from v . and lakefront edges the song of the own Thrasher stands orus of twice-r phrases is truly unique. ensive vocal re s of any North American able of up to stinctive combinations of ely large si rown Thrasher often goes pical sighti is thrasher consists of nothing ps from ngle to another. • The Brown und, m s eggs and nestlings particularly weasel ks and other animals. Although lant enders, sometimes to the point of is ays enough to protect their young. er kingbird (*Mimus polyglottos*) and the hrasher prefers to live well away from

r,
l; incubates 4 bluish white to pale blue eggs, dotted with reddish brown, for 11–14 days.

Feeding: gleans the ground and vegetation for larval and adult invertebrates; occasionally tosses leaves aside with its bill; also eats seeds and berries.

Voice: sings a large variety of phrases, with each phrase usually repeated twice: *dig-it dig-it, hoe-it hoe-it, pull-it-up pull-it-up;* calls include a loud, crackling note, a harsh *shuck,* a soft *churr* and a whistled, 3-note *pit-cher-ee.*

Similar Species: *Wood Thrush* (p. 122): dark brown eyes; much shorter bill; gray brown back; short tail; lacks wing bars.

Best Sites: found statewide in appropriate habitat; more common in northeastern and southern Iowa.

EUROPEAN STARLIN

Sturnus vulgaris

The European Starling was introduced to N
about 100 of these birds were released into
local Shakespeare society's plan to intro
favorite author's writings. The European Starlin
York landscape, then spread rapidly across th
many native cavity-nesting birds, such as the
Red-headed Woodpecker. Despite many concert
this species, the European Starling will no doubt
than 200 million individuals in North Americ
from these first 100 birds. • Courting European St
reproduce the sou
Red-tailed Haw

breeding

ID: dark eyes; short, square tail. *Breeding:* blackish, iridescent plumage; yellow bill. *Nonbreeding:* blackish wings; feather tips are heavily spotted with white and buff. *Juvenile:* gray brown plumage; brown bill. *In flight:* pointed, triangular wings.

Size: *L* 8½ in; *W* 16 in.

Status: abundant resident.

Habitat: agricultural areas, townsites, woodland and forest edges, landfills and roadsides.

Nesting: in an abandoned woodpecker cavity, natural cavity, nest box or other
arti
and
blui
Fee
dive
berr
Voi
gur
Sim
(p.
darl
juve
and
Blac
tail
Bes
hab

CEDAR WAXWING

Bombycilla cedrorum

Flocks of handsome Cedar Waxwings gorge on ripe berries in late summer and fall. Waxwings have a remarkable ability to digest a wide variety of berries, some of which are inedible or even poisonous to humans. If the fruits have fermented, these birds will show definite signs of tipsiness. Native berry-producing trees and shrubs planted in your backyard can attract Cedar Waxwings and will often encourage them to nest in your area. • Cedar Waxwing pairs perform a wonderful courtship dance: the male first lands slightly away from the female, then tentatively hops toward her and offers her a berry. The female accepts the berry and hops away from the male, then she stops, hops back, and offers him the berry. This gentle ritual can last for several minutes. Cedar Waxwings are late nesters, which ensures that the berry crops will be ripe when nestlings are ready to be fed. • Practiced observers learn to recognize this bird by its high-pitched, trilling calls.

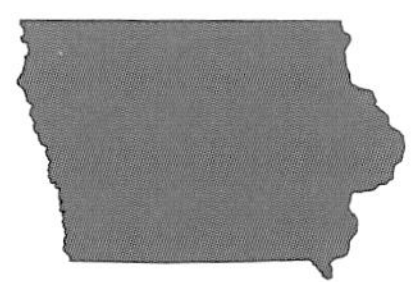

ID: black "mask"; cinnamon crest; brown upperparts; yellow wash on belly; gray rump; white undertail coverts; small red "drops" on wings; yellow terminal tail band. *Juvenile:* no "mask"; streaked underparts; gray brown body.

Size: *L* 7 in; *W* 12 in.

Status: abundant migrant from mid-March to early May and from late September through late November; common breeder; rare in winter.

Habitat: wooded residential parks and gardens, overgrown fields, forest edges, second-growth, riparian and open woodlands. *Winter:* berry or crab apple trees.

Nesting: in a coniferous or deciduous tree or shrub; cup nest of twigs, grass, moss and lichen is lined with fine grass; female incubates 3–5 pale gray to bluish gray eggs, with fine dark spotting, for 12–16 days.

Feeding: catches flying insects on the wing or gleans vegetation; also eats large amounts of berries and wild fruit, especially in fall and winter.

Voice: faint, high-pitched, trilled whistle: *tseee-tseee-tseee.*

Similar Species: *Bohemian Waxwing:* winter visitor; larger; chestnut undertail coverts; small, white, red and yellow markings on wings; juvenile has chestnut undertail coverts and white wing patches.

Best Sites: found statewide in appropriate habitat.

YELLOW WARBLER

Dendroica petechia

Yellow Warblers usually arrive here in early May in search of caterpillars, aphids, beetles and other invertebrates. Flitting from branch to branch among open woodland edges and riparian shrubs, these inquisitive birds seem to be in perpetual motion. • Yellow Warblers are among the most frequent victims of Brown-headed Cowbirds, but a pair often evades nest parasitism when it recognizes foreign eggs and abandons its nest or builds a new one on top of the old. Some persistent Yellow Warblers rebuild many times, creating bizarre, multilayered, high-rise nests. • In their fall migration plumage, silent Yellow Warblers can be difficult to identify, but they have unique yellow flashes on the sides of their tails that can help to distinguish them from other similar-looking warblers. • Because of their bright yellow plumage, Yellow Warblers are often mistakenly called "Wild Canaries."

♂ ♀

breeding

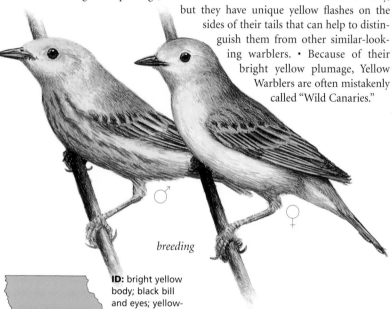

ID: bright yellow body; black bill and eyes; yellowish legs; bright yellow highlights on dark yellow-olive tail and wings. *Breeding male:* red breast streaks. *Breeding female:* faint, red breast streaks.

Size: *L* 5 in; *W* 8 in.

Status: uncommon to locally common migrant and breeder from May through July.

Habitat: shrubby meadows, willow tangles, shrubby fencerows and riparian woodlands; usually near water along rivers and lakes; also moist, open woodlands with dense, low scrub.

Nesting: in a fork in a deciduous tree or small shrub; female builds a compact cup nest of grass, weeds and shredded bark, lined with plant down and fur; female incubates 4–5 speckled or spotted, greenish white eggs for 11–12 days.

Feeding: gleans foliage and vegetation for invertebrates, especially caterpillars, inchworms, beetles, aphids and cankerworms; occasionally hover-gleans.

Voice: *Male:* song is a fast, frequently repeated *sweet-sweet-sweet summer sweet.*

Similar Species: *American Goldfinch* (p. 163): black wings and tail; male often has black forehead. *Common Yellowthroat* (p. 135): darker face and upperparts; female lacks yellow highlights on wings. *Blue-winged Warbler:* black line through eye; gray wings with wing bars. *Orange-crowned Warbler:* darker olive plumage overall; lacks reddish breast streaks. *Wilson's Warbler:* shorter, darker tail; male has black "cap"; female has darker crown and upperparts.

Best Sites: widespread in appropriate habitat; especially in the northeast and around lakes in the northwest.

YELLOW-RUMPED WARBLER

Dendroica coronata

The Yellow-rumped Warbler is the most abundant and widespread wood-warbler in North America. Your greatest chance of meeting it in Iowa comes each spring from late April to late May. Sightings are most common during the first few hours after dawn, when most Yellow-rumps forage among streamside and lakeshore trees. • Two subspecies of the Yellow-rumped Warbler, which were once considered to be two separate species, occur: the white-throated, eastern subspecies, formerly called "Myrtle Warbler," and the yellow-throated, western subspecies, formerly called "Audubon's Warbler," which is very rarely seen here. • The yellow rump is prominent, even on the plumage of the drab brown fall birds, and not only is reflected in their common name, but in the nickname, "butterbutts." • The scientific name *coronata*, Latin for "crowned," refers to this bird's yellow crown.

breeding

ID: dark "cheek"; thin "eyebrow"; yellow foreshoulder patches and rump; white underparts; faint white wing bars. *Male:* yellow crown; black "cheek," breast and streaking along sides and flanks; blue gray upperparts with black streaking. *Female* and *nonbreeding:* gray brown upperparts with dark streaking; dark streaking on breast, sides and flanks.

Size: *L* 5–6 in; *W* 9 in.

Status: abundant migrant from late April to late May and from late September through October; rare winter resident.

Habitat: *In migration:* woodlands or shrubby areas. *Winter:* protected areas often near open water.

Nesting: does not nest in Iowa.

Feeding: hawks and hovers for beetles, flies, wasps, caterpillars, moths and other insects; also gleans vegetation; sometimes eats berries.

Voice: *Male:* song is a tinkling trill, often given in 2-note phrases that rise or fall at the end (there can be much variation among individuals); call is a sharp *chip* or *check*.

Similar Species: *Cape May Warbler:* heavily streaked, yellow throat, breast and sides; lacks yellow crown. *Magnolia Warbler:* bold, white "eyebrow"; yellow throat and underparts; white patches on tail; lacks yellow crown. *Chestnut-sided Warbler:* chestnut sides on clean white underparts; lacks yellow rump. *Yellow-throated Warbler:* yellow throat; bold, white "eyebrow," "ear" patch and wing bars; lacks yellow crown and rump.

Best Sites: found statewide in appropriate habitat.

PALM WARBLER

Dendroica palmarum

The Palm Warbler, which does not forage in palm trees, was apparently named to indicate its subtropical winter range. Based on its summer habitat, however, it could just as easily have been named "Bog Warbler" because of its preference for northern bogs and fens of sphagnum moss and black spruce. Despite its name, the Palm Warbler nests farther north than all other wood-warblers, except the Blackpoll. In migration they sometimes join flocks of other warblers, especially Yellow-rumps. • Palm Warblers are unusual in their preference for foraging on the ground, or in low shrubs and vegetation. • The Palm Warbler incessantly bobs its tail, a prominent field mark for this bird, particularly in fall, when its distinctive chestnut crown fades to olive brown. The paler, eastern Palm Warbler and the more yellow western form are both found in Iowa.

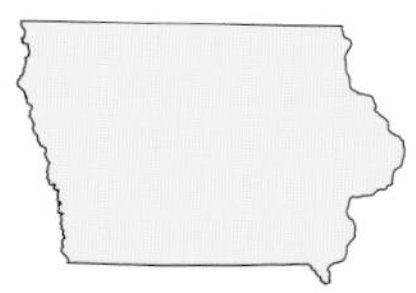

ID: chestnut brown "cap" (may be inconspicuous in fall); yellow "eyebrow"; yellow throat and undertail coverts; yellow or white breast and belly; dark streaking on breast and sides; olive brown upperparts; may show dull yellowish rump; frequently bobs its tail.
Size: *L* 4–5½ in; *W* 8 in.
Status: common migrant from mid-April to mid-May and from mid-September to mid-October.
Habitat: most often found in open areas.
Nesting: does not nest in Iowa.
Feeding: gleans the ground and vegetation for a variety of insects and berries when perched or hovering; occasionally hawks for insects; may take some seeds.
Voice: song is a weak, buzzy trill with a quick finish; call is a sharp *sup* or *check*.
Similar Species: *Yellow-rumped Warbler* (p. 129): white wing bars, throat and undertail coverts. *Prairie Warbler:* dark jaw stripe; darker eye line; dark streaking on yellow breast restricted to the sides; lacks chestnut crown. *Pine Warbler:* head more uniformly yellow; no obvious "cap"; faint, whitish wing bars; white undertail coverts. *Chipping Sparrow* (p. 139) and *American Tree Sparrow* (p. 138): stouter body; unstreaked, grayish underparts; lack yellow plumage.
Best Sites: found statewide.

BLACK-AND-WHITE WARBLER

Mniotilta varia

The foraging behavior of the Black-and-white Warbler stands in sharp contrast to that of most of its kin. Rather than dancing or flitting quickly between perches, Black-and-white Warblers behave like creepers and nuthatches—a distantly related group of birds. • Birders, tired from trying to observe other energetic birds, will be refreshed by the sight of this slower-moving warbler, methodically creeping up and down tree trunks, probing bark crevices. • Novice birders can easily identify this unique, two-tone bird, which retains its standard plumage throughout its stay in our state. Even a trip to its wintering grounds will reveal the Black-and-white Warbler in the same outfit. A keen ear also helps to identify this forest dweller: its gentle oscillating song—like a wheel in need of greasing—is easily recognized and remembered.

breeding

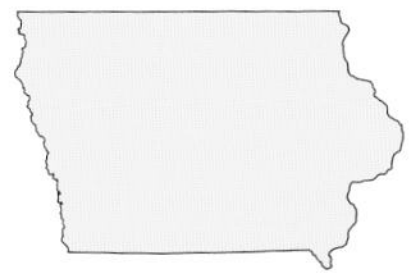

ID: black-and-white-striped crown; dark upperparts with white streaking; 2 white wing bars; white underparts with black streaking on sides, flanks and undertail coverts; black legs. *Male:* black "cheek" and throat. *Female:* gray "cheek"; white throat.

Size: *L* 4½–5½ in; *W* 8 in.

Status: common migrant from late April to mid-May and from late August to September; rare breeder.

Habitat: deciduous or mixed forests, often near water.

Nesting: usually on the ground next to a tree, log or large rock; in a shallow scrape, often among a pile of dead leaves; female builds a cup nest with grass, leaves, bark strips, rootlets and pine needles and lines it with fur and fine grasses; female incubates 5 creamy white eggs, with brown flecks toward the larger end, for 10–12 days.

Feeding: creeps along tree trunks and branches; gleans insect eggs, larval insects, beetles, spiders and other invertebrates.

Voice: series of high, thin, 2-syllable notes: *weetsee weetsee weetsee weetsee weetsee weetsee;* call is a sharp *pit* and a soft, high *seet.*

Similar Species: *Blackpoll Warbler:* breeding male has solid black "cap" and clean white undertail coverts.

Best Sites: found statewide in appropriate habitat.

AMERICAN REDSTART

Setophaga ruticilla

American Redstarts are a consistent favorite among birders. These supercharged birds flit from branch to branch in a dizzying pursuit of prey. Even when perched, their tails sway rhythmically back and forth. Few birds can rival a mature male redstart for his contrasting black-and-orange plumage and amusing behavior. A common foraging technique used by the American Redstart is to flash its wings and tail patches to flush prey. If a concealed insect tries to flee, the redstart will give chase. On its Central American wintering grounds, the American Redstart is known locally as "candelita," meaning "little candle." • Although redstarts are common here, their beautiful, trilling songs are so variable that many birders use the common rule of assumption that "if the song cannot be identified, it must be a redstart."

ID: *Male:* black overall; red orange shoulder, wing and tail patches; white belly and undertail coverts. *Female* and *immature:* gray green head; olive brown upperparts; clean white underparts; yellow shoulder, wing and tail patches.
Size: *L* 5 in; *W* 8 in.
Status: common migrant and breeder, arriving in mid-May and departing in September.
Habitat: shrubby woodland edges, open and semi-open deciduous and mixed forests with a regenerating deciduous understory of shrubs and saplings; often near water.
Nesting: in the fork of a shrub or sapling, usually 3–23 ft above the ground; female builds an open cup nest of plant down, bark shreds, grass and rootlets, lined with feathers; female incubates 4 whitish eggs, marked with brown or gray, for 11–12 days.
Feeding: actively gleans foliage and hawks for insects and spiders on leaves, buds and branches; often hover-gleans.
Voice: male's song is a highly variable series of *tseet* or *zee* notes, often given at different pitches; call is a sharp, sweet *chip*.
Similar Species: none.
Best Sites: found statewide in appropriate habitat.

PROTHONOTARY WARBLER

Protonotaria citrea

The Prothonotary Warbler is an unusual wood-warbler because it nests in cavities. Standing dead trees and stumps and woodpecker excavations provide perfect nesting habitat for this bird, especially if the site is near stagnant water. Most of the time its swampy habitat is inaccessible to birders, but if you are in the right place at the right time, you might be lucky enough to come across a Prothonotary Warbler, foraging for insects. • A breeding pair of Prothonotary Warblers will often return to the same nest cavity year after year. The male can be very aggressive when defending his territory and often resorts to combative aerial chases when songs and warning displays fail to intimidate an intruder. Unfortunately, other cavity-nesting birds such as woodpeckers, wrens and bluebirds are often victims of this fury. • This bird acquired its unusual name because its plumage resembled the yellow hoods worn by protonotaries, high-ranking clerics in the Catholic Church. At one time it was called the Golden Swamp Warbler, an apt name.

breeding

ID: large, dark eyes; long bill; unmarked, yellow head; yellow underparts except for white undertail coverts; olive green back; unmarked, bluish gray wings and tail.

Size: *L* 5½ in; *W* 8½ in.

Status: locally rare migrant and breeder from early May into August.

Habitat: wooded deciduous swamps.

Nesting: cavities in standing dead trees, rotten stumps, birdhouses or abandoned woodpecker nests, found from water level to 10 ft above the ground; often reuses nest sites; mostly the male builds a cup nest of twigs, leaves, moss and plant down, lined with soft plant material; female incubates 4–6 brown-spotted, creamy to pinkish eggs for 12–14 days.

Feeding: gleans vegetation for a variety of insects and small mollusks; may hop on floating debris or creep along tree trunks.

Voice: song is a loud, ringing series of *sweet* or *zweet* notes issued on a single pitch; flight song is *chewee chewee chee chee;* call is a brisk *tink*.

Similar Species: *Yellow Warbler* (p. 128): yellow undertail coverts; wings and tail have yellow highlights; male has reddish streaking on breast. *Hooded Warbler:* female has yellow undertail coverts and yellow olive upperparts. *Blue-winged Warbler:* black eye line; white wing bars; yellowish white undertail coverts.

Best Sites: Mississippi backwaters; swampy areas along Mississippi, Iowa, Des Moines, Chariton and Little Sioux rivers.

OVENBIRD

Seiurus aurocapilla

The Ovenbird's loud and joyous "ode to teachers" is a common sound that echoes through deciduous and mixed forests in spring. Unfortunately, pinpointing the exact location of this resonating call is not always easy. An Ovenbird rarely exposes itself, and even when it does, active searching and patience is necessary to get a good look at it. What may sound like one long-winded Ovenbird may actually be two neighboring males singing and responding on the heels of each other's song. • This bird's name refers to its unusual, dome-shaped ground nest. An incubating female nestled within her woven dome usually feels so secure that she will choose to sit tight rather than flee when approached. The nest is so well camouflaged that few people ever find one, even though nests are often located near hiking trails and bike paths. • Robert Frost was so moved by this bird's spring songs that he wrote a poem entitled "Ovenbird."

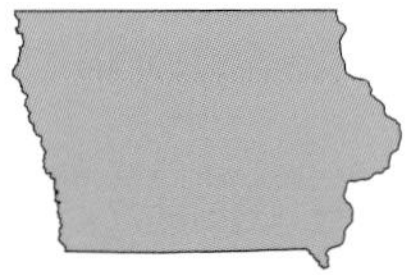

ID: white eye ring; heavy, dark streaking on white breast, sides and flanks; rufous crown has black border; olive brown upperparts; pink legs; white undertail coverts.

Size: *L* 6 in; *W* 9½ in.

Status: common migrant and breeder from May to September.

Habitat: *Breeding:* undisturbed, mature forests with a closed canopy and very little understory; often in ravines and riparian areas. *In migration:* dense riparian shrubbery and thickets and a variety of woodlands.

Nesting: on the ground; female builds an oven-shaped, domed nest of grass, weeds, bark, twigs and dead leaves and lines it with animal hair; female incubates 4–5 white eggs, spotted with gray and brown, for 11–13 days.

Feeding: gleans the ground for worms, snails, insects and occasionally seeds.

Voice: loud, distinctive *tea-cher tea-cher Tea-CHER Tea-CHER,* increasing in speed and volume; night song is an elaborate series of bubbly, warbled notes, often ending in *teacher-teacher;* call is a brisk *chip, cheep* or *chock.*

Similar Species: *Northern Waterthrush* and *Louisiana Waterthrush:* bold, yellowish or white "eyebrow"; darker upperparts; lack rufous crown. *Thrushes* (pp. 121–123): all are larger and lack rufous crown outlined in black.

Best Sites: found statewide in appropriate habitat.

COMMON YELLOWTHROAT

Geothlypis trichas

This energetic songster of our wetlands is a favorite among birders—its small size, bright plumage and spunky disposition quickly endear it to all observers. • The Common Yellowthroat favors shrubby marshes and wet, overgrown meadows, shunning the forest habitat preferred by most of its wood-warbler relatives. In May and June, the male Common Yellowthroat issues his distinctive *witchity-witchity-witchity* songs while perched atop tall cattails or shrubs. Observing a male in action will reveal the location of his favorite singing perches, which he visits in rotation. These strategic outposts mark the boundary of his territory, which is fiercely guarded from intrusion. • The Common Yellowthroat is often parasitized by Brown-headed Cowbirds.

ID: yellow throat, breast and undertail coverts; dingy white belly; olive green to olive brown upperparts; orangy legs. *Breeding male:* broad, black "mask" with white, upper border. *Female:* no "mask"; may show faint, white eye ring. *Immature:* duller overall.

Size: *L* 5 in; *W* $6\frac{1}{2}$ in.

Status: abundant migrant and breeder from early May through September; rare in early winter.

Habitat: cattail marshes, riparian willow clumps, sedge wetlands, beaver ponds and wet, overgrown meadows; occasionally dry, abandoned fields.

Nesting: on or near the ground, often in a small shrub or among emergent aquatic vegetation; female builds a bulky, open cup nest of weeds, grass, sedges and other materials and lines it with hair and soft plant fibers; female incubates 3–5 creamy white eggs, spotted with brown and black, for 12 days.

Feeding: gleans vegetation and hovers for adult and larval insects, including dragonflies, spiders and beetles; occasionally eats seeds.

Voice: song is a clear, oscillating *witchity-witchity-witchity;* call is a sharp *tcheck* or *tchet.*

Similar Species: male's black "mask" is distinctive. *Kentucky Warbler:* yellow spectacles; half "mask"; all-yellow underparts. *Yellow Warbler* (p. 128): brighter yellow overall; all-yellow underparts; yellow highlights on wings. *Wilson's Warbler:* bright yellow forehead, "eyebrow," "cheek" and underparts; may show dark "cap." *Orange-crowned Warbler:* dull, yellow olive overall; faint breast streaks. *Nashville Warbler:* bold, complete eye ring; blue gray crown.

Best Sites: found statewide in appropriate habitat.

SCARLET TANAGER

Piranga olivacea

Each spring, birders eagerly await the sweet, rough-edged song of the lovely Scarlet Tanager, which is often the only thing that gives away this unobtrusive forest denizen. The return of the brilliant red male to wooded ravines and traditional migrant stopover sites is always a much-anticipated event in our state. • During the cold and rainy weather that often dampens spring migration, you may find yourself observing a Scarlet Tanager at eye level, foraging in the forest understory. At other times, however, this bird can be surprisingly difficult to spot as it works through the forest canopy in pursuit of insect prey. • The Scarlet Tanager migrates farther than any other tanager, most of which are sedentary birds in Central and South American forests. In its wintering range, there are over 200 tanager species representing every color of the rainbow.

♂ ♀

breeding

ID: *Breeding male:* bright red overall with black wings and tail; pale bill. *Fall male:* patchy, red and greenish yellow plumage; black wings and tail. *Nonbreeding male:* olive upperparts; yellow underparts; black wings and tail. *Female:* uniformly olive upperparts; yellowish underparts; gray-brown wings.

Size: *L* 7 in; *W* 11½ in.

Status: common migrant and breeder in the east and south from mid-May to early October; local elsewhere.

Habitat: mature, upland deciduous and mixed forests and large woodlands.

Nesting: on a high branch, usually in a deciduous tree well away from the trunk; female builds a flimsy, shallow cup nest of grass, weeds and twigs and lines it with rootlets and fine grass; female incubates 2–5 pale, blue green eggs, spotted with reddish brown, for 12–14 days.

Feeding: gleans, hover-gleans or hawks insects from a tree canopy; may forage at lower levels during cold weather; also takes some seasonally available berries.

Voice: song is a series of 4–5 sweet, clear, whistled phrases like a hoarse version of the American Robin's song; call is a *chip-burrr* or *chip-churrr*.

Similar Species: *Summer Tanager:* larger bill; male has red wings and tail; female has paler wings and duskier overall, often with orange or reddish tinge. *Northern Cardinal* (p. 150): red bill, wings and tail; prominent head crest; male has black "mask" and "bib." *Orchard Oriole* and *Baltimore Oriole* (p. 160): females have wing bars and sharper bills.

Best Sites: Yellow River Forest/Effigy Mounds; Shimek SF; Stephen's SF.

EASTERN TOWHEE

Pipilo erythrophthalmus

Eastern Towhees are often heard before they are seen. These noisy foragers rustle about in dense undergrowth, craftily scraping back layers of dry leaves to expose the seeds, berries or insects hidden beneath. They employ an unusual two-footed technique to uncover food items—a strategy that is especially important in winter when virtually all of their food is taken from the ground. • Although you wouldn't guess it, this colorful bird is a member of the American Sparrow family—a group that is usually drab in color. • The Eastern Towhee and its similar western relative, the Spotted Towhee, were once grouped together as a single species called the "Rufous-sided Towhee." Watch for the Eastern Towhee's spotted cousin on the ground below bird feeders in winter. • The scientific name *Pipilo* is derived from the Latin *pipo*, meaning "to chirp or peep." *Erythrophthalmus* is derived from Greek words that mean "red eye."

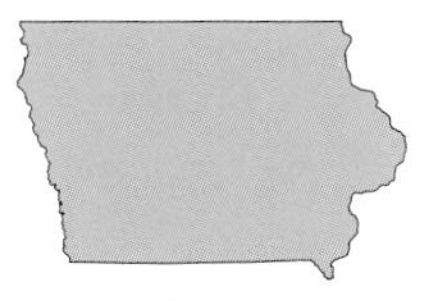

ID: red eyes; dark bill; white lower breast and belly; rufous sides and flanks; buff undertail coverts; white outer tail corners. *Male:* black "hood" and upperparts. *Female:* brown "hood" and upperparts.

Size: *L* 7–8½ in; *W* 10½ in.

Status: common migrant and breeder from April through October; rare in winter.

Habitat: along woodland edges and in shrubby, abandoned fields.

Nesting: on the ground or low in a dense shrub; female builds a camouflaged cup nest of twigs, bark strips, grass and animal hair; mostly the female incubates 3–4 creamy white to pale gray eggs, spotted with brown toward the larger end, for 12–13 days.

Feeding: scratches at leaf litter for insects, seeds and berries; sometimes forages in low shrubs and saplings.

Voice: song is 2 high, whistled notes followed by a trill: *drink your teeeee;* call is a scratchy, slurred *cheweee!* or *chewink!*

Similar Species: *Dark-eyed Junco* (p. 147): much smaller; pale bill; black eyes; white outer tail feathers. *Spotted Towhee:* rare; white spots on wings and back

Best Sites: found statewide in appropriate habitat.

AMERICAN TREE SPARROW

Spizella arborea

Many of us know these rufous-capped, spot-breasted sparrows as visitors to backyard feeders, but they are much more common along scrubby roadsides during our state's colder months. Even in the dead of winter, these tough little northerners offer bubbly, bright songs between bouts of foraging. • Although its name suggests a close relationship with trees or forests, the American Tree Sparrow actually prefers open fields and semi-open, shrubby habitats. • This bird got its name because of a superficial resemblance to the Eurasian Tree Sparrow *(Passer montanus)*, familiar to early settlers. Perhaps a more appropriate name for this bird would be "Subarctic Shrub Sparrow." With adequate food supplies, the American Tree Sparrow can survive temperatures as cold as –28° F.

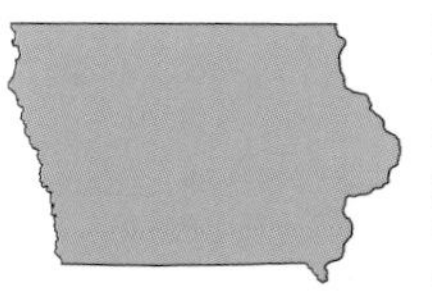

ID: pale rufous "cap"; rufous stripe behind eye; gray face; dark, central breast spot; dark upper mandible; yellow lower mandible; mottled brown upperparts; gray, unstreaked underparts; dark legs; notched tail; 2 white wing bars. *Nonbreeding:* gray central crown stripe. *Juvenile:* streaky breast and head.

Size: *L* 6–6½ in; *W* 9½.

Status: abundant migrant and winter resident, decreasing northward; arrives in mid-October and leaves by early to mid-April.

Habitat: brushy thickets, roadside shrubs, semi-open fields, croplands and feeders in rural areas.

Nesting: does not nest in our region.

Feeding: scratches exposed soil or snow for seeds; picks over weed heads in winter; eats mostly insects in summer; takes some berries; regularly visits feeders.

Voice: a high, whistled *tseet-tseet* is followed by a short, sweet, musical series of slurred whistles; song may be given in late winter and during spring migration; call is a 3-note *tsee-dle-eat*.

Similar Species: *Chipping Sparrow* (p. 139): black eye line and white "eyebrow"; lacks dark breast spot. *Swamp Sparrow:* white throat; lacks dark breast spot and white wing bars. *Field Sparrow:* white eye ring; orange pink bill; lacks dark breast spot.

Best Sites: found statewide in appropriate habitat.

CHIPPING SPARROW

Spizella passerina

The rapid trill of the Chipping Sparrow is one of the most common sounds associated with summer in Iowa. Virtually every town park, cemetery or wooded neighborhood has a pair or more. • Chipping Sparrows commonly nest at eye level, so you can easily watch their breeding and nest-building rituals. They are well known for their preference of coniferous nesting sites and for lining their nests with hair. By planting conifers in your backyard and offering samples of your pet's hair—or even your own—when they arrive in spring, you could attract nesting Chipping Sparrows to your area. • The Chipping Sparrow is the smallest and tamest of sparrows. "Chipping" refers to this bird's call.

breeding

ID: *Breeding:* prominent rufous "cap"; white "eyebrow"; black eye line; all-dark bill; mottled brown upperparts; light gray, unstreaked underparts; pale legs; 2 faint wing bars. *Nonbreeding:* brown "eyebrow" and "cheek"; pale lower mandible; paler crown with dark streaks. *Juvenile:* pale lower mandible; brown gray overall with dark brown streaking.

Size: *L* 5–6 in; *W* 8½ in.

Status: common migrant and breeder from April through October; rare in winter.

Habitat: mature stands of conifers or mixed woodland edges; yards and gardens with tree and shrub borders.

Nesting: usually at mid-level in a coniferous tree; female builds a compact cup nest of woven grass and rootlets, often lined with hair; female incubates 4 pale blue eggs for 11–12 days.

Feeding: gleans seeds from the ground and from the outer branches of trees or shrubs; prefers seeds from grass, dandelions and clovers; also eats adult and larval invertebrates; occasionally visits feeders.

Voice: song is a rapid, dry trill of *chip* notes; call is a high-pitched *chip*.

Similar Species: *American Tree Sparrow* (p. 138): dark central breast spot; narrow rufous eye line; lacks bold, white "eyebrow." *Swamp Sparrow:* lacks white "eyebrow," white wing bars and dark eye line. *Field Sparrow:* white eye ring; orange pink bill; lacks bold, white "eyebrow."

Best Sites: found statewide in appropriate habitat.

VESPER SPARROW

Pooecetes gramineus

For birders who live near grassy fields and agricultural lands with multitudes of confusing, little brown sparrows, the Vesper Sparrow offers welcome relief—white outer tail feathers and a bold eye ring help to reveal its identity. The Vesper Sparrow is also known for its bold and easily distinguished song, which begins with two sets of unforgettable, double notes: *here-here! there-there!* and ends in a jumble of trills. • When the business of nesting begins, the Vesper Sparrow scours the neighborhood for a potential nesting site. It usually settles in a grassy hollow at the base of a clump of weeds or small shrub. This setup provides camouflage and protection from the wind to keep the young safe. • "Vesper" is Latin for "evening," the time of day when this bird often sings. *Pooecetes* is Greek for "grass dweller."

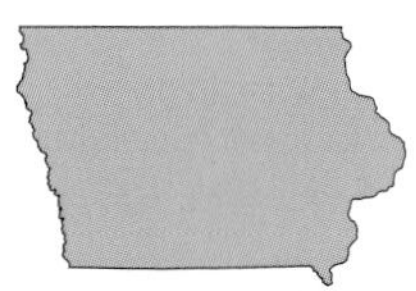

ID: white eye ring; inconspicuous, chestnut shoulder patch; white outer tail feathers; weak flank streaking; pale legs.

Size: *L* 6 in; *W* 10 in.

Status: common migrant and breeder from April through October; rare in winter; abundance increases northward.

Habitat: open fields bordered or interspersed with shrubs, semi-open shrub lands and grasslands; also in agricultural areas, open, dry conifer plantations and scrubby gravel pits.

Nesting: in a scrape on the ground, often under a canopy of loosely woven grass or at the base of a shrub; cup nest is lined with rootlets, fine grass and hair; mostly the female incubates 3–5 whitish to greenish white eggs, blotched with brown and gray, for 11–13 days.

Feeding: walks and runs along the ground; eats seeds, grasshoppers, beetles, cutworms and other invertebrates.

Voice: song is 4 characteristic, preliminary notes, with the 2nd higher in pitch, followed by a bubbly trill: *here-here! there-there! everybody-down-the-hill.*

Similar Species: *Lark Sparrow* (p. 141): bold face pattern; white corners on tail. *Other sparrows* (pp. 137–149): lack white outer tail feathers and eye ring. *Horned Lark* (p. 106): long, blackish tail with white sides; little if any streaking; lacks eye ring. *American Pipit:* thinner bill; grayer upperparts lacks brown streaking; lacks chestnut shoulder patch. *Lapland Longspur* (p. 148): blackish or buff wash on upper breast; nonbreeding has broad, pale "eyebrow" and reddish edgings on wing feathers.

Best Sites: found statewide in appropriate habitat.

LARK SPARROW

Chondestes grammacus

Most sparrows share the same basic head plumage pattern, with a mixture of less highly contrasting browns and grays, but the Lark Sparrow's is distinctively bold. • Although these birds are typically seen in open, shrubby areas, they occasionally venture into meadows, grassy forest openings and wooded areas. • Male Lark Sparrows are known for their "turkey walk." Fluffing their chestnut feathers, they lift their beaks to the sky, spread their tails, droop their wings to the ground and boldly strut back and forth in front of potential mates, all the while bubbling with song. During courtship, the male Lark Sparrow employs the common gift-giving technique of the bird world, offering a twig to his mate. • It was this bird's beautiful aria that reminded early naturalists of the famed Sky Lark of Europe, and earned this bird its name.

ID: white throat, "eyebrow" and crown stripe; black eye line and jawline; chestnut red crown and "cheek"; unstreaked, pale breast with central spot; black tail with white corners; mottled brown back and wings; light-colored legs.

Size: *L* 6 in; *W* 11 in.

Status: uncommon migrant and local breeder from late April to early September.

Habitat: semi-open shrub lands, sand hills and sandy soils, prairies, cropland and fallow fields; occasionally pastures.

Nesting: on the ground or in a low bush; occasionally reuses an abandoned thrasher nest; female builds a bulky cup nest of grass and twigs and lines it with finer material; female incubates 4–5 white eggs, marked with black, gray and lavender, for 11–12 days.

Feeding: gleans seeds while walking or hopping along the ground; also eats grasshoppers and other invertebrates.

Voice: melodious, variable song that consists of short trills, buzzes, pauses and clear notes.

Similar Species: no other sparrow has the distinctive head pattern or white tail corners. *Eastern Towhee* (p. 137): male has black head; female is larger and all-brown.

Best Sites: found statewide in appropriate habitat, especially in western and southern Iowa.

SAVANNAH SPARROW

Passerculus sandwichensis

The Savannah Sparrow is one of the most common open-country birds in northeast Iowa, becoming less common heading southwest. Although most people have probably seen or heard the Savannah Sparrow, they may not have been aware of it—this bird's streaky, dull brown, buff-and-white plumage resembles so many of the other grassland sparrows that it is easily overlooked. • From early spring to early summer, male Savannah Sparrows belt out their distinctive, buzzy tunes while perched atop prominent shrubs, tall weeds or strategic fence posts. Later in the summer and throughout early fall, they are most often seen darting across roads, highways and open fields in search of food. When danger appears, they take flight only as a last resort, preferring to run swiftly and inconspicuously through the grass, like feathered voles.

ID: dull brown, buff-and-white plumage; yellow lores; light jawline; pale legs and bill; may show dark breast spot; finely streaked breast, sides and flanks; mottled brown upperparts; pale, streaked underparts.

Size: *L* 5–6 in; *W* 6½ in.

Status: common migrant and uncommon breeder from April through October; rare in winter.

Habitat: *Breeding:* agricultural fields, especially hay and alfalfa. *In migration:* moist sedge and grass meadows, pastures, beaches, bogs and fens.

Nesting: on the ground in a shallow scrape, concealed by grass or a shrub; female builds a woven, open cup nest, lined with grass; female incubates 3–6 brown-marked, whitish to greenish or pale tan eggs for 10–13 days.

Feeding: gleans insects and seeds while walking or running along the ground; occasionally scratches.

Voice: song is a 2-tone, clear trill, usually with 2 introductory notes: *tea tea teeeee taaaay;* call is a high, thin *tsit.*

Similar Species: *Vesper Sparrow* (p. 140): eye ring; white outer tail feathers. *Lincoln's Sparrow:* broad, gray "eyebrow"; buff jawline; buff wash across breast. *Grasshopper Sparrow* (p. 143): unstreaked breast; short tail. *Song Sparrow* (p. 144): triangular "mustache" stripes; bold, blurry breast streaking; long, rounded tail; lacks yellow lores.

Best Sites: *Breeding:* primarily in the northeast. *In migration:* found statewide in appropriate habitat.

GRASSHOPPER SPARROW

Ammodramus savannarum

The Grasshopper Sparrow is named not for its diet, but rather for its buzzy, insectlike song. During courtship flights, males chase females through the air, buzzing at a frequency that is usually inaudible to human ears. The males sing two different versions of their songs: one ends in a short trill and the other is a prolonged series of high trills that vary in pitch and speed. • The Grasshopper Sparrow is an open-country bird that prefers grassy expanses free of trees and shrubs. Wide, well-drained, grassy ditches occasionally attract nesting Grasshopper Sparrows. Mowing or harvesting these grassy margins early in the nesting season may be detrimental to these birds, and convincing local landowners and state governments to delay cutting until mid-August or September would benefit this bird.

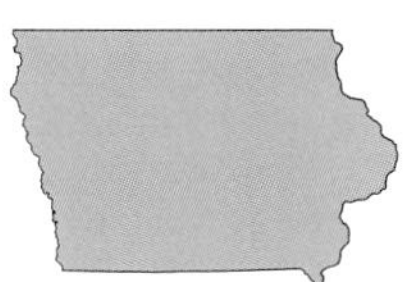

ID: unstreaked, white underparts; buff wash on breast, sides and flanks; flattened head profile; dark crown with pale, central stripe; buff "cheek"; mottled brown upperparts; beady, black eyes; narrow or pointed tail; pale legs; may show small, yellow patch on edge of forewing. *Immature:* less buff on underparts; faint streaking across breast.

Size: *L* 5–5½ in; *W* 7½ in.

Status: common migrant and breeder from May through September, decreasing in abundance from south to north.

Habitat: grasslands and grassy fields with little or no shrub or tree cover.

Nesting: in a shallow depression on the ground, usually concealed by grass; female builds a small cup nest of grass and lines it with rootlets, fine grass and hair; female incubates 4–5 creamy white eggs, spotted with gray and reddish brown, for 11–13 days.

Feeding: gleans a variety of insects, including grasshoppers; eats seeds from the ground and grass.

Voice: song is a high, wiry trill preceded by 1–3 high, thin, whistled notes: *tea-tea-tea zeeeeeeeeee;* may add a long series of varying trills to the end.

Similar Species: *Le Conte's Sparrow:* buff-and-black-striped head with white central crown stripe; gray "cheek"; dark streaking on sides and flanks. *Nelson's Sharp-tailed Sparrow:* buff orange face and breast; gray, central crown stripe; gray "cheek" and shoulders. *Henslow's Sparrow:* similar to immature Grasshopper Sparrow, but with darker breast streaking, small, dark ear and "whisker" marks and rusty wings.

Best Sites: found statewide in appropriate habitat.

SONG SPARROW

Melospiza melodia

The Song Sparrow's heavily streaked, low-key plumage does not prepare you for its symphonic song. Although some birders will argue that the Fox Sparrow and Lincoln's Sparrow carry the best tunes, this well-named bird is known for the complexity and rhythm of its spring-time rhapsodies. • Young Song Sparrows and many other songbirds learn to sing by eavesdropping on their fathers or on rival males. By the time a young male Song Sparrow is a few months old, he will have formed the basis of his own courtship tune. • Most songbirds are lucky if they can produce one brood per year, but in some years Song Sparrows in our region can successfully raise three. There are about 31 different subspecies of the Song Sparrow, from the pale, desert birds to the larger and darker Alaskan forms. • The scientific name *melodia* means "melody" in Greek.

ID: grayish face; dark eye line; pale jawline is bordered by dark "whisker" and "mustache" stripes; dark crown with a pale, central stripe; whitish underparts with heavy, brown streaking that converges into a central breast spot; mottled brown upperparts; rounded tail tip.
Size: *L* 5½–7 in; *W* 8½ in.
Status: abundant migrant and common breeder; uncommon in winter.
Habitat: shrubby areas, often near water, including riparian thickets, forest openings and pastures. *Winter:* open streams and ditches.
Nesting: usually on the ground or low in a shrub or small tree; female builds an open cup nest of weeds, leaves and bark shreds, lined with rootlets, fine grass and hair; female incubates 3–5 greenish white eggs, heavily spotted with reddish brown, for 12–14 days; may raise 2–3 broods.
Feeding: gleans the ground, shrubs and trees for seeds, cutworms, beetles, grasshoppers, ants and other invertebrates; also eats wild fruit and visits feeders.
Voice: song is 1–4 bright, distinctive introductory notes, such as *sweet, sweet, sweet,* followed by a buzzy *towee,* then a short, descending trill; calls include a short *tsip* and a nasal *tchep.*
Similar Species: *Fox Sparrow:* heavier breast spotting and streaking; reddish upperparts; lacks pale, central crown stripe and dark "mustache." *Lincoln's Sparrow:* lightly streaked breast with buff wash; buff jawline. *Savannah Sparrow* (p. 142): finely streaked breast; yellow lores; notched tail; lacks dark, triangular "mustache."
Best Sites: found statewide in appropriate habitat.

WHITE-THROATED SPARROW

Zonotrichia albicollis

The handsome White-throated Sparrow presents itself in two color morphs throughout the state: one has black-and-white stripes on the head; the other has brown-and-tan stripes. White-striped males are more aggressive than the tan-striped, and tan-striped females tend to be more nurturing than the white-striped. These two color morphs are perpetuated because each one almost always breeds with the other. • In spring and fall, White-throated Sparrows can appear anywhere in our region in great abundance. Urban backyards dressed with brushy fence-line tangles and a bird feeder brimming with seeds can attract numbers of these delightful sparrows. • *Zonotrichia* means "hairlike," a reference to the striped heads of birds in this genus; *albicollis* is Latin for "white neck," which is not quite an accurate description, as it is the bird's throat and not its neck that is white.

white-striped morph

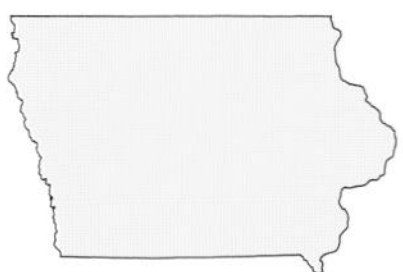

ID: black-and-white (or brown-and-tan) stripes on head; white throat; gray "cheek"; yellow lores; black eye line; grayish bill; mottled brown upperparts; unstreaked, gray underparts.

Size: *L* 6½–7½ in; *W* 9 in.

Status: abundant migrant from March to mid-May and from mid-September into November; rare in winter.

Habitat: woodlots, wooded parks and riparian brush.

Nesting: does not nest in Iowa.

Feeding: scratches the ground to expose invertebrates, seeds and berries; also gleans insects from vegetation and while in flight; visits feeders in winter.

Voice: variable song is a clear, distinct, whistled *Old Sam Peabody, Peabody, Peabody;* call is a sharp *chink*.

Similar Species: *White-crowned Sparrow:* pinkish bill; gray "collar"; lacks bold, white throat and yellow lores. *Swamp Sparrow:* smaller; gray and chestnut on crown; streaked underparts; lacks head pattern.

Best Sites: found statewide in appropriate habitat.

HARRIS'S SPARROW

Zonotrichia querula

The Harris's Sparrow is an unassuming migrant that visits Iowa in small, isolated trickles, frequently mixing with flocks of White-throated Sparrows and White-crowned Sparrows (*Zonotrichia leucophrys*). Occasionally, a few Harris's Sparrows can be seen picking through the seed offerings at backyard feeders. • The Harris's Sparrow breeds in the far north of Canada, where the treeline fades to tundra. Because of such remote breeding grounds, there is little information about this species' breeding habits, nests and eggs. • John J. Audubon named this sparrow after his friend and amateur naturalist, Edward Harris, with whom he traveled up the Missouri River in 1843. • The scientific name *querula* means "plaintive" in Latin and refers to this bird's quavering, whistled song.

nonbreeding

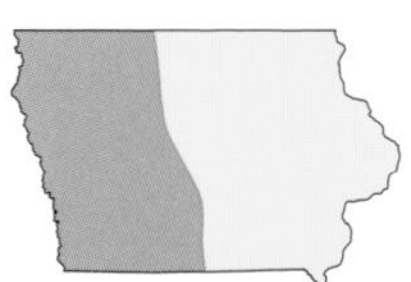

ID: pink orange bill; mottled brown-and-black upperparts; white underparts. *Breeding:* black crown, "ear" patch, throat and "bib"; gray face; black streaks on sides and flanks; white wing bars. *Nonbreeding:* brown face; white flecks on black crown; brownish sides and flanks. *Immature:* white throat; mostly brownish crown with some black streaking.

Size: *L* 7–7½ in; *W* 10½ in.

Status: common migrant in the west and rare in the east from mid-April to mid-May and in October; rare, but regular winter visitor in the west.

Habitat: brushy roadsides, shrubby vegetation, forest edges and riparian thickets.

Nesting: does not nest in Iowa.

Feeding: gleans the ground and vegetation for seeds, fresh buds, insects and berries; occasionally takes seeds from bird feeders.

Voice: song is a series of 2–4 long, quavering whistles; each series may be sung at the same or at a different pitch; call is a *jeenk* or *zheenk;* flocks in flight may give a rolling *chug-up chug-up*.

Similar Species: *House Sparrow* (p. 164): gray crown; broad, brown band behind eye; broad, whitish jaw band; dark bill; male is brownish overall. *White-throated Sparrow* (p. 145): grayish bill; yellow lores; black-and-white or brown-and-tan stripes on crown. *White-crowned Sparrow:* black-and-white stripes on crown; gray "collar"; immature has broad, gray "eyebrow" bordered by brown eye line and crown.

Best Sites: found statewide in appropriate habitat, especially in western half of the state.

DARK-EYED JUNCO

Junco hyemalis

Juncos usually congregate in backyards where there are bird feeders and sheltering conifers. With such amenities at their disposal, more and more are appearing in urban areas around Iowa. Juncos rarely perch at feeders, preferring to snatch up seeds that are knocked to the ground by other visitors. • Juncos spend most of their time on the ground, and they flash their distinctive, white outer tail feathers when they are flushed from wooded trails and backyard feeders. • In 1973, the American Ornithologists' Union grouped five junco species into a single species called the Dark-eyed Junco. The five subspecies are closely related and have similar habits, but differ in coloration and range, interbreeding where their ranges meet. The "Slate-colored" subspecies is the one most commonly found in Iowa; western forms do occur, but are much more rare.

Slate-colored Junco

ID: pale bill; white outer tail feathers. *Male:* dark, slate gray plumage; white lower breast, belly and undertail coverts; flanks and back may be variably brownish. *Female:* brown rather than gray. *Juvenile:* brown, like female, but streaked with darker brown.
Size: *L* 5½–7 in; *W* 9½ in.
Status: abundant migrant and winter resident from October through April.
Habitat: shrubby woodland borders, backyard feeders.
Nesting: does not nest in Iowa.
Feeding: scratches the ground for invertebrates; also eats berries and seeds.
Voice: song is a long, dry trill, very similar to that of the Chipping Sparrow, but more musical; call is a smacking *chip* note, often given in series.
Similar Species: *Eastern Towhee* (p. 137): larger; female has rufous sides, red eyes and grayish bill.
Best Sites: found statewide, with abundance decreasing from south to north.

LAPLAND LONGSPUR

Calcarius lapponicus

Throughout winter, Lapland Longspurs wheel about in large numbers over our fields, typically appearing wherever there is an abundance of seeds or waste grain. Flocks of longspurs can be surprisingly inconspicuous, but if a group is approached, the flash of their white outer tail feathers when they erupt into the sky is an awing sight. • In fall, these birds arrive from their breeding grounds looking like mottled, brownish sparrows, and they retain their drab plumage throughout the winter months. When farmers work their fields in early spring, lingering Lapland Longspurs have already molted into their bold, breeding plumage, which they will wear throughout summer. • The Lapland Longspur breeds in northern polar regions, including the area of northern Scandinavia known as Lapland.

ID: pale bill; white outer tail feathers. *Breeding male:* black crown, face and "bib"; chestnut nape; broad, white stripe curving down to shoulder from eye (may be tinged with buff behind eye). *Breeding female:* mottled brown-and-black upperparts; lightly streaked flanks; narrow, lightly streaked, buff breast band. *Nonbreeding male:* similar to female, but with faint chestnut on nape and black breast.

Size: *L* 6½ in; *W* 11½ in.

Status: abundant migrant and common winter resident from October through mid-April.

Habitat: pastures, meadows and croplands, especially in corn and bean stubble; roadsides after a snowfall.

Nesting: does not nest in Iowa.

Feeding: gleans the ground and snow for seeds and waste grain.

Voice: flight song is a rapid, slurred warble; musical calls; flight calls include a rattled *tri-di-dit* and a descending *teew.*

Similar Species: *Horned Lark* (p. 106): longer, blackish tail; long, thin bill; unstreaked back. *Snow Bunting* (p. 149): bold, white patches on wings. *Smith's Longspur:* rare; completely buff to buff orange underparts; male has black-and-white face and buff orange nape.

Best Sites: found statewide in appropriate habitat.

SNOW BUNTING

Plectrophenax nivalis

In early winter, when flocks of Snow Buntings fly across rural fields, their startling black-and-white plumage flashes against a dazzling snow-covered backdrop. It may seem strange that Snow Buntings are whiter in summer than in winter, but the darker winter plumage may help these birds to absorb heat on clear, cold winter days. • Snow Buntings venture farther north than any other songbird in the world. A single individual, likely misguided and lost, was recorded near the North Pole in May 1987. • In winter, Snow Buntings prefer expansive areas, including grain croplands, fields and pastures where they scratch and peck at exposed seeds and grains. They also ingest small grains of sand or gravel from roadsides as a source of minerals and to help digestion. • Snow Buntings are definitely cold-weather songbirds, often bathing in snow in early spring and burrowing into it during bitter cold snaps to stay warm. They commonly flock at roadsides with Horned Larks and Lapland Longspurs after a snowfall.

♂ *breeding* ♀

♂ *nonbreeding* ♀

ID: white underparts; black-and-white wings and tail. *Breeding male:* black bill; black back; all-white head and rump. *Breeding female:* streaky, brown-and-whitish crown and back; dark bill. *Nonbreeding male:* yellowish bill; golden brown crown and rump. *Nonbreeding female:* similar to male, but with blackish forecrown and dark-streaked, golden back.

Size: *L* 6–7½ in; *W* 14 in.

Status: erratic winter visitor; more common in the north.

Habitat: manured fields, feedlots, pastures, agricultural areas, grassy meadows, lakeshores, major reservoirs, roadsides and railroads.

Nesting: does not nest in Iowa.

Feeding: gleans the ground and snow for seeds and waste grain; also takes insects when available.

Voice: call is a whistled *tew*.

Similar Species: *Lapland Longspur* (p. 148), *Smith's Longspur* and *American Pipit:* overall brownish upperparts; all lack white wing patches. *Horned Lark* (p. 106): uniform brown color; no white wing patches.

Best Sites: found statewide in appropriate habitat; more common in the north.

NORTHERN CARDINAL

Cardinalis cardinalis

The striking Northern Cardinal rarely fails to capture our attention and admiration: it is often the first choice of bird chosen to adorn calendars and Christmas cards. Most people can easily recognize this delightful, year-round neighbor, even without the help of a field guide. • These birds prefer the tangled, shrubby edges of woodlands and are easily attracted to backyards with feeders and sheltering trees and shrubs. • Northern Cardinals form one of the most faithful pair bonds among birds. The male and female remain in close contact year-round, singing to one another through the seasons with soft, bubbly whistles. The female usually sings while on the nest, and it is believed that she is informing her partner whether or not she and the young need food. The male is highly territorial and will even challenge his own reflection in a window or shiny hubcap! • The Northern Cardinal owes its name to the vivid red plumage of the male, which resembles the red robes of Roman Catholic cardinals.

ID: *Male:* red overall; red, conical bill; pointed crest; black "mask" and throat. *Female:* shaped like male; brown buff to buff olive overall; red bill; reddish crest, wings and tail. *Juvenile male:* similar to female, but has dark bill and crest.
Size: *L* 7½–9 in; *W* 12 in.
Status: abundant resident in the south and east; less common in the northwest.
Habitat: brushy thickets and shrubby tangles along forest and woodland edges; riparian habitats; also in backyards and suburban and urban parks.
Nesting: in a dense shrub, thicket, vine tangle or low in a coniferous tree; female builds an open cup nest of twigs, bark shreds, weeds, grass, leaves and rootlets, lined with hair and fine grass; female incubates 3–4 whitish to bluish or greenish white eggs, marked with gray, brown and purple, for 12–13 days.
Feeding: gleans seeds, insects and berries from low shrubs or while hopping along the ground.
Voice: song is a variable series of clear, bubbly, whistled notes: *what cheer! what cheer! birdie-birdie-birdie what cheer!;* call is a metallic *chip.*
Similar Species: *Summer Tanager* and *Scarlet Tanager* (p. 136): lack head crest, red conical bill and black "mask" and throat; Scarlet Tanager has black wings and tail.
Best Sites: found statewide in appropriate habitat, especially in southern and eastern Iowa.

ROSE-BREASTED GROSBEAK

Pheucticus ludovicianus

It is easy to miss the quiet warble of the Rose-breasted Grosbeak, but once this bird's robinlike song is learned, it is one of the more common sounds heard in our deciduous forests throughout spring and summer. The female lacks the magnificent colors of the male, but she shares his talent for beautiful song, which sounds like an American Robin that has taken singing lessons. • Mating grosbeaks appear pleasantly affectionate toward each other, often touching bills during courtship and after absences. They usually build their nests low in a tree or tall shrub, but typically forage high in the canopy where they can be difficult to spot. Luckily for birders, the abundance of berries in fall often draws these birds to ground level.

♂ ♀

breeding

ID: large, pale, conical bill; dark wings with small white patches; dark tail. *Male:* black "hood" and back; red breast and inner underwings; white underparts and rump. *Female:* bold, whitish "eyebrow"; thin crown stripe; brown upperparts; buff underparts with dark brown streaking.

Size: *L* 7–8½ in; *W* 12½ in.

Status: common migrant and breeder from early May to late September; rare in winter.

Habitat: deciduous and mixed forests.

Nesting: fairly low in a tree or tall shrub, often near water; mostly the female builds a flimsy cup nest of twigs, bark strips, weeds, grass and leaves and lines it with rootlets and hair; pair incubates 3–5 pale, greenish blue eggs, spotted with reddish brown, for 13–14 days.

Feeding: gleans vegetation for insects, seeds, buds, berries and some fruit; occasionally hover-gleans or catches flying insects on the wing; may also visit feeders.

Voice: song is a long, melodious series of whistled notes, much like a run-on version of a robin's song; call is a distinctive squeak, resembling the sound of shoes against a gym floor.

Similar Species: male is distinctive. *Purple Finch* (p. 161) and *House Finch* (p. 162): females are much smaller and have heavier streaking on underparts. *Sparrows* (pp. 137–149): smaller; all lack large conical bill.

Best Sites: found statewide in appropriate habitat, but most abundant in the east and south.

INDIGO BUNTING

Passerina cyanea

In the shadow of a towering tree, a male Indigo Bunting can look almost black. If possible, move quickly to a place from which you can see the sun strike and enliven its incomparable plumage—the rich shade of blue is rivaled only by the sky. • Raspberry thickets are a favored nesting location for many of our Indigo Buntings. The dense, thorny stems provide the nestlings with protection from many predators, and the berries are a convenient source of food. • The Indigo Bunting employs a clever and comical foraging strategy to reach the grass and weed seeds upon which it feeds. The bird lands midway on a stem and then shuffles slowly toward the seed head, which eventually bends under the bird's weight, giving the bunting easier access to its target. • Only male Indigo Buntings sing, and they do not learn their musical warble from their fathers, but from neighboring males during their first spring.

ID: stout, gray, conical bill; beady, black eyes; black legs; no wing bars. *Male:* blue overall; black lores; wings and tail may show some black. *Female:* soft brown overall; brown streaks on breast; whitish throat. *Nonbreeding male:* similar to female, but usually with some blue in wings and tail.

Size: *L* 5½ in; *W* 8 in.

Status: abundant migrant and breeder from mid-May to September.

Habitat: deciduous forest and woodland edges, regenerating forest clearings, shrubby fields, orchards, abandoned pastures and hedgerows; occasionally along mixed woodland edges.

Nesting: within a vine tangle or in the upright fork of a small tree or shrub; female builds a cup nest of grass, leaves and bark strips, lined with rootlets, hair and feathers; female incubates 3–4 white to bluish white eggs, rarely spotted with brown or purple, for 12–13 days.

Feeding: gleans low in vegetation and on the ground for insects, especially grasshoppers, beetles, weevils, flies and larvae; also eats the seeds of thistles, dandelions, goldenrods and other native plants.

Voice: song consists of paired, warbled whistles: *fire-fire, where-where, here-here, see-it see-it;* call is a quick *spit*.

Similar Species: *Blue Grosbeak:* larger overall; larger, more robust bill; 2 rusty wing bars; male has black around base of bill; female lacks streaking on breast. *Eastern Bluebird* (p. 121): slimmer bill; reddish breast and white belly.

Best Sites: found statewide in appropriate habitat.

DICKCISSEL

Spiza americana

The perky Dickcissel is an ubiquitous presence on Iowa farmlands. Territorial males arrive before the females in spring to set up suitable nesting habitats. They perch atop tall blades of grass, fence posts or rocks to scan their turf for signs of potential mates or unwelcome males. Dickcissels are polygynous, and males may mate with up to eight females in a single breeding season, providing no assistance in nesting or raising the brood. • This miniature meadowlark has a special fondness for fields of alfalfa. Although Dickcissels eat mostly insects on their breeding grounds, seeds and grain form the main part of their diet on their South American wintering grounds, making them unpopular with local farmers. Each year large numbers of these birds are killed by pesticides in efforts to reduce crop losses, which may partially explain the Dickcissel's pattern of alternating absence and abundance in parts of North America.

♂

♀

breeding

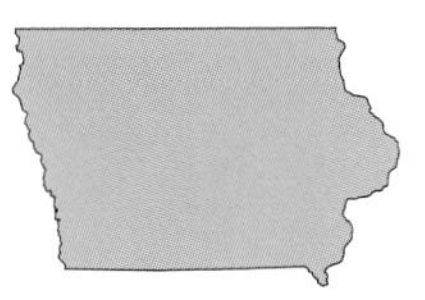

ID: yellow "eyebrow"; gray head, nape and sides of yellow breast; rufous shoulder patch; dark, conical bill; brown upperparts; pale, grayish underparts. *Male:* white "chin" and black "bib." *Female* and *nonbreeding:* duller colors than breeding male; pale yellow breast and underparts; chestnut on shoulder; white throat. *Immature:* similar to female, but has very faint "eyebrow" and dark streaking on crown, breast, sides and flanks.

Size: *L* 6–7 in; *W* 9½ in.

Status: abundant migrant and breeder from May to September; occasionally lingers into early October.

Habitat: abandoned fields dominated by forbs, weedy meadows, croplands, grasslands and grassy roadsides.

Nesting: on or near the ground, concealed in tall, dense vegetation; female builds a bulky, open cup nest of grass, weed stems and leaves, lined with rootlets, fine grass or hair; female incubates 4 pale blue eggs for 11–13 days.

Feeding: gleans insects and seeds from the ground and low vegetation.

Voice: song consists of 2–3 single notes followed by a trill, often paraphrased as *dick dick ciss-cissel;* flight call is a buzzerlike *bzrrrrt.*

Similar Species: *Eastern Meadowlark* and *Western Meadowlark* (p. 156): much larger; long, pointed bill; yellow "chin" and throat with black "necklace." *American Goldfinch* (p. 163): white or buff yellow bars on dark wings; may show black forecrown; lacks black "bib." *House Sparrow* (p. 164): lacks any yellow plumage.

Best Sites: found statewide in appropriate habitat.

BOBOLINK

Dolichonyx oryzivorus

During the nesting season, male and female Bobolinks rarely interact with one another. For the most part, males perform aerial displays and sing their bubbly, tinkling songs from exposed, grassy perches while the females carry out the nesting duties. Once the young have hatched, males become scarce, spending much of their time on the ground hunting for insects. • At first glimpse, the female Bobolink resembles a sparrow, but the male, with his dark belly and his buff, black-and-white upperparts, is colored like no other bird in our region. • Bobolinks once benefited from increased agriculture in the state, but modern practices, such as harvesting hay early in the season, thwart the reproductive efforts of these birds. • The Bobolink's name is thought to be an abbreviation of the title of William Cullen Bryant's poem, "Robert of Lincoln." Others believe it is a reference to the bird's song.

breeding

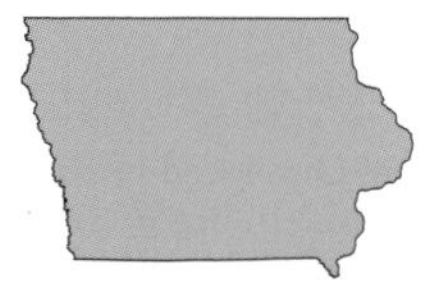

ID: *Breeding male:* black bill, head, wings, tail and underparts; buff nape; white rump and wing patch. *Breeding female:* buff brown overall; yellowish bill; pale "eyebrow"; dark eye line; pale, central crown stripe bordered by dark stripes; whitish throat; streaked back, sides, flanks and rump. *Nonbreeding male:* similar to breeding female, but darker above and rich golden buff below.

Size: *L* 6–8 in; *W* 11½ in.

Status: locally common migrant and breeder from May to late summer.

Habitat: tall, grassy meadows and ditches, hayfields and some croplands.

Nesting: on the ground, usually in a hay field, concealed in a shallow depression; female builds a cup nest of grass and weed stems, lined with fine grass; female incubates 5–6 grayish to light reddish brown eggs, heavily blotched with lavender and brown, for 11–13 days.

Feeding: gleans the ground and low vegetation for adult and larval invertebrates; also eats seeds.

Voice: song is a bubbly series of notes: *bobolink bobolink spink spank spink,* often given in flight; also issues a *pink* call in flight.

Similar Species: male is distinctive. *Le Conte's Sparrow:* much smaller; more pronounced "cheek" patch; white belly. *Savannah Sparrow* (p. 142): dark breast streaking; yellow lores. *Vesper Sparrow* (p. 140): breast streaking; white outer tail feathers. *Grasshopper Sparrow* (p. 143): white belly; unstreaked sides and flanks.

Best Sites: found statewide in appropriate habitat, but more common in the north and east.

RED-WINGED BLACKBIRD

Agelaius phoeniceus

Red-winged Blackbirds get an early start on the season, congregating in our marshes and wetlands in late winter. • The male's flashy red shoulders and short, raspy song are his most important tools in the strategy he employs to defend his territory from rivals and attract several mates. A flashy and richly voiced male who has managed to establish a large and productive territory can attract several mates to his cattail kingdom. In field experiments, males whose red shoulders were painted black soon lost their territories to rivals they had previously defeated. • After the male has wooed the female, she starts the busy work of weaving a nest amid the cattails. Cryptic coloration allows the female to sit inconspicuously upon her nest, blending in perfectly with the surroundings. • *Agelaius* is a Greek word meaning "flocking," which is an accurate description of this bird's winter behavior. The species name *phoeniceus* is a reference to the color red, which was introduced as a dye to the Greeks by the ancient Phoenicians.

ID: *Male:* all black, except for large, red shoulder patch edged in yellow (occasionally concealed). *Female:* faint, red shoulder patch; light "eyebrow"; mottled brown upperparts; heavily streaked underparts.

Size: *L* 7–9½ in; *W* 13 in.

Status: abundant migrant and breeder from March through November; small flocks and individuals overwinter.

Habitat: cattail marshes, wet meadows and ditches, croplands, fields and shoreline shrubs.

Nesting: colonial; in cattails or shoreline bushes; female weaves an open cup nest of dried cattail leaves and grass and lines it with fine grass; female incubates 3–4 darkly marked, pale blue green eggs for 10–12 days.

Feeding: gleans the ground for seeds, waste grain and invertebrates; gleans vegetation for seeds, insects and berries; occasionally catches insects in flight; may visit feeders.

Voice: song is a loud, raspy *konk-a-ree* or *ogle-reeeee;* calls include a harsh *check* and a high *tseert;* female may give a loud *che-che-che chee chee chee.*

Similar Species: male is distinctive when shoulder patch shows. *Brewer's Blackbird* and *Rusty Blackbird:* females lack streaked underparts. *Brown-headed Cowbird* (p. 159): juvenile is smaller and has a stubbier, conical bill.

Best Sites: found statewide in appropriate habitat.

WESTERN MEADOWLARK

Sturnella neglecta

Both Western and Eastern Meadowlarks occur in Iowa, and telling them apart, especially when they are not singing, is a constant challenge for birders. These birds are very similar, differing only in a few subtle characteristics, such as the amount of yellow on the face, so birders usually listen for their songs to distinguish one from the other. The song of the Western Meadowlark is a fluty series of notes, while the Eastern Meadowlark *(Sturnella magna)* usually gives a four-part whistle. • Birders are encouraged to use extreme caution when walking through a meadowlark's nesting habitat. Their grassy domed nests are difficult to locate, and are so well concealed that they are often accidentally crushed before they are seen. • Eastern Meadowlarks are predominant in the southeast and south central part of the state, whereas the Western Meadowlark is found throughout most of Iowa. Where their ranges overlap, the two species will occasionally interbreed, but their offspring are thought to be infertile. • The Western Meadowlark was overlooked by members of the Lewis and Clark expedition, who mistakenly thought it was the same species as the Eastern Meadowlark. This oversight is represented in the scientific name *neglecta.*

breeding

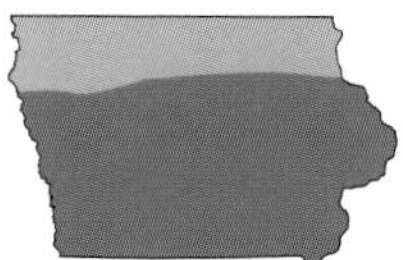

ID: yellow lores; brown crown stripes and eye line border; pale "eyebrow" and median crown stripe; broad, black breast band; long, sharp bill; mottled brown upperparts; yellow underparts; dark streaking on white sides and flanks; long, pinkish legs; short, wide tail with white outer tail feathers. *Breeding:* yellow on throat extends onto lower "cheek."

Size: *L* 9–9½ in; *W* 14½ in.

Status: abundant resident from March to November; rare in winter.

Habitat: grassy meadows and roadside ditches, pastures, some croplands and weedy fields.

Nesting: in a depression or scrape on the ground, concealed by dense grass or low shrubs; female builds a domed grass nest with a side entrance, which is woven into surrounding vegetation; female incubates 3–7 white eggs, heavily spotted with brown and purple, for 13–15 days.

Feeding: gleans grasshoppers, crickets, beetles, other insects and spiders from the ground and vegetation; extracts grubs and worms by probing its bill into the soil; also eats seeds.

Voice: song is a rich, melodic series of bubbly, flutelike notes; calls include a low, loud *chuck* or *chup*. Eastern's song is usually a 4-part whistle and its call is a buzzy *jzzzrt*. Both species may give a dry rattle or a few whistled notes in flight.

Similar Species: *Eastern Meadowlark:* darker upperparts, especially crown stripes and eye line; yellow on throat does not extend onto lower "cheek"; simpler whistled song and buzzy call. *Dickcissel* (p. 153): much smaller; solid dark crown; conical bill; white throat; lacks brown streaking on sides and flanks.

Best Sites: found statewide in appropriate habitat, especially in the west.

YELLOW-HEADED BLACKBIRD

Xanthocephalus xanthocephalus

You might expect a bird as handsome as the Yellow-headed Blackbird to have a song as splendid as its gold-and-black plumage. Unfortunately, a trip to a favored wetland will quickly reveal the shocking truth: when the male arches his golden head backward, his struggles produce only a painful grinding noise, possibly North America's poorest song. • But few sights can match a colony of Yellow-headed Blackbirds perched atop the cattails in the evening sun—they light up the marsh like candle flames. Where Yellow-headed Blackbirds occur together with Red-winged Blackbirds, the larger Yellow-heads dominate, commandeering the center of the wetland and pushing the red-winged competitors to the periphery. • Yellow-heads often nest in small colonies of about 30 pairs.

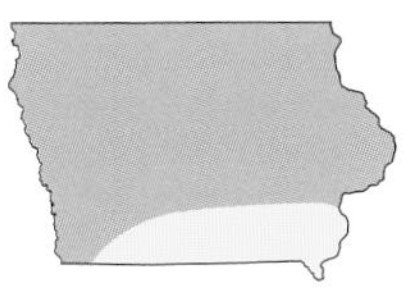

ID: *Male:* yellow head and breast; black lores, bill and body; white wing patches; long tail. *Female:* dusky brown overall; yellow breast, throat and "eyebrow"; hints of yellow on face.
Size: *L* 8–11 in; *W* 15 in.
Status: common migrant and breeder in the north and west, arriving in late April to early May and departing by late summer; local elsewhere; a few overwinter.
Habitat: deep marshes, sloughs, lakeshores and river impoundments where cattails dominate.
Nesting: loosely colonial; female builds a bulky, deep basket of emergent aquatic plants, lined with dry grass and other vegetation; nest is woven into emergent vegetation over water; female incubates 4 pale green to pale gray eggs, marked with gray or brown, for 11–13 days.
Feeding: gleans the ground for seeds, beetles, snails, water bugs and dragonflies; also probes cattail heads for larval invertebrates.
Voice: song is a strained, metallic grating note followed by a descending buzz; call is a deep *krrt* or *ktuk;* low quacks and liquidy *clucks* may be given during the breeding season.
Similar Species: male is distinctive. *Rusty Blackbird* and *Brewer's Blackbird:* females lack yellow throat and face.
Best Sites: marshes in the Prairie Pothole Region.

COMMON GRACKLE

Quiscalus quiscula

The Common Grackle is a poor, but spirited singer. Usually perching in a shrub or tree, a male grackle will slowly take a deep breath to inflate his breast, causing his feathers to spike outward, then close his eyes and give out a loud, strained *tssh-schleek.* Despite his lack of musical talent, the male remains smug and proud, posing with his bill held high. • In fall, large flocks of Common Grackles are common in rural areas where they forage for waste grain in open fields. Smaller bands occasionally venture into urban neighborhoods, asserting their dominance at backyard bird feeders—even Blue Jays will yield feeding rights to these cocky, aggressive birds. • The Common Grackle is easily distinguished from the Rusty Blackbird (*Euphagus carolinus*) and Brewer's Blackbird (*Euphagus cyanocephalus*) by its long, heavy bill and lengthy, wedge-shaped tail. In flight, the grackle's long tail trails behind it. • At night, grackles commonly roost in mixed groups of European Starlings, Red-winged Blackbirds and Brown-headed Cowbirds.

ID: iridescent, purple blue head and breast; bronze back and sides; purple wings and tail; often looks blackish; yellow eyes; long, heavy bill; long, keeled tail. *Female:* smaller, duller and browner than male. *Juvenile:* dull brown overall; dark eyes.

Size: *L* 11–13½ in; *W* 17 in.

Status: abundant migrant and breeder from March to November; uncommon in winter.

Habitat: wetlands, hedgerows, fields, wet meadows, riparian woodlands and at the edges of coniferous forests and woodlands; also shrubby urban and suburban parks and gardens.

Nesting: singly or in small colonies; in dense tree or shrub branches or emergent vegetation; often near water; female builds a bulky, open cup nest of twigs, grass, plant fibers and mud, lined with fine grass or feathers; female incubates 4–5 brown-blotched, pale blue eggs for 12–14 days.

Feeding: slowly struts along the ground, gleaning, snatching and probing for insects, earthworms, seeds, waste grain and fruit; also catches insects in flight and eats small vertebrates; may take some bird eggs.

Voice: song is a series of harsh, strained notes ending with a metallic squeak: *tssh-schleek* or *gri-de-leeek;* call is a quick, loud *swaaaack* or *chaack.*

Similar Species: *Great-tailed Grackle:* larger; purple overall. *Rusty Blackbird* and *Brewer's Blackbird:* smaller; shorter tails. *Red-winged Blackbird* (p. 155): shorter tail; male has red shoulder patch and dark eyes. *European Starling* (p. 126): speckled appearance; dark eyes; long, thin bill (yellow in summer); very short tail.

Best Sites: found statewide in appropriate habitat.

BROWN-HEADED COWBIRD

Molothrus ater

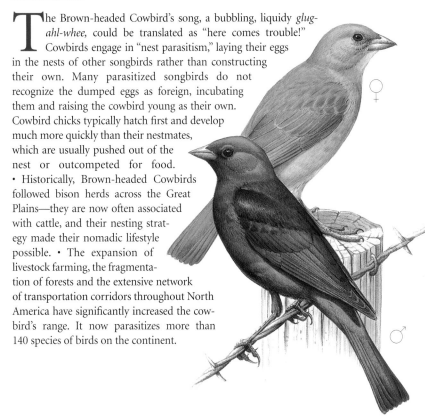

The Brown-headed Cowbird's song, a bubbling, liquidy *glug-ahl-whee,* could be translated as "here comes trouble!" Cowbirds engage in "nest parasitism," laying their eggs in the nests of other songbirds rather than constructing their own. Many parasitized songbirds do not recognize the dumped eggs as foreign, incubating them and raising the cowbird young as their own. Cowbird chicks typically hatch first and develop much more quickly than their nestmates, which are usually pushed out of the nest or outcompeted for food. • Historically, Brown-headed Cowbirds followed bison herds across the Great Plains—they are now often associated with cattle, and their nesting strategy made their nomadic lifestyle possible. • The expansion of livestock farming, the fragmentation of forests and the extensive network of transportation corridors throughout North America have significantly increased the cowbird's range. It now parasitizes more than 140 species of birds on the continent.

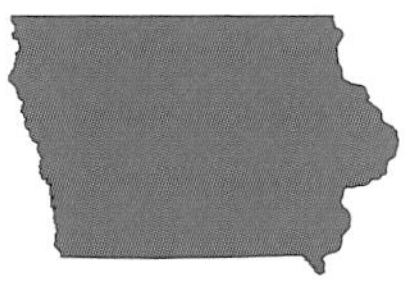

ID: thick, conical bill; dark eyes; short, squared tail. *Male:* iridescent, green blue body plumage usually looks glossy black; dark brown head. *Female:* brown plumage overall; pale throat; faint streaking on light brown underparts.

Size: *L* 6–8 in; *W* 12 in.

Status: common migrant and breeder from mid-March through mid-October; rare to uncommon in winter.

Habitat: open agricultural and residential areas, including fields, woodland edges, utility cutlines, roadsides, fencelines, landfills, campgrounds, picnic areas and areas near cattle. *Winter:* feedlots.

Nesting: does not build a nest; each female may lay up to 40 eggs per year in the nests of other birds, usually laying 1 egg per nest; whitish eggs, marked with gray and brown, hatch after 10–13 days.

Feeding: gleans the ground for seeds, waste grain and invertebrates, especially grasshoppers, beetles and bugs.

Voice: song is a high, liquidy gurgle: *glug-ahl-whee* or *bubbloozeee;* call is a squeaky, high-pitched *seep, psee* or *wee-tse-tse,* often given in flight; also a fast, chipping *ch-ch-ch-ch-ch-ch.*

Similar Species: *Rusty Blackbird* and *Brewer's Blackbird:* longer, slimmer bills; longer tails; all have yellow eyes except for female Brewer's Blackbird; lack contrasting brown head and darker body. *Common Grackle* (p. 158): much larger overall; longer bill; longer keeled tail.

Best Sites: found statewide in appropriate habitat.

BALTIMORE ORIOLE

Icterus galbula

The male Baltimore Oriole has striking black-and-orange plumage that flickers like smoldering embers in our neighborhood treetops. As if his brilliant plumage was not enough to secure our admiration, he also sings a rich flutelike courtship song and vocalizes almost continuously until he finds a mate. • Baltimore Orioles are fairly common in our state, but they are often difficult to find because they inhabit the forest heights. Developing an ear for their clear whistled tune and frequently scanning local deciduous trees will undoubtedly produce enchanting views of these beloved orioles. • This oriole doesn't suffer as much as the Orchard Oriole from nest parasitism. Female Baltimore Orioles will eject Brown-headed Cowbird eggs, and both male and female orioles will react aggressively toward any intruder approaching their nest. • The city of Baltimore was first established as a colony by Irishman George Calvert, the Baron of Baltimore. Mark Catesby, one of America's first naturalists, chose this bird's name because the male's plumage mirrored the colors of the baron's coat of arms.

♀

♂

ID: *Male:* black "hood," back, wings and central tail feathers; bright orange underparts, shoulder, rump and outer tail feathers; white wing patch and feather edgings. *Female:* olive brown upperparts with dark head; dull yellow orange underparts and rump; white wing bar.

Size: *L* 7–8 in; *W* 11½ in.

Status: common migrant and breeder from May to early September.

Habitat: deciduous and mixed forests, particularly riparian woodlands, natural openings, shorelines, roadsides, orchards, gardens and parklands.

Nesting: high in a deciduous tree, suspended from a branch; female builds a hanging pouch nest made of grass, bark shreds, rootlets, plant stems and grapevines and lines it with fine grass, rootlets and fur; occasionally adds string or fishing line; female incubates 4–5 darkly marked, pale gray to bluish white eggs for 12–14 days.

Feeding: gleans canopy vegetation and shrubs for caterpillars, beetles, wasps and other invertebrates; eats some fruit and nectar; may visit hummingbird feeders and feeders with orange halves.

Voice: song consists of loud, clear whistles, occasionally with scolding notes interspersed; calls include a 2-note *tea-too* and a rapid chatter: *ch-ch-ch-ch-ch.*

Similar Species: *Orchard Oriole:* male has darker chestnut plumage; female is olive yellow and lacks orange overtones. *Summer Tanager* and *Scarlet Tanager* (p. 136): females have thicker, pale bills and lack wing bars.

Best Sites: found statewide in appropriate habitat.

PURPLE FINCH

Carpodacus purpureus

The Purple Finch's gentle nature and simple, but stunning plumage endear it to many birdwatchers. Its arrival at your backyard bird feeder is a sure sign that winter is approaching. It settles in and shares space at the table with the resident House Finches. • Flat, table-style feeding stations with nearby tree cover may attract Purple Finches, and erecting one may keep a small flock in your area over winter. • "Purple" (*purpureus*) is simply a false description of this bird's reddish coloration. Roger Tory Peterson said it best when he described the Purple Finch as "a sparrow dipped in raspberry juice." Only the male is brightly colored, though—the female is a rather drab, unassuming bird by comparison.

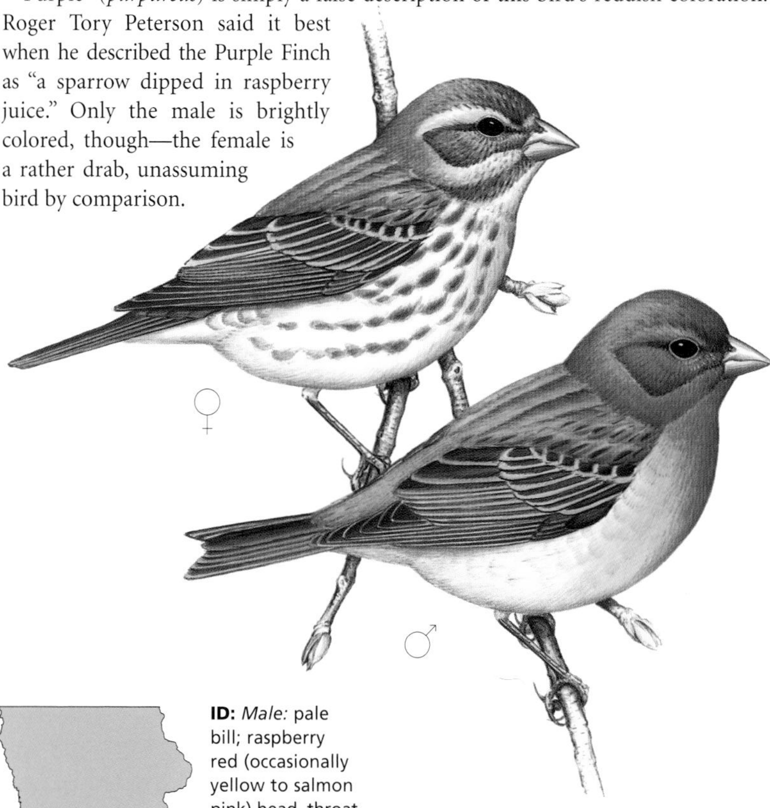

ID: *Male:* pale bill; raspberry red (occasionally yellow to salmon pink) head, throat, breast and nape; back and flanks are streaked with brown and red; reddish brown "cheek"; red rump; pale, unstreaked belly and undertail coverts. *Female:* dark brown "cheek" and jawline; white "eyebrow" and lower "cheek" stripe; boldly streaked underparts; unstreaked undertail coverts.

Size: *L* 5–6 in; *W* 10 in.

Status: common migrant and uncommon winter resident from October to early May.

Habitat: forests, shrubby open areas and feeders with nearby tree cover.

Nesting: does not nest in Iowa.

Feeding: gleans the ground and vegetation for seeds, buds, berries and insects; feeding stations.

Voice: song is a bubbly, continuous warble; call is a single metallic *cheep* or *weet*.

Similar Species: *House Finch* (p. 162): blurry streaking on tan breast, flanks and belly; male has brown "cap" and less red coloring; female lacks distinct pale "eyebrow." *Red Crossbill:* larger bill with crossed mandibles; male has more red overall and dark "V"s on whitish undertail coverts.

Best Sites: found statewide in appropriate habitat.

HOUSE FINCH

Carpodacus mexicanus

A native to western North America, the House Finch was brought to eastern parts of the continent as an illegally captured cage bird known as the "Hollywood Finch." In the early 1940s, New York pet shop owners released their birds to avoid prosecution and fines, and it is the descendants of those birds that have colonized our area. In fact, the House Finch is now commonly found throughout the continental U.S. and southern Canada. • The resourceful House Finch is one of the few birds aggressive and stubborn enough to successfully out-compete the House Sparrow. In the western U.S. this bird is often found in natural settings, but in the east it is seldom found outside of urban and suburban settings. House Finches seem to thrive on human companionship, often nesting in hanging plants on patios. • The male House Finch's plumage varies in color from light yellow to bright red, but females seem to choose the reddest males with which to breed.

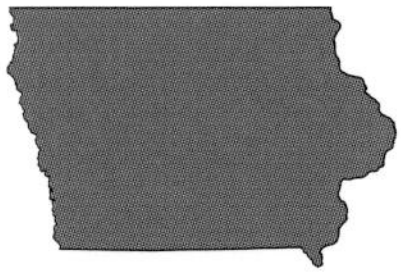

♂

♀

ID: streaked breast, flanks and belly; brown-streaked back; square tail. *Male:* brown "cap"; bright red "eyebrow," forecrown, throat and breast; heavily streaked flanks. *Female:* indistinct facial patterning; underparts marked with blurry streaks.

Size: *L* 5–6 in; *W* 9½ in.

Status: common resident, but more often seen in winter.

Habitat: cities, towns and agricultural areas.

Nesting: in a cavity, building, or abandoned bird nest, especially in evergreens and ornamental shrubs near buildings; mostly the female builds an open cup nest of grass, twigs and leaves, often adding string and other debris; female incubates 4–5 pale blue eggs, dotted with lavender and black, for 12–14 days.

Feeding: gleans vegetation and the ground for seeds; also takes berries, buds and some flower parts; often visits feeders.

Voice: song is a bright, disjointed warble lasting about 3 seconds, often ending with a harsh *jeeer* or *wheer;* flight call is a sweet *cheer*, given singly or in series.

Similar Species: *Purple Finch* (p. 161): unstreaked, pale belly; male has more burgundy red "cap," upper back and flanks; female has distinct "eyebrow" and clean streaking on underparts. *Red Crossbill:* bill has crossed mandibles; male has more red overall and darker wings.

Best Sites: found statewide in appropriate habitat.

AMERICAN GOLDFINCH

Carduelis tristis

American Goldfinches are bright, cheery songbirds that are commonly seen fluttering through weedy fields, along roadsides and among backyard shrubs. • These birds rain down to ground level to poke and prod the heads of dandelions, and can look quite comical as they attempt to crawl down a bouncing flower stem to reach the seedhead. A dandelion-covered lawn always seems a lot less weedy with a flock of glowing goldfinches hopping through it. • The scientific name *tristis*, Latin for "sad," refers to the goldfinch's voice, but seems a rather unmatched choice for such a pleasing and playful bird. • This bird has also been referred to as "Eastern Goldfinch" or "Wild Canary." In 1933, in a campaign led by school children, the Iowa legislature designated the goldfinch Iowa's state bird.

ID: *Breeding male:* black "cap" (extends onto forehead), wings and tail; bright yellow body; white wing bars, undertail coverts and tail base; orange bill and legs. *Female:* yellow throat and breast; yellow green upperparts and belly. *Nonbreeding:* yellow-tinged head; gray underparts; dark wings with wingbars.

Size: *L* 4½–5½ in; *W* 9 in.

Status: common resident.

Habitat: weedy fields, woodland edges, meadows, riparian areas, parks and gardens.

Nesting: in late summer and early fall; in a fork in a deciduous shrub or tree, often in hawthorn, serviceberry or sapling maple; female builds a compact cup nest of plant fibers, grass and spider silk, lined with plant down and hair; female incubates 4–6 pale bluish white eggs, occasionally spotted with light brown, for about 12–14 days.

Feeding: gleans vegetation for seeds, primarily thistle, birch and alder, as well as for insects and berries; commonly visits feeders.

Voice: song is a long, varied series of trills, twitters, warbles and hissing notes; calls include *po-ta-to-chip* or *per-chic-or-ee,* often delivered in flight, and a whistled *dear-me, see-me*.

Similar Species: *Evening Grosbeak:* much larger; massive bill; lacks black forehead. *Wilson's Warbler:* thin, dark bill; olive upperparts and wings; no wing bars; black "cap" does not extend onto forehead.

Best Sites: found statewide in appropriate habitat.

HOUSE SPARROW

Passer domesticus

For most of us, the House Sparrow was the first bird we met and recognized in our youth. Although it is one of our state's most abundant and conspicuous birds, many generations of House Sparrows live out their lives in our backyards with few of us ever knowing much about this omnipresent neighbor. • House Sparrows were introduced to North America in the 1850s around Brooklyn, New York, as part of a plan to control the numbers of insects that were damaging grain and cereal crops. Contrary to popular opinion at the time, this sparrow's diet is largely vegetarian, so its effect on crop pests proved to be minimal. Since then, this Eurasian sparrow has managed to colonize most human-altered environments on the continent and has benefited greatly from a close association with humans. Unfortunately, its early breeding season and aggressive behavior have helped it to usurp territory from many native bird species. • House Sparrows are not closely related to the other North American sparrows, but belong to the family of Old World Sparrows, or "Weaver Finches."

breeding

ID: *Breeding male:* gray crown; black "bib" and bill; light gray "cheek"; chestnut nape; white wing bar; dark, mottled upperparts; gray underparts. *Female:* plain gray brown overall; buffy "eyebrow"; indistinct facial patterns; streaked upperparts; grayish, unstreaked underparts. *Nonbreeding male:* smaller, black "bib"; pale bill.

Size: *L* 5½–6½ in; *W* 9½ in.

Status: abundant year-round resident.

Habitat: urban and suburban areas, farmyards, agricultural areas, railroad yards, farm buildings and fast-food restaurants.

Nesting: often communal; in a human-made structure, ornamental shrub or natural cavity; pair builds a large, dome-shaped nest of grass, twigs, plant fibers and litter, lined with feathers; pair incubates 4–6 whitish to greenish white eggs, dotted with gray and brown, for 10–13 days.

Feeding: gleans the ground and vegetation for seeds, insects and fruit; frequently visits feeders for seeds.

Voice: song is a plain, familiar *cheep-cheep-cheep-cheep;* call is a short *chill-up*.

Similar Species: *Eurasian Tree Sparrow:* brown crown; black ear spot on white "cheek." *Dickcissel* (p. 153): female has some yellow tint around the breast. *Harris's Sparrow* (p. 146): gray face; black "cap"; pink orange bill.

Best Sites: found statewide in appropriate habitat.

GLOSSARY

accipiter: a forest hawk (genus *Accipiter*), characterized by a long tail and short, rounded wings; feeds mostly on birds.

brood: *n.* a family of young from one hatching; *v.* to incubate the eggs.

brood parasite: a bird that lays its eggs in other birds' nests.

buteo: a high-soaring hawk (genus *Buteo*), characterized by broad wings and a short, wide tail; feeds mostly on small mammals and other land animals.

cere: on birds of prey, a fleshy area at the base of the bill that contains the nostrils.

clutch: the number of eggs laid by the female at one time.

dabbling: a foraging technique used by some ducks, in which the head and neck are submerged, but the body and tail remain on the water's surface; dabbling ducks can usually walk easily on land, can take off without running and have brightly colored speculums.

"eclipse" plumage: a cryptic plumage, similar to that of females, worn by some male ducks in autumn when they molt their flight feathers and, consequently, are unable to fly.

endangered: a species that is facing extirpation or extinction in all or part of its range.

extinct: a species that no longer exists.

extirpated: a species that no longer exists in the wild in a particular region, but occurs elsewhere.

flushing: when frightened birds explode into flight in response to a disturbance.

flycatching: a feeding behavior in which the bird leaves a perch, snatches an insect in midair and returns to the same perch; also known as "hawking" or "sallying."

hawking: attempting to capture insects through aerial pursuit.

irruption: a sporadic mass migration of birds into an unusual range.

peep: sandpipers of the *Calidris* genus.

polyandry: a mating strategy in which one female breeds with many males.

polygyny: a mating strategy in which one male breeds with many females.

precocial: a bird that is relatively well developed upon hatching; precocial birds usually have open eyes, extensive down and are fairly mobile.

riparian: refers to habitat along riverbanks.

sexual dimorphism: a difference in plumage, size, or other characteristics between males and females of the same species.

speculum: a brightly colored patch on the wings of many dabbling ducks.

stage: to gather in one place during migration, usually when birds are flightless or partly flightless during molting.

stoop: a steep dive through the air, usually performed by birds of prey while foraging or during courtship displays.

syrinx: a bird's voice organ.

threatened: a species likely to become endangered in the near future in all or part of its range.

vagrant: a bird that has wandered outside of its normal range.

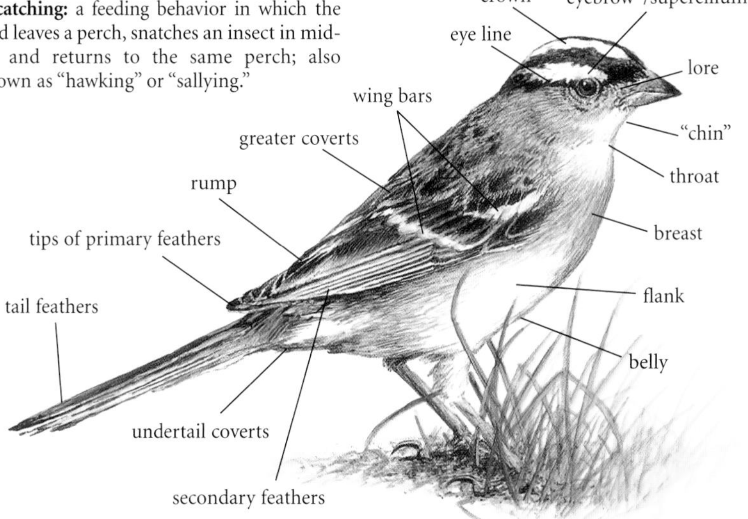

SELECT REFERENCES

American Ornithologists' Union. 1998. *Check-list of North American Birds.* 7th ed. (and its supplements). American Ornithologists' Union, Washington, D.C.

Black, Gladys. 1992. *Iowa Birdlife.* University of Iowa Press, Iowa City, IA.

Butler, Elaine. 1991. *Attracting Birds.* Lone Pine Publishing, Edmonton, Alberta.

Choate, E.A. 1985. *The Dictionary of American Bird Names.* Rev. ed. Harvard Common Press, Cambridge, MA.

Cox, R.T. 1996. *Birder's Dictionary.* Falcon Publishing Inc., Helena, Montana.

Pileated Woodpecker

Elphick, C., J.B. Dunning, Jr., and D.A. Sibley, eds. 2001. *National Audubon Society The Sibley Guide to Bird Life & Behavior.* Alfred A. Knopf, New York.

Erlich, P.R., D.S. Dobkin and D. Wheye. 1988. *The Birder's Handbook.* Simon & Schuster Inc., New York.

Iowa Ornithologists' Union. *Iowa Bird Life.* Published quarterly.

Jones, J.O. 1990. *Where the Birds Are.* William Morrow and Company, Inc., New York.

Kaufman, K. 1996. *Lives of North American Birds.* Houghton Mifflin Co., Boston.

Kaufman, K. 2000. *Birds of North America.* Houghton Mifflin Co., New York.

Kent, T.H. and J.J. Dinsmore. 1996. *Birds in Iowa.* Published by the authors, Iowa City and Ames, Iowa.

National Geographic Society. 2002. *Field Guide to the Birds of North America.* 4th ed. National Geographic Society, Washington, D.C.

Peterson, R.T. 2002. *A Field Guide to the Birds of Eastern and Central North America.* 5th ed. Houghton Mifflin Co., Boston.

Roth, Sally. 1998. *Attracting Birds to Your Backyard 536 Ways to Turn Your Yard and Garden into a Haven for Your Favorite Birds.* Rodale Press, Inc. Emmaus, Pennsylvania.

Sibley, D.A. 2000. *National Audubon Society The Sibley Guide to Birds.* Alfred A. Knopf, New York.

Sibley, D.A. 2002. *Sibley's Birding Basics.* Alfred A. Knopf, New York.

Tekiela, Stan. 2000. *Birds of Iowa Field Guide.* Adventure Publications, Cambridge, MN.

CHECKLIST

The following list of 410 species of birds is based on the Official Checklist of Iowa Birds (published in 1998, with updates through December 2004), as maintained by the Iowa Ornithologists' Union Records Committee. The risk factors are taken from the draft of the *Iowa Comprehensive Wildlife Conservation Plan* (2004) and the criteria species established by the Iowa Important Bird Areas program. Species are grouped by family and listed in taxonomic order in accordance with the A.O.U. *Check-list of North American Birds* (7th ed.) and its supplements.

Accidental and casual species (those not seen annually) are listed in *italics*. An asterisk (*) denotes a species with at least one nesting record in Iowa (some are historical). In addition, the following risk categories for breeding species are noted: extinct or extirpated (ex), endangered (en), threatened (th) and conservation concern (cc).

Waterfowl (Anatidae)

- ❑ *Black-bellied Whistling-Duck*
- ❑ *Bean Goose*
- ❑ Greater White-fronted Goose
- ❑ Snow Goose
- ❑ Ross's Goose
- ❑ *Brant*
- ❑ Cackling Goose
- ❑ Canada Goose*
- ❑ Mute Swan
- ❑ Trumpeter Swan (cc)*
- ❑ Tundra Swan
- ❑ Wood Duck*
- ❑ Gadwall*
- ❑ *Eurasian Wigeon*
- ❑ American Wigeon*
- ❑ American Black Duck*
- ❑ Mallard*
- ❑ Blue-winged Teal*
- ❑ Cinnamon Teal
- ❑ Northern Shoveler*
- ❑ Northern Pintail (cc)*
- ❑ *Garganey*
- ❑ Green-winged Teal*
- ❑ Canvasback (cc)*
- ❑ Redhead (cc)*
- ❑ Ring-necked Duck*
- ❑ Greater Scaup
- ❑ Lesser Scaup*
- ❑ *King Eider*
- ❑ *Common Eider*
- ❑ *Harlequin Duck*
- ❑ Surf Scoter
- ❑ White-winged Scoter
- ❑ Black Scoter
- ❑ Long-tailed Duck
- ❑ Bufflehead*
- ❑ Common Goldeneye
- ❑ *Barrow's Goldeneye*
- ❑ Hooded Merganser*
- ❑ Common Merganser
- ❑ Red-breasted Merganser
- ❑ Ruddy Duck*

Grouse & Allies (Phasianidae)

- ❑ Gray Partridge*
- ❑ Ring-necked Pheasant*
- ❑ Ruffed Grouse (cc)*
- ❑ Sharp-tailed Grouse (ex)
- ❑ Greater Prairie-Chicken (cc)*
- ❑ Wild Turkey*

New World Quail (Odontophoridae)

- ❑ Northern Bobwhite (cc)*

Loons (Gaviidae)

- ❑ Red-throated Loon
- ❑ Pacific Loon
- ❑ Common Loon*
- ❑ *Yellow-billed Loon*

Grebes (Podicipedidae)

- ❑ Pied-billed Grebe*
- ❑ Horned Grebe
- ❑ Red-necked Grebe*
- ❑ Eared Grebe*
- ❑ Western Grebe*
- ❑ *Clark's Grebe*

Pelicans (Pelecanidae)

- ❑ American White Pelican
- ❑ *Brown Pelican*

Cormorants (Phalacrocoracidae)

- ❑ *Neotropic Cormorant*
- ❑ Double-crested Cormorant*

Darters (Anhingidae)

- ❑ *Anhinga*

Frigatebirds (Fregatidae)

- ❑ *Magnificent Frigatebird*

Herons & Allies (Ardeidae)

- ❑ American Bittern (cc)*
- ❑ Least Bittern (cc)*
- ❑ Great Blue Heron*
- ❑ Great Egret*
- ❑ Snowy Egret
- ❑ Little Blue Heron
- ❑ *Tricolored Heron*
- ❑ *Reddish Egret*
- ❑ Cattle Egret*
- ❑ Green Heron*
- ❑ Black-crowned Night-Heron (cc)*

- ❑ Yellow-crowned Night-Heron (cc)*

Ibises & Spoonbills (Threskiornithidae)

- ❑ *White Ibis*
- ❑ *Glossy Ibis*
- ❑ White-faced Ibis*
- ❑ *Roseate Spoonbill*

Storks (Ciconiidae)

- ❑ *Wood Stork*

Vultures (Cathartidae)

- ❑ *Black Vulture*
- ❑ Turkey Vulture*

Kites, Hawks & Eagles (Accipitridae)

- ❑ Osprey (cc)*
- ❑ *Swallow-tailed Kite**
- ❑ Mississippi Kite*
- ❑ Bald Eagle (en)*
- ❑ Northern Harrier (en)*
- ❑ Sharp-shinned Hawk*
- ❑ Cooper's Hawk*
- ❑ Northern Goshawk
- ❑ Red-shouldered Hawk (en)*
- ❑ Broad-winged Hawk (cc)*
- ❑ Swainson's Hawk (cc)*
- ❑ Red-tailed Hawk*
- ❑ *Ferruginous Hawk*
- ❑ Rough-legged Hawk
- ❑ Golden Eagle

Caracaras & Falcons (Falconidae)

- ❑ *Crested Caracara*
- ❑ American Kestrel*
- ❑ Merlin*
- ❑ *Gyrfalcon*
- ❑ Peregrine Falcon (en)*
- ❑ Prairie Falcon

Rails & Coots (Rallidae)

- ❑ Yellow Rail
- ❑ *Black Rail*
- ❑ *King Rail* (en)*
- ❑ Virginia Rail*
- ❑ Sora*
- ❑ *Purple Gallinule*
- ❑ Common Moorhen (cc)*
- ❑ American Coot*

Cranes (Gruidae)

- ❑ Sandhill Crane (cc)*
- ❑ *Whooping Crane**

Plovers (Charadriidae)

- ❑ Black-bellied Plover
- ❑ American Golden-Plover
- ❑ *Snowy Plover*
- ❑ Semipalmated Plover
- ❑ Piping Plover (en)*
- ❑ Killdeer*

Stilts & Avocets (Recurvirostridae)

- ❑ Black-necked Stilt
- ❑ American Avocet

Sandpipers & Allies (Scolopacidae)

- ❑ Greater Yellowlegs
- ❑ Lesser Yellowlegs
- ❑ Solitary Sandpiper
- ❑ Willet
- ❑ Spotted Sandpiper*
- ❑ Upland Sandpiper (cc)*
- ❑ Eskimo Curlew (ex)
- ❑ *Whimbrel*
- ❑ *Long-billed Curlew**
- ❑ Hudsonian Godwit
- ❑ Marbled Godwit*
- ❑ Ruddy Turnstone
- ❑ *Red Knot*
- ❑ Sanderling
- ❑ Semipalmated Sandpiper
- ❑ Western Sandpiper
- ❑ Least Sandpiper
- ❑ White-rumped Sandpiper
- ❑ Baird's Sandpiper
- ❑ Pectoral Sandpiper
- ❑ *Sharp-tailed Sandpiper*
- ❑ Dunlin
- ❑ *Curlew Sandpiper*
- ❑ Stilt Sandpiper
- ❑ Buff-breasted Sandpiper
- ❑ *Ruff*
- ❑ Short-billed Dowitcher
- ❑ Long-billed Dowitcher
- ❑ Wilson's Snipe*
- ❑ American Woodcock (cc)*
- ❑ Wilson's Phalarope (cc)*
- ❑ Red-necked Phalarope
- ❑ *Red Phalarope*

Gulls & Allies (Laridae)

- ❑ *Pomarine Jaeger*
- ❑ *Parasitic Jaeger*
- ❑ *Long-tailed Jaeger*
- ❑ *Laughing Gull*
- ❑ Franklin's Gull*
- ❑ *Little Gull*
- ❑ *Black-headed Gull*
- ❑ Bonaparte's Gull
- ❑ *Mew Gull*
- ❑ Ring-billed Gull*
- ❑ *California Gull*
- ❑ Herring Gull
- ❑ Thayer's Gull
- ❑ *Iceland Gull*
- ❑ Lesser Black-backed Gull
- ❑ *Slaty-backed Gull*
- ❑ Glaucous Gull
- ❑ *Great Black-backed Gull*
- ❑ Sabine's Gull
- ❑ *Black-legged Kittiwake*
- ❑ *Ross's Gull*
- ❑ *Ivory Gull*
- ❑ Caspian Tern
- ❑ Common Tern
- ❑ *Arctic Tern*
- ❑ Forster's Tern (cc)*
- ❑ Least Tern (en)*
- ❑ Black Tern (cc)*

Auks, Murres & Puffins (Alcidae)

- ❑ *Thick-billed Murre*
- ❑ *Long-billed Murrelet*
- ❑ *Ancient Murrelet*

Pigeons & Doves (Columbidae)

- ❑ Rock Pigeon*
- ❑ Eurasian Collared-Dove*
- ❑ *White-winged Dove*
- ❑ Mourning Dove*
- ❑ Passenger Pigeon (ex)*
- ❑ *Common Ground-Dove*

Parakeets (Psittacidae)

- ❑ Carolina Parakeet (ex)

Cuckoos (Cuculidae)
❑ Black-billed Cuckoo (cc)*
❑ Yellow-billed Cuckoo (cc)*
❑ *Groove-billed Ani*

Barn Owls (Tytonidae)
❑ Barn Owl (en)*

Owls (Strigidae)
❑ Eastern Screech-Owl*
❑ Great Horned Owl*
❑ Snowy Owl
❑ *Northern Hawk Owl*
❑ *Burrowing Owl* (cc)*
❑ Barred Owl*
❑ *Great Gray Owl*
❑ Long-eared Owl (th)*
❑ Short-eared Owl (en)*
❑ Boreal Owl
❑ Northern Saw-whet Owl

Nightjars (Caprimulgidae)
❑ Common Nighthawk (cc)*
❑ Chuck-will's-widow (cc)*
❑ Whip-poor-will (cc)*

Swifts (Apodidae)
❑ Chimney Swift*

Hummingbirds (Trochilidae)
❑ Ruby-throated Hummingbird*
❑ *Rufous Hummingbird*

Kingfishers (Alcedinidae)
❑ Belted Kingfisher*

Woodpeckers & Allies (Picidae)
❑ *Lewis's Woodpecker*
❑ Red-headed Woodpecker (cc)*
❑ Red-bellied Woodpecker*
❑ Yellow-bellied Sapsucker*
❑ Downy Woodpecker*
❑ Hairy Woodpecker*
❑ *Black-backed Woodpecker*
❑ Northern Flicker*
❑ Pileated Woodpecker (cc)*

Flycatchers (Tyrannidae)
❑ Olive-sided Flycatcher
❑ *Western Wood-Pewee*
❑ Eastern Wood-Pewee*
❑ Yellow-bellied Flycatcher
❑ Acadian Flycatcher (cc)*
❑ Alder Flycatcher
❑ Willow Flycatcher (cc)*
❑ Least Flycatcher (cc)*
❑ *Western Flycatcher*
❑ Eastern Phoebe*
❑ *Say's Phoebe**
❑ *Vermilion Flycatcher*
❑ Great Crested Flycatcher*
❑ Western Kingbird*
❑ Eastern Kingbird*
❑ *Scissor-tailed Flycatcher**

Shrikes (Laniidae)
❑ Loggerhead Shrike (cc)*
❑ Northern Shrike

Vireos (Vireonidae)
❑ White-eyed Vireo (cc)*
❑ Bell's Vireo (cc)*
❑ Yellow-throated Vireo*
❑ Blue-headed Vireo
❑ Warbling Vireo*
❑ Philadelphia Vireo
❑ Red-eyed Vireo*

Jays, Crows & Magpies (Corvidae)
❑ *Gray Jay*
❑ Blue Jay*
❑ *Pinyon Jay*
❑ *Clark's Nutcracker*
❑ Black-billed Magpie*
❑ American Crow*
❑ *Fish Crow*
❑ *Common Raven*

Larks (Alaudidae)
❑ Horned Lark*

Swallows (Hirundinidae)
❑ Purple Martin*
❑ Tree Swallow*
❑ Northern Rough-winged Swallow*
❑ Bank Swallow*
❑ Cliff Swallow*
❑ Barn Swallow*

Chickadees & Titmice (Paridae)
❑ Black-capped Chickadee*
❑ *Boreal Chickadee*
❑ Tufted Titmouse*

Nuthatches (Sittidae)
❑ Red-breasted Nuthatch*
❑ White-breasted Nuthatch*
❑ *Pygmy Nuthatch*

Creepers (Certhiidae)
❑ Brown Creeper (cc)*

Wrens (Troglodytidae)
❑ *Rock Wren**
❑ Carolina Wren*
❑ Bewick's Wren (cc)*
❑ House Wren*
❑ Winter Wren*
❑ Sedge Wren (cc)*
❑ Marsh Wren*

Kinglets (Regulidae)
❑ Golden-crowned Kinglet
❑ Ruby-crowned Kinglet

Gnatcatchers (Sylviidae)
❑ Blue-gray Gnatcatcher*

Thrushes (Turdidae)
❑ Eastern Bluebird*
❑ *Mountain Bluebird*
❑ *Townsend's Solitaire*
❑ Veery (cc)*
❑ Gray-cheeked Thrush
❑ Swainson's Thrush
❑ Hermit Thrush
❑ Wood Thrush (cc)*
❑ American Robin*
❑ Varied Thrush

Mockingbirds & Thrashers (Mimidae)
❑ Gray Catbird*
❑ Northern Mockingbird (cc)*

- ❑ *Sage Thrasher*
- ❑ Brown Thrasher*
- ❑ *Curve-billed Thrasher*

Starlings (Sturnidae)

- ❑ European Starling*

Pipits (Motacillidae)

- ❑ American Pipit
- ❑ *Sprague's Pipit*

Waxwings (Bombycillidae)

- ❑ Bohemian Waxwing
- ❑ Cedar Waxwing*

Wood-Warblers (Parulidae)

- ❑ Blue-winged Warbler (cc)*
- ❑ Golden-winged Warbler*
- ❑ Tennessee Warbler
- ❑ Orange-crowned Warbler
- ❑ Nashville Warbler
- ❑ Northern Parula*
- ❑ Yellow Warbler*
- ❑ Chestnut-sided Warbler*
- ❑ Magnolia Warbler
- ❑ Cape May Warbler
- ❑ Black-throated Blue Warbler
- ❑ Yellow-rumped Warbler
- ❑ *Black-throated Gray Warbler*
- ❑ Black-throated Green Warbler
- ❑ *Townsend's Warbler*
- ❑ Blackburnian Warbler
- ❑ Yellow-throated Warbler*
- ❑ Pine Warbler*
- ❑ *Prairie Warbler**
- ❑ Palm Warbler
- ❑ Bay-breasted Warbler
- ❑ Blackpoll Warbler
- ❑ Cerulean Warbler (cc)*
- ❑ Black-and-white Warbler (cc)*
- ❑ American Redstart*
- ❑ Prothonotary Warbler (cc)*
- ❑ Worm-eating Warbler (cc)*
- ❑ Ovenbird*
- ❑ Northern Waterthrush
- ❑ Louisiana Waterthrush (cc)*
- ❑ Kentucky Warbler (cc)*
- ❑ Connecticut Warbler
- ❑ Mourning Warbler
- ❑ *MacGillivray's Warbler*
- ❑ Common Yellowthroat*
- ❑ Hooded Warbler (cc)*
- ❑ Wilson's Warbler
- ❑ Canada Warbler
- ❑ Yellow-breasted Chat (cc)*

Tanagers (Thraupidae)

- ❑ Summer Tanager*
- ❑ Scarlet Tanager*
- ❑ *Western Tanager*

Sparrows & Allies (Emberizidae)

- ❑ *Green-tailed Towhee*
- ❑ Spotted Towhee
- ❑ Eastern Towhee (cc)*
- ❑ American Tree Sparrow
- ❑ Chipping Sparrow*
- ❑ Clay-colored Sparrow*
- ❑ Field Sparrow (cc)*
- ❑ Vesper Sparrow*
- ❑ Lark Sparrow (cc)*
- ❑ *Black-throated Sparrow*
- ❑ *Lark Bunting*
- ❑ Savannah Sparrow*
- ❑ Grasshopper Sparrow (cc)*
- ❑ *Baird's Sparrow*
- ❑ Henslow's Sparrow (th)*
- ❑ Le Conte's Sparrow
- ❑ Nelson's Sharp-tailed Sparrow
- ❑ Fox Sparrow
- ❑ Song Sparrow*
- ❑ Lincoln's Sparrow
- ❑ Swamp Sparrow*
- ❑ White-throated Sparrow
- ❑ Harris's Sparrow
- ❑ White-crowned Sparrow
- ❑ *Golden-crowned Sparrow*
- ❑ Dark-eyed Junco
- ❑ Lapland Longspur
- ❑ Smith's Longspur
- ❑ *Chestnut-collared Longspur*
- ❑ Snow Bunting

Grosbeaks & Buntings (Cardinalidae)

- ❑ Northern Cardinal*
- ❑ Rose-breasted Grosbeak*
- ❑ *Black-headed Grosbeak*
- ❑ Blue Grosbeak*
- ❑ *Lazuli Bunting*
- ❑ Indigo Bunting*
- ❑ *Painted Bunting*
- ❑ Dickcissel (cc)*

Blackbirds & Allies (Icteridae)

- ❑ Bobolink (cc)*
- ❑ Red-winged Blackbird*
- ❑ Eastern Meadowlark (cc)*
- ❑ Western Meadowlark*
- ❑ Yellow-headed Blackbird*
- ❑ Rusty Blackbird
- ❑ Brewer's Blackbird
- ❑ Common Grackle*
- ❑ Great-tailed Grackle*
- ❑ Brown-headed Cowbird*
- ❑ Orchard Oriole*
- ❑ *Hooded Oriole*
- ❑ *Bullock's Oriole*
- ❑ Baltimore Oriole*

Finches & Allies (Fringillidae)

- ❑ *Gray-crowned Rosy-Finch*
- ❑ *Pine Grosbeak*
- ❑ Purple Finch
- ❑ House Finch*
- ❑ Red Crossbill*
- ❑ White-winged Crossbill
- ❑ Common Redpoll
- ❑ *Hoary Redpoll*
- ❑ Pine Siskin*
- ❑ *Lesser Goldfinch*
- ❑ American Goldfinch*
- ❑ *Evening Grosbeak*

Old World Sparrows (Passeridae)

- ❑ House Sparrow*
- ❑ Eurasian Tree Sparrow*

INDEX OF SCIENTIFIC NAMES

This index references only the primary species accounts.

INDEX OF COMMON NAMES

Page numbers in boldface type refer to the primary, illustrated species accounts.

ABOUT THE AUTHORS

Photograph by Reid Allen

ANN JOHNSON has been birding for most of her life. A past officer of the Iowa Ornithologists' Union and current Secretary of the Iowa Rare Bird Records Committee, Ann is a frequent contributor to the state journal, *Iowa Bird Life*. She is involved in Iowa's Important Bird Areas program and acts as an advisor to the Iowa Department of Natural Resources' Comprehensive Wildlife Conservation Plan. Ann has led birding trips throughout the United States and Mexico for many years, and when not out birding, she can be found at her computer where she administers the Iowa Ornithologists' Union website: www.iowabirds.org.

Photograph by Cathy Lindsay

JIM BANGMA began adding Iowa birds to his life list at age 13 while on family vacations. He has traveled extensively throughout both the eastern and western hemispheres, and since 1985, he has led tours for New Jersey Audubon and several other organizations. Participants of his many tours will attest to his ability to not only find the birds but also have fun doing so. As an accomplished nature photographer and author, he has contributed to various national and international birding publications. His current project is the New Jersey Odonata Survey website: www.njodes.com

GREGORY KENNEDY has been an active naturalist and adventurer since he was a young boy. He is the author of many books on natural history and has produced film and television work on environmental issues and indigenous concerns in Southeast Asia, New Guinea, South and Central America and the High Arctic. His involvement in numerous research projects around the world ranges from studies in the upper canopy of tropical and temperate rainforests to deepwater marine investigations.